D1297510

HORATIO NELSON

A CONTROVERSIAL HERO

MARIANNE CZISNIK

Hodder Arnold

A MEMBER OF THE HODDER HEADLINE GROUP

First published in Great Britain in 2005 by
Hodder Education, a member of the Hodder Headline Group,
338 Euston Road, London NW1 3BH

www.hoddereducation.com

Distributed in the United States of America by
Oxford University Press Inc.
198 Madison Avenue, New York, NY10016

The advice and information in this book are believed to be true and
accurate at the date of going to press, but neither the authors nor the publisher
can accept any legal responsibility or liability for any errors or omissions.

British Library Cataloguing in Publication Data
A catalogue record for this book is available from the British Library

Library of Congress Cataloging-in-Publication Data
A catalog record for this book is available from the Library of Congress

ISBN-10: 0-340-90021-0
ISBN-13: 978-0-340-90021-5

1 2 3 4 5 6 7 8 9 10

Typeset in 10.5/12.5pt Monotype Apollo by Servis Filmsetting Ltd, Manchester
Printed and bound in Malta

What do you think about this book? Or any other
Hodder Education title? Please send your comments to
the feedback section on www.hoddereducation.com.

To the memory
of
Marie Elisabeth Zimmermann,
née Graef

Contents

Illustrations

Colour plates in central section

Black and white illustrations

Acknowledgements

Many people have supported the development of this book in many ways. First and foremost among them stands the supervisor of my doctoral thesis, Professor H. T. Dickinson of the University of Edinburgh. First my thesis and then this book took shape mostly thanks to his guidance. He was ready to advise me at every stage, and patiently read and commented in detail on my drafts. Since my very inspiring viva, conducted by Dr Michael Duffy (University of Exeter), Dr Frances Dow and Mr Geoffrey Carnall (both of the University of Edinburgh), I have received considerable additional support from Dr Michael Duffy. Another source of constant inspiration over the years was talking to Jane and Professor Roger Knight, who also granted me the most generous hospitality. Long before I knew any of these academic supporters, and even before I had contemplated the study of history, my friend Dr Alberto Lena Ordóñez insisted I would one day write a book about Nelson. I was never able to convince him of the contrary.

Advice, hospitality and inspiration needed to be complemented by pecuniary support, which I was very pleased to receive through the Jeremiah Dalziel Prize of the Department of History of the University of Edinburgh (awarded for my master's dissertation), and different scholarships from the Faculty of Arts of the University of Edinburgh, the Student Awards Agency for Scotland (and later from the Arts and Humanities Research Board), the Carnegie Trust for the Universities of Scotland, the Faculty of Arts of the University of Edinburgh with its 'George Scott Travelling Fellowship' and the Deutsches Historisches Institut, Paris.

Last but not least I am indebted to several members of my family for having had enough confidence in my project to give me their financial support at the beginning, when there was not yet much proof of my progress. These relatives who helped me financially were my parents, Karin and Ulrich Czisnik, my grandmother, Marie Elisabeth Zimmermann, and after her death my uncle, Jürgen Zimmermann-Hallier. My grandmother also furthered my research indirectly through her professional achievements. She had been the librarian of the German naval officers' school for about a quarter of a century since the refoundation of the German navy after the Second World War and she left behind a thoroughly organized and well-catalogued library that enabled me to trace sources about Nelson that I did not find anywhere else. In gratitude for her heartfelt generosity and in admiration for her dedicated professionalism, this book is dedicated to her memory.

Introduction

Horatio Nelson has left many traces in the public memory, in visual imagery and even in the English language: these include the one-armed figure on top of the column in London's Trafalgar Square; the famous order, 'England expects that every man will do his duty'; his ship, HMS *Victory*, in her dry dock in Portsmouth; the death scene with the immortal phrase, 'Kiss me, Hardy'; the passionate love affair with Lady Hamilton; the often seasick sailor; and the one-eyed admiral turning his blind eye to his superior's order, declaring: 'I do not see the signal.' How Horatio Nelson could excite such public curiosity in the first place and how the enduring fascination that he exerts has been forged during the 200 years since his death is explored in this book.

The prologue deals with Nelson's funeral. It introduces the event that connects the two main subjects that follow: on the one hand, the appeal of the man himself and, on the other, the way in which his image was shaped and disputed by others. The public reaction to the death of Nelson shows the enormous hold he had over the public imagination during his lifetime and, at the same time, it forms the starting point for the posthumous interest in him. Having established the massive interest in Nelson at his death, this book sets out to assess the nature of the man himself and then to show how he became and has remained ever afterwards a focal point of national consciousness.

The first part of the book presents views of Nelson himself. In order to get closer to the historic Nelson, the most controversial aspects of his life and death are examined. On the basis of primary research and the work of numerous other scholars, this first part explores the key aspects of Nelson's career in a roughly chronological fashion. First, Nelson's acts of disobedience are examined, since they not only shaped him as an officer, but also seized the attention of his superiors and eventually aroused the interest of the public. The next chapter assesses Nelson as a commander, the role that ultimately made him famous. The following two chapters deal with those aspects of his life that are usually regarded as the major blemishes on his heroic image: his involvement in the defeat of the Neapolitan revolution in 1799 and his love affair with

Lady Hamilton. The last two chapters of this first part examine accounts of Nelson's death and the main features of his personal character. In each chapter historical analysis is followed by an overview of how historians have dealt with the respective aspects of Nelson's life in the course of the last 200 years.

The second part goes on to explore how aspects of Nelson's life and career have been used to shape his image over the last 200 years, to this very day. The first chapter in this part of the book examines the early visual representations of Nelson, at a time when monuments, pictures and ceramics dominated the means of representation of the hero. The next chapter shows how, later in the nineteenth century, commemorations of the image and achievements of Nelson were transferred to new media, such as exhibitions and anniversary celebrations of the battle of Trafalgar. This is followed by a chapter exploring the twentieth-century image of Nelson. In this century, though earlier forms of representation were perpetuated, different forms of fictional representation of Nelson appeared, such as novels, plays and films. The final chapter in this part looks at views of Nelson from across the Channel, from France, Spain and Germany.

The material for this book has been assembled in great part from my doctoral dissertation at the University of Edinburgh on *Admiral Nelson. Image and Icon*. The text, however, has been substantially rewritten and the notes and bibliography have been much reduced.

Prologue: Nelson's funeral

The death of Nelson was felt in England as something more than a public calamity: men started at the intelligence, and turned pale; as if they had heard of the loss of a dear friend. An object of our admiration and affection, of our pride and of our hopes, was suddenly taken from us; and it seemed as if we had never, till then, known how deeply we loved and reverenced him.[1]

This is how Robert Southey remembered the reaction to the death of Nelson eight years after the event. Newspapers commented at the time that the 'deep and universal affliction' following news of Nelson's death, 'though it is visible to every eye, and is felt in every heart, baffles the efforts of description', and they further observed how 'one universal sentiment of sorrow, and deep regret, pervades the public mind, as it reflects that the nation's "glory and its pride" have fallen!'[2]

How was this 'sentiment of sorrow, and deep regret' at Nelson's death expressed among the British public? This prologue will show how the emotional response to the news of Nelson's death evolved into a profound public mourning: a process that helped people to face the fact that Nelson was dead and also a process that began the public commemoration of the hero. This process began when the news of the battle of Trafalgar and of Nelson's death were first published in Britain on 6 November 1805; it culminated in Nelson's funeral on 9 January 1806, but it took several months before it ceased to be a major topic of discussion and commemoration.

At first the public seemed uncertain how to express its sadness at the shocking news of Nelson's death, particularly as it was received at the same time as the news of the great naval victory off Cape Trafalgar. The sombre feelings were not easily reflected in the brightness of the illuminations that commonly marked any event of national importance. Loyal citizens, intent on celebrating the victorious battle, sought to include references to Nelson in their illuminations, either in the form of 'illuminated initials of the gallant Nelson, or transparent medallions of his head, with suitable inscriptions'. More elaborate designs included symbols of death, such as urns, or a wreath of palm and laurel. Many people believed that illuminations were inappropriate after the death of Nelson, however, so that they either did not participate in the illuminations at all or 'displayed black with the lights, others hung bay-leaves round the windows, while some transparencies, expressing the general feeling, repeated, in large letters, "Britons lament! Your Nelson is no more"'.[3] Not surprisingly, the illuminations were not accompanied by the usual expressions of joy, common even for much less decisive naval victories.

The sombre mood that the news of Nelson's death produced also affected other events, such as the Lord Mayor's Day in London, which was traditionally celebrated in November. In 1805 the whole event appeared rather to be a celebration exclusively dedicated to Nelson, since the room in which a sumptuous dinner was held on the occasion was decorated with the portrait and bust of Nelson, and speeches were made with ample reference to Nelson. Immediately after the toast to members of the royal family, 'The immortal Memory of Lord Nelson' was drunk,[4] a toast that has since become a tradition, particularly on the anniversary of the battle of Trafalgar.

The fifth of December 1805, appointed as a day of public thanksgiving, gave an opportunity for the spiritual expression of grief for those who had died in the battle of Trafalgar, Nelson in particular; it was an opportunity which was 'observed with remarkable, and, perhaps, unexampled attention'.[5] Ministers of religion tried to soothe the harsh reality of Nelson's death by interpreting the significance of his life on earth. The great majority of clergymen appear to have seen Nelson as an 'instrument in the hand of God' chosen to deliver the country from danger.[6] Taken to its logical conclusion, this line of argument made Nelson appear as a mere tool of the divine will, rather than someone whose death could be presented as a deliberate sacrifice for the benefit of his country. Comforting as the notion was that God found the human instrument needed to protect Britain in this crisis, ministers did not show how Nelson became such an instrument. Certain ministers, among them Nelson's influential biographer, James Stanier Clarke, therefore divided their argument and claimed, on the one hand, that 'our naval power has been selected by Providence', while, on the other hand, the specific individuals 'willingly offered themselves' as instruments of this Providence.[7] The combination of a nation under God's special protection and individuals within it who were willing to sacrifice themselves enabled believers in God to see his will manifested on earth and at the same time allow for human acts of sacrifice, if not martyrdom, as the result of an individual's own free will.

Now that Nelson was regarded as a martyr for his nation, his dead body prompted similar veneration to that given to a martyred saint. Newspapers recorded the means of its preservation (in spirits) on board the *Victory*, and noted the different stages of its journey home. It took some time before the body arrived in Britain, because 'the crew of the Victory [Nelson's flagship] . . . manifested the strongest reluctance to part with the precious relic', and thus stopped it from being brought home on a fast-sailing frigate.[8] Interest in the body's whereabouts and in its treatment rose as it approached England on board Nelson's flagship. The first sighting of the *Victory* 'off the Lizard' was reported with excitement, even more so the arrival of 'the remains' at Portsmouth, where all 'pendants [were] half-mast high' and 'there was scarcely a person of any description who did not hasten to obtain a sight of the vessel which contained all that was mortal of the hero of their affection'.[9] Nelson's biographers, James Stanier Clarke and John M'Arthur, recorded meticulously, and with the veneration normally shown to a martyr, how the body was treated in order to preserve it as long as possible: 'His sacred remains were . . . wrapped in cotton vestments, and rolled from head to foot with bandages after the ancient mode of embalming, and the body was then placed in a leaden coffin filled with brandy holding a strong solution of camphor and myrrh'.[10] It was reported that subsequently this provisional coffin 'was cut in pieces, which were distributed as relics of Saint Nelson – so the gunner of the *Victory* called them'.[11]

Nelson's final coffins attracted great attention in themselves. Following a pattern that had developed during the eighteenth century, Nelson's body was placed into several shells of flat-lidded coffins. The innermost of these shells was Nelson's most famous trophy: the coffin which Captain Hallowell had presented to him in 1799 and which was made out of the mainmast of *L'Orient*, the French flagship that had blown up at the battle of the Nile. While this innermost shell of Nelson's multi-layered coffin had the greatest emotional resonance as a relic, the most sumptuous part of the coffin was naturally the outer wooden case. This was covered with black velvet, which was decorated with patterns in gold. The design of the outer coffin included national symbols (Britannia and the lion) and naval imagery (dolphins and trophies), as well as emblems specifically referring to the battle of the Nile (a crocodile and sphinx); and it also gave expression to the nation's grief (through reclining female figures). Its lid was decorated with a golden plate that bore as inscription Nelson's titles. The whole design attracted so much attention that it was depicted on a print, in newspapers and in other publications. Many members of the public were now naturally keen to see it displayed. Ten days before the official lying-in-state began, 'an immense crowd' assembled at Greenwich to see the coffin with its most valued contents arrive.[12]

The public, particularly the inhabitants of London, had been waiting for Nelson's funeral ever since the news of his death had reached Britain. In the issue that reported the first news about the battle of Trafalgar, *The Times* emphatically declared:

> If ever there were a hero who merited the honours of a public funeral, and a public mourning, it is the pious, the modest, and the gallant Nelson; the darling of the British navy, whose death has plunged a whole nation into the deepest grief.[13]

Since no public announcement to the effect was made known, the same newspaper insisted six days later:

> His Majesty has shewn so much regret for the loss of this gallant Chief, that it is not to be doubted that it will be the Royal wish to have all possible respect shewn to his memory, and to have his remains sepulchred among the most exalted Characters this country ever boasted.[14]

The *Sun* went even further and began to comment on how the funeral procession should be organized.[15] If the government had not yet made up its mind, it took the broad hint of public opinion and let it be known what 'His Majesty has been pleased to order' for Nelson's funeral. The solemnities were to consist of three major stages: the lying-in-state in the Painted Hall of Greenwich Hospital, a procession by water to Whitehall, and a procession by land to St Paul's Cathedral (in the City of London) where Nelson was to be interred. The preparations for the funeral did not proceed smoothly, however, so that when *The Times* reported two weeks later, at the end of November, that Nelson's coffin was to be let down directly into the crypt through a hole in its ceiling, instead of 'down the steps', it also remarked rather impatiently: 'We do not learn that any other arrangements are finally determined upon.'[16] This aside, and the suggestion in another newspaper that the funeral should include members of *Victory*'s crew who had fought next to the fallen hero, was shortly afterwards followed by an appeasing official declaration that a 'detachment of able seamen of the Victory' would take part in the procession.[17] Since no further information about the funeral was made known, *The Times* took the initiative and presented its own ideas. Observing an 'uncommon interest in the obsequies of the Hero' among 'the lower classes', *The Times* stated what it perceived to be the current taste about some details of a public funeral.[18] When more arrangements for the different aspects of the funeral were made known, *The Times* commented on them in a tone of impatience: 'It is finally determined. . .'[19] Clearly, the press was informing the government that the public wanted a splendid funeral for Nelson.

As to the official response to the death of Nelson, it did indeed take some time to emerge. Nothing is recorded before the date of 13 November, when the Lord Chamberlain was informed about the 'Royal Wish' for a public funeral.[20] The College of Arms and a funeral committee of the City of London began their preparations for the funeral on 23 December 1805, only a day before Nelson's body arrived at Greenwich. During the next two and a half weeks there was much to prepare. The City of London arranged for its own participation, mobilizing the livery companies to take part in the procession by water and ensuring the necessary order for the procession both by water and land. The Office of Works used the days before the procession on land in order to organize the gravelling of the streets, while the main task of organizing the procession itself fell to the College of Arms.

The College of Arms, an institution of medieval origin which gained the authority to regulate 'outward marks of gentility' from Henry VIII, has the exclusive right to organize heraldic funerals in England.[21] Street processions and 'the chivalric element of the service within the church building' followed long-standing traditions about the display of chivalric emblems and the order of the procession, as well as certain symbolic acts.[22] Within this framework there was scope for decisions about each particular funeral. In the case of Nelson's funeral these mainly concerned the choice of participants in and the order of the procession, as well as the form of the funeral car. Sir Isaac Heard, Garter King of Arms, the herald in charge of the arrangements for Nelson's funeral, caused some friction at the planning stage when he positioned the lord mayor of the City of London behind the royal princes who intended to take part in the procession. This in itself was an innovation, because it had been 'the tradition that royalty did not attend funerals of subjects, however distinguished'.[23] The new lord mayor stated that only the sovereign had the right to be placed ahead of him in the City. In the end, the king intervened in favour of the lord mayor. The king himself never thought of participating in the procession, and it would be more than another hundred years before a British sovereign attended a funeral; but George III would watch Nelson's funeral procession from St James's Palace.

The most significant elements in Nelson's funeral procession were, however, the different representatives of his profession. The government and the College of Arms chose them to stand out in the procession. The government did so by choosing Admiral Peter Parker, Nelson's early mentor, as the chief mourner. Traditionally this position, honourably placed in the procession directly behind the coffin, was filled by the successor in the title of the deceased in order to emphasize the 'continuation of the family's power'. Timothy Jenks has convincingly argued that by replacing Nelson's aristocratic successor by a leading member of his profession, Pitt and Lord Hawkesbury (who decided on the chief mourner) tried to stress instead 'the continuation of Britain's naval superiority'.[24] The College of Arms also gave members of the naval profession prominent places in the funeral procession. Instead of the usual group of the deceased's tenants, the College of Arms decided to include in the procession some Greenwich pensioners and, probably in response to public demand, some members of the crew of the *Victory*.

Sir Isaac Heard also made sure that the funeral car would bear ample reference to Nelson's professional achievements. He appointed the College of Arms' herald painter, Ange Denis Macquin, a French immigrant, to design the hearse. The most obvious feature of the funeral car was that it was shaped in the form of the *Victory*, Nelson's flagship at the battle of Trafalgar. The ship-shaped hearse was decorated with a personification of fame as a figurehead, holding a laurel wreath in her outstretched hand. Apart from heraldic imagery on the sides of the 'ship', the emblematic decoration of the funeral car consisted of elements that would be understood by contemporary onlookers:

imitations of palm trees (for the battle of the Nile) supported a canopy that was decorated with Nelson's motto (*Palmam qui meruit ferat* – those who merit it shall bear the palm) and black feathers (since the mid-eighteenth century these were traditional elements of a hearse). Additional inscriptions on the canopy and on the car itself read 'Nile' and 'Trafalgar' and also listed were the four most famous ships Nelson had taken or sunk. In bearing such imagery, instead of merely intricate heraldic devices, the hearse could appeal to the aesthetics of many more onlookers.

As the preparations for the funeral developed, the public began to expect it to be unequalled 'in point of grandeur and pomp' in British history and they were keen to witness the event.[25] The newspaper columns filled with advertisements either looking for or offering seats with good views of the processions by water or land. The architect responsible for the fabric of St Paul's Cathedral informed the press that the 'applications for seats are so extremely numerous, that . . . [he] gave directions for seats to be made to the top of the arches, which was not originally intended', and that he would create additional seating inside and outside the cathedral so that the whole would be 'upon a larger scale than ever yet was known'.[26] Thousands of people visited St Paul's Cathedral to see the preparations for Nelson's grave; by 6 January 1806 *The Times* reported that 'the door-money . . . has amounted for several days to more than 40l. each day!!' and that it was calculated the cathedral would make in all £1,000 from these admissions.[27] The immense public interest in the event can be explained not only by curiosity, but by a desire to be involved in some small way in an appropriate tribute to a great naval hero, since it was the public will itself, expressed in newspapers, which had urged that the funeral should be celebrated appropriately, long before any details were known about official plans for it. The nature of the public's response to the news of the death of Nelson, particularly the sombre mood that dominated the whole country, clearly indicates a strong emotional reaction to Nelson's death. It is well known that individuals need a mourning process in order to adapt 'to the loss of the object, as well as the readjustment to an external environment wherein this object no longer exists in reality'. This mourning process helps 'to detach the survivors' memories and hopes from the dead'.[28] In view of the fact that Nelson's reputation had reached a peak just before his death, that his last feted visit to Britain (particularly to London) had been little more than a month before his death, that many hopes for the averting of a French invasion had been connected with his last mission and – last, but not least – that the nation felt indebted for his last great victory, it appears likely that the first reactions to his death as well as the extreme interest in his funeral were genuine expressions of collective national grief.

The intense public grief at the news of Nelson's death is also reflected in a massive production of mourning imagery. Mourning figures, as displayed already in the illuminations in immediate response to the news of Nelson's death, became staple illustrations in different media. Prints of all kinds of quality showed mourning female figures or 'Britannia consecrating the Ashes of the Immortal Nelson'.[29] Of the very simple and affordable glass pictures alone, fourteen different designs have survived that represent the public mourning. They all follow the same pattern, which consists of a monument to Nelson (a plinth with a bust or portrait of Nelson) flanked with mourning figures, often weeping sailors. Similar motifs can be found on an immense number of ceramic items, textiles and other pieces, such as jewellery, glasses and boxes, and even on privately produced pieces of needlework. Cabinetmakers went so far as to produce mourning furniture, with the wood inlaid with a black line.

The public interest in mourning Nelson's death naturally found its strongest expression in the different stages of the funeral itself. The event attracted people from many different parts of the country. The rush to see the coffin in the Painted Hall at Greenwich surpassed all expectations. *The Times* reported that so many people pressed to see the lying-in-state that those who got into the hall were 'pushed onward with such rapidity, as to afford none of them the opportunity of having more than a short and transient glance of the solemn object of their curiosity'. The same account estimated that 'above twenty thousand persons were unable to gratify themselves'.[30] The situation on the second day of the three-day lying-in-state, though supported by 'Volunteers', was no better:

> the rushing torrent of the multitude was so impetuous, that . . . many were crushed in a dreadful manner, in the competition for entrance . . . others were beaten down by the impetuosity of those who rushed forward from behind, and very severely trampled – in many cases, almost to death. Shoes, pattens, muffs, tippets, coat sleeves, skirts of pelices and gowns, without number were despoiled from their owners, and trampled in the mud.

The Times insisted, however, that inside the hall the best order prevailed and the 'distinctions of rank were forgotten in the general avidity to pay the last melancholy honours to the Hero's remains'.[31] It was only on the third and last day of the lying-in-state that, with the help of 'the King's Life Guards', some order could be established in the crowds that pressed forward for admission to the Painted Hall, although even then some 'Ladies . . . were so severely squeezed, that . . . [they] fainted'. Within the hall only now was the pall taken from the coffin to display it completely and the six mourners grouped parallel to the coffin facing towards it, so that 'the effect was much more solemn and impressive'.[32] The last act of the lying-in-state was an exclusive visit by the seamen and marines of the *Victory*, who had been chosen to take part in the procession. 'After this part of the ceremony, the doors and gates were closed, and an immense concourse of people, extending almost from Greenwich to

London, were under the necessity of returning, ungratified with the sight for which they had so anxiously pressed forward.'[33]

The procession by water was the first occasion for the wider public to see the coffin and large numbers seized this opportunity. The *Gentleman's Magazine* described how the 'decks, yards, rigging, and masts of the numerous ships on the river, were all crowded with spectators; and the number of ladies was immense'.[34] Like the remark in *The Times* about the 'Ladies' who struggled for admission to the lying-in-state, it appears that the high proportion of female participants from a respectable social background was regarded as unusual for such large crowds. Perhaps women of elegant society felt more encouraged to participate in something that could be expected to develop peacefully and which could be interpreted as an emotional rather than a political statement. *The Times* remarked about the 'immense' crowd that 'their conduct every where marked their affection for the departed hero'.[35] An eye-witness who had mingled with the crowds wrote to a friend about those assembled: 'Every post of vantage wherever the procession could be seen was swarming with living beings, all wearing mourning, the very beggars having a bit of crape on their arms'.[36] The aquatic procession reached its climax with the landing of Nelson's coffin at Whitehall stairs. The effect was not only underlined by the playing of Handel's 'Dead March in Saul', but also by the sudden appearance of a 'tremendous hailstorm' that finished as suddenly as it had appeared, as soon as the body was landed.[37] In Whitehall, where it was possible to get a closer view of the coffin, the 'windows, as well as the streets . . . were crowded, and even the front wall of the Admiralty, and the roofs of the houses, were crowded with spectators'.[38]

During the night before 9 January 1806, the day of the procession by land to the funeral service in St Paul's Cathedral, Nelson's body was to stay at the Admiralty. Though it had been announced that there would not be another lying-in-state, many people stayed until late at night or waited from the early hours of the morning in the hope of getting a glimpse of the coffin, either inside the Admiralty or on its first appearance. Along the route of the funeral procession crowds started assembling from six o'clock in the morning. According to one eye-witness:

> while it was still dark hundreds more than what are usually seen at mid-day, were assembled . . . It would be impossible to convey an adequate idea of the multitude of persons who crowded from all quarters of town and country to witness this interesting spectacle.'[39]

Even those who had found places at the beginning of the processional route had to wait until twelve o'clock for the procession to begin and even longer for the funeral car to appear. When it finally left the Admiralty, the coffin was ceremonially covered by a pall. This disappointed the waiting spectators so much that, at their urgent request, the coffin was exposed to general view and remained so during the rest of the procession. The effect that it produced on the avidly waiting crowds is famously described in Lady Bessborough's words:

> Amongst many touching things the silence of that immense Mob was not the least striking; they had been very noisy. I was in a House in Charing Cross, which look'd over a mass of heads. The moment the Car appear'd which bore the body, you might have heard a pin fall, and without any order to do so, they all took off their hats. I cannot tell you the effect this simple action produc'd; it seem'd one general impulse of respect beyond any thing that could have been said or contriv'd.[40]

Less known is the account of someone who witnessed the same event from within the crowd and thus could also report on what was said: 'As it [the funeral car] passed, all uncovered, and many wept. I heard a great deal said among the people about "poor Emma" [Lady Hamilton], and some wonder whether she will get a pension or not.'[41] It appears that Nelson had an appeal among the wider public not only as a hero, but also as a lover.

The actual interment was celebrated with a grand service at St Paul's Cathedral. The cathedral had filled up shortly after it opened at seven o'clock in the morning, but 'the interest was so deep, that no uneasiness whatever appeared to be produced by the time which it became necessary to wait, exposed to a great severity of cold'.[42] The impressively staged service included music by Handel and Purcell, as well as music specially composed for the occasion. It also used new techniques to illuminate the cathedral and to lower the coffin into the crypt by a mechanism invisible to the spectators. While the body was being deposited, an anthem by Handel was sung, finishing with: 'His body is bury'd in peace. But his name liveth evermore',[43] an expression which might be interpreted as referring to Nelson as well as to Christ. As soon as the body was laid to rest, 'the troops being drawn up in Moorfield, the Artillery fired their guns, and the Infantry gave vollies, by corps, three times repeated'.[44] After this climax to the funeral, Sir Isaac Heard of the College of Arms made the traditional proclamation of the 'Styles' of the deceased to which he added an individual ending: 'and the hero who, in the moment of Victory, fell covered with mortal Glory! Let us humbly trust, that he is now raised to bliss ineffable, and to a glorious immortality!'[45] After another heraldic tradition, the breaking and throwing into the grave of staves, had been completed, the men from the *Victory* gave the scene a final personal touch. They were supposed to lay flags of the *Victory* into the grave, but 'desirous of retaining some mementoes of their great and favourite commander, [they] tore off a considerable part of the largest flag, of which most, if not all, of them, obtained a small portion'.[46] The ceremony was finally concluded a little before six o'clock, but the church was not entirely vacated until past nine.[47]

After the funeral, which had been celebrated with great order throughout London, Nelson's grave became a great attraction for visitors. So far the coffin had merely been sunk into its walled resting place and had not yet been covered by the sarcophagus. Since, moreover, the hole through which the coffin had been lowered into the crypt was not yet closed, spectators could look down onto the coffin: a practice described in a letter to the editor of *The Times* as a 'disgraceful exhibition'.[48] Another attraction was the funeral car, which was first exhibited for two days in the King's Mews (later replaced by Trafalgar Square) and then conveyed to Greenwich Hospital.

The funeral prompted a boom in the printing business. Part of the printed output about the funeral consisted not only of newspaper accounts of the event, mostly filling several columns, but also complete publications dedicated solely to the funeral. Other printed works on offer to the mourning public included prints of the coffin, the armorial bearings, the funeral barge and car, as well as different stages of the funeral. The *Naval Chronicle* published a print of the funeral car opposite the title page of its volume for the first half of 1806 and *The Times* dedicated nearly one whole page of its four pages on 10 January 1806 to illustrations and descriptions of the funeral car and coffin. Glass pictures, which were produced in great numbers for less well-off customers, instead of focusing on the coffin with its emblematical decorations, showed the funeral barge and the funeral car, elements that anybody present at the funeral could have seen, even from a distance.

Most varied are the prints that include the celebration of the funeral, particularly the processions, because they also give some idea of the public reaction to what was going on. It needs to be kept in mind, however, that the documentary value of these prints is often diminished, because some of them clearly reflect the kind of customer their producers wished to attract. In his representation of the procession by water, Edward Orme, for example, chose to represent spectators in the foreground that he may have regarded as representative of his customers in elegant society: ladies and gentlemen in their Sunday dress walk leisurely along the riverside, with the procession by water unfolding before the skyline of London. There is only a small group of less elegant people on the right of the picture, where they appear more as decorative elements than actual participants of the scene, because their view of the procession by water is blocked by buildings (see plage 1). J. T. Smith, on the other hand, showed from a similar perspective (the procession in front of the City of London with St Paul's Cathedral depicted) crowds of ordinary people set in a typical port scene; around a crane on the shore and on barges they look at the procession, holding up their children; a scene that reminds us much more of the written contemporary accounts and that reflects much better the character of Southwark as the industrial side of the river Thames than does Orme's elegant engraving. G. Thompson added drama to the assembled crowds; instead of choosing an impressive background, he presented a view of Blackfriars Bridge, with onlookers standing behind and even in front

1 *View from the House of W. Tunnard, Esq., when the remains of the great Admiral Lord Nelson were conveyed from Greenwich to Whitehall, drawn & etched by* J. T. Smith (1806) © National Maritime Museum, London

of the balustrade, a hat falling down from the bridge and a spectator being pulled out of the water at the moment Nelson's funeral barge passes.

Beyond such mere pictorial representations, people who had missed parts or all of the funeral wished to have a similar experience and so efforts were made to re-enact the event by different means. The Foundling's Hospital performed the programme of the funeral service. In Bristol the day of the funeral itself was celebrated from 'early in the morning . . . [when] the funeral knell began tolling, which continued throughout the day'; 'on the Exchange, where three or four thousand persons were assembled [t]he military band of the North-Gloucester Militia appeared in full dress uniform, with mourning, . . . [and] performed a solemn dirge'.[49]

The *Glasgow Herald* pointed out that 'though prevented, by local situation, from bearing our part in this enviable tribute, the citizens of Glasgow have still the means of evincing the liberal spirit for which they are eminent' by subscribing to a Nelson monument. When the foundation stone to the monument was laid in the summer of the same year, this was celebrated with a procession and service, as if in imitation of the funeral.[50] 'An "exact copy" of the coffin was exhibited at the Assembly Room in Lincoln, in order to "gratify" country families', and in Hull a businessman even rebuilt the whole lying-in-state.[51] Some theatres presented entire re-enactments of the funeral processions with 'moving figures', though the performance in the Manchester Theatre failed when the figures, representing the participants, fell from the stage and caused laughter among the spectators and a rebuke from a reviewer as 'improper' behaviour.[52]

2 *A View of the Funeral Procession by Water from Greenwich to Whitehall*, G. Thompson (1806) ©
National Maritime Museum, London

The funeral, therefore, afforded an outlet for the nation's grief at the death
of Nelson. It was a means of coming to terms with a traumatic national shock
and of paying public tribute to the great hero.[53] How this strong emotional
response can be explained by an examination of the person of Nelson himself
will be the subject of the first part of this book, and how the emotional
response was subsequently exploited and transformed will be described in
the second part.

Part I

A controversial life

1

The disobedient officer

Horatio Nelson's early career in the navy did not show much of those traits that might reveal a distinct individuality, let alone a most promising one. Instead, his career followed a pattern that could have been true for any young man of his social background. Born on 29 September 1758 as the sixth of a Norfolk clergyman's eleven children, Horatio Nelson began his professional life at the age of twelve, when he joined the Royal Navy. His uncle, Maurice Suckling, using the then common system of patronage, made his nephew a midshipman on his own ship. In the following years this uncle took care that his young relative would get opportunities to gain experience in his profession by serving on different ships. Whenever possible the uncle gave his support and before his own death he managed to arrange his nephew's lieutenant's examination and to ensure that his protégé would get a promising posting on a man-of-war in the West Indies. This last favour proved to be the ideal step on the career ladder to the rank of captain.

If anything particularly marked the start of Nelson's career it was his great zeal: a zeal not only for whatever task the young man was set, but also to take on challenges in the first place. As a fourteen-year-old the young Horatio Nelson had successfully insisted on joining a polar expedition on which 'no boys' were allowed. As a lieutenant, he later volunteered to take a prize in a storm. He even defined his own task, when, as a captain of only twenty-one years of age, he was ordered to transport a military expedition to the coast of central America. On landing the troops he noticed that the expedition was lacking the necessary equipment and so he decided to support it with his ship's crew and boats, although this was not covered by his orders. Nelson had correctly assessed that the expedition would have been doomed without his support; but, in giving it, tropical illnesses had the opportunity to spread among more people. In the course of this risky undertaking most of his men lost their lives and Nelson himself saw his own health severely damaged. The aspiring young Captain Nelson appears therefore to have been rather over-zealous in fulfilling whatever task was given him, even helping others to fulfil their tasks. Soon he proved also that his enthusiasm could lead him to decisions that were uncomfortably independent of those taken by his superior.

In 1784, when still only twenty-five years of age, Nelson found himself senior captain of the Leeward Islands station under Admiral Hughes and in command of its northern division. In this position Nelson noticed that – following old commercial links – a considerable amount of trade was going on between the islands and the newly independent United States of America. Nelson knew that this trade benefited the inhabitants of the islands and 'filled their pockets',[1] but, at the same time, it contravened the Navigation Acts which prohibited these British colonies from having direct commerce with foreign countries; and the United States of America, although former colonies, had now to be seen as a foreign country. Nelson felt a strong need to defend the Navigation Acts, because, in his view, it was necessary to 'preserve the Carrying Trade to our Country, as it encouraged British artificers, manufacturers, and seamen'.[2] To disregard the Navigation Acts meant in his view to reduce the government's revenue and possibly lose the islands: 'The residents of these Islands are Americans by connexion and by interest, and are inimical to Great Britain.'[3] Consequently, Nelson convinced his superior, Admiral Hughes, to issue an order against these practices. The fact that Nelson obeyed this order unreservedly caused outrage among the islanders, which was forcibly expressed by Governor Shirley.[4] Admiral Hughes, of whom Nelson had said several months previously that he 'bows and scrapes too much', reacted to this protest by issuing a revised order that left the judgement of the trade to the civil authorities.[5] In answer to this new order Nelson wrote to Admiral Hughes: 'Whilst I have the honour to command an English Man of War, I never shall allow myself to be subservient to the will of any Governor, nor co-operate with him in doing *illegal* acts. Presidents of Council I feel myself superior to.' On the opinion of the attorney-general, who had taken Governor Shirley's view, Nelson commented in the same letter: 'How the King's Attorney-General conceives he has a right to give an illegal Opinion, which I assert the above is, he must answer for. I know the Navigation Law.'[6]

Having decided to disregard his superior's order, Nelson carried on defending his cause. Supported by his friends, the Collingwood brothers (both captains), he continued to pursue this line and interrupted the illegal inter-American trade for a period of about three years. At the beginning of this period he wrote to an old friend: 'I have given my answer to the Admiral upon the subject; how he will like it I know not: but I am determined to suppress the admission of Foreigners.'[7] Nelson informed the Admiralty about the illegal trade in the West Indies, reported to the secretary of state, Lord Sydney, and wrote to his brother: 'I feel I am perfectly right, you know upon those occasions I am not famous for giving up a point.'[8] The fact that Nelson acted according to his principles, even interrupting trade with the USA, caused him some trouble with the local merchants. 'Having done what was my duty' – as Nelson called it – 'some people in these Colonies . . . have taken the first opportunity of making me suffer pecuniary Punishment, although what they have charged me with they know is as false as anything can possibly be'.[9] Nevertheless, these accusations kept Nelson from going ashore and forced him to remain a 'close prisoner [on board his ship] for eight weeks'.[10] Fortunately, 'His Majesty has been pleased to direct that the Law Officers of the Crown should defend the suit' against Nelson and as a result 'all the prosecutions against me [Nelson] were dropped'.[11] Some months later Nelson described his dilemma:

> I must either disobey my orders, or disobey Acts of Parliament, which the Admiral was disobeying. I determined upon the former, trusting to the uprightness of my intention, and believed that my Country would not allow me to be ruined, by protecting her Commerce.[12]

This remark, like his whole action to enforce the Navigation Acts, demonstrates that Nelson had developed an independent judgement that enabled him, first, to see where his superior acted against clear rules and, second, to dare to counteract his decision in such a case. The remark also illustrates that he was hoping for recognition of his superior judgement by those on a higher level ('my Country would not allow me to be ruined, by protecting her Commerce'). These hopes were only partly fulfilled, when the Admiralty finally approved of his proceedings – praising Admiral Hughes for it! As a result Nelson regarded himself as confirmed in what he did, while he was disappointed in his hopes of gaining recognition for it.

Nelson's acts of disobedience in the West Indies have attracted much controversy among his biographers, not only because it was his first major act of insubordination, but also because it was by far the most persistent and therefore so much more difficult to ignore. Nelson's consistency in insisting on the implementation of the Navigation Acts against his superior's wishes was particularly hard to accept for Nelson's early biographers. They rather wished to present their hero as a model of obedience. One of them went even further than merely asserting Nelson's obedience. He invented a little story about Nelson's ideals of subordination and political loyalty. Nelson's political message was said to have been summarized in the following set of rules given to a midshipman:

> 'There are three things, young gentleman', said he, 'which you are constantly to bear in mind: first, you must always implicitly obey orders, without attempting to form any opinion of your own respecting their propriety; secondly, you must consider every man as your enemy who speaks ill of your king; and, thirdly, you must hate a Frenchman as you do the devil.'[13]

This passage, fanciful as it was, was copied into the influential biography of Nelson written later by Robert Southey, and through him it gained wide currency thereafter.[14]

Later in the nineteenth century Nelson's acts of disobedience in the West Indies were addressed more directly. Over time two ways of interpreting them emerged. One approach was used by authors of biographies aimed at the wider market, while the other was more thoroughly argued by scholarly naval historians. The former approach uniformly praised Nelson for disobeying his admiral in the West Indies. In justification of Nelson's actions, writers referred to Nelson's highly developed concept of duty, without explaining how such an act of insubordination can be regarded as the fulfilment of his 'duty'.[15] The fascination that Nelson's act of disobedience exerted on later historians was probably due less to any feasible concept of 'duty', than to the single-mindedness he displayed in the face of adversity. Nelson was now regarded as 'a law unto himself', and as a maverick who went his own way, overcoming all odds, without due recognition from the establishment.[16]

The famous naval historians, Laughton and Mahan, investigated Nelson's acts of disobedience in the West Indies more thoroughly than earlier writers. Laughton, though acknowledging that Nelson was 'right in his contention', insisted on the formalities of a hierarchically structured organization:

> The first duty of an officer is to obey orders, to submit his doubts to the Commander-in-Chief, and in a becoming manner to remonstrate against any order he conceives to be improper; but for an officer to settle a moot-point himself, and to act in contravention of an order given under presumably adequate knowledge of the circumstances, is subversive of the very first principles of discipline.[17]

Mahan was more generous. In a letter to Laughton he pointed out that he thought 'Nelson's course towards Hughes [was] justified upon the whole', because 'Nelson owed it to . . . his country's interest . . . to do as he did'.[18]

Authors in the twentieth century did not pursue this line of argument about whether Nelson's acts of disobedience in the West Indies might be justified or even necessary. Instead of investigating these acts within their professional context, authors preferred to explore them from a psychological viewpoint. Following this approach, C. S. Forester, in his biography of 1929, searched for Nelson's motives. He observed a general restlessness in Nelson and a dislike of Admiral Hughes that combined to explain 'the attraction the disobeying of ill-conceived orders had for Nelson'.[19] Even biographies written by naval officers now viewed Nelson's acts of disobedience more as attempts to challenge those in higher social positions than as decisions dictated by naval circumstances. Nelson's disobedience in the West Indies was described as performed notwithstanding 'social ostracism'.[20] In the second half of the twentieth century Nelson's zeal for the implementation of the Navigation Acts in the West Indies tended still to be treated in the same fashion. Nelson is described as 'socially ostracized' and his action is interpreted as a reflection of Nelson's 'contempt' for his superior.[21] More recent biographies do not use this psychological approach any more. Instead they tend to maintain that Nelson acted in a 'self-righteous' manner as an 'immature firebrand'.[22]

Not all of Nelson's acts of disobedience, however, can be interpreted as expressions of youthful defiance of authority. Ten years after his prolonged insubordination in the West Indies, Nelson committed what came to be regarded as one of his most famous acts of disobedience. During the battle of Cape St Vincent, on 14 February 1797, Nelson, by now already a commodore, moved his ship out of the rear of the British line of battle and sailed directly towards the Spanish line. His superior at the time, Sir John Jervis, had supported Nelson's career in the previous year and he went on to do so – even against resistance from within the navy – in the years that followed this battle, which earned him the title of Earl St Vincent. In view of Jervis's reaction, can Nelson's manoeuvre on this occasion have been an act of disobedience at all? Historians disagree on the matter.

Nelson himself stated in his own report about the battle of Cape St Vincent: 'the Admiral made the signal to "tack in succession"; but I . . . ordered the ship to be wore'.[23] Consequently, most biographers assumed that Nelson had acted independently of his superior's order, if not directly against it. The daring manoeuvre was generally praised, because as a result of it Nelson managed to take two much larger ships, although his move was not immediately followed by any other ships from his part of the fleet (the rear portion of the British line). Only fairly recently has it been claimed that Nelson did not only achieve a pleasing result for his superior, but that he actually followed his commander's orders. The argument goes that the signalling code did not allow Jervis to express exactly what he intended to say, so that he had to combine two different orders, hoping that in their entirety they would be understood in just the way Nelson executed them.[24] That explains why Jervis was content with what Nelson did, but it does not prove that Nelson actually saw both signals, particularly since they are not recorded in his ship's log-book. Even supposing Nelson had seen both signals, however, it is accepted that only he interpreted them (if not the whole situation) in the right way and possessed the daring to execute what was required.

There is no doubt whatsoever about the character of another act of disobedience, committed in the Bay of Naples in the summer of 1799 against the then commander-in-chief in the Mediterranean, Admiral Keith. By now Nelson had established his reputation as a famous admiral, thanks to the battle of the Nile, fought on 1 August 1798. At the end of June 1799 Nelson had just accomplished the reconquest of the city of Naples,[25] and he had sent men ashore to defeat the French garrisons in Capua and Gaeta, two towns north of Naples, when he received Keith's order to join him with his force. Keith, assuming Nelson to be still in Sicily, needed these forces to protect Minorca (at that time in the hands of the British) against an attack by the French fleet which was at large in the Mediterranean. Nelson's squadron was needed even more if the French should manage to combine with the Spanish fleet. Nelson could not have reacted immediately to Keith's order, because he had employed too many men ashore, but, in any case, he decided to keep them there. Weighing the likely loss (or at least relapse into chaos) of Naples, if his forces should retire, against the danger to Minorca, Nelson decided 'that it is better to save the Kingdom of Naples and risk Minorca, than to risk the Kingdom of Naples to save Minorca'.[26] Although an attack on Minorca was not attempted and the French fleet did not combine forces with the Spanish fleet, the Admiralty disapproved of Nelson's conduct for two reasons: first, he should not have sent so many sailors inland (to Capua), thereby weakening his own force, and, second, he should not have employed his whole squadron in the reconquest of the kingdom of Naples.[27] Nelson complained to a friend that he had been 'censured': 'My conduct is measured by the Admiralty, by the narrow rule of law, when I think it should have been done by that of common sense. I restored a faithful Ally by breach of orders'.[28] Nelson had become so convinced of his own ability to judge a situation and to decide competently and honourably that he dared to use his own standards, even when they contravened what he acknowledged as 'the law', again hoping for subsequent recognition of his superior judgement by those on a higher level.

The complexity of the situation Nelson was in at Naples in 1799 is rarely assessed properly by those who judge his disobedience at the time. Nelson's defenders have often been hero-worshippers, among them Theodore Roosevelt and Admiral John Fisher, who defended Nelson's disobedience against Keith as an act of a 'great soldier [who] may disregard rules which must be binding upon all save those of transcendent ability'.[29] Most authors, however, agree in condemning Nelson for disobeying Keith in 1799, though they do not offer much better arguments than the Nelson-worshippers have done. The critics of Nelson's disobedience against Keith often merely state that Nelson was enthralled by Lady Hamilton at the time, thereby assuming that his decision cannot have been justifiable. The search for motives for Nelson's decision to disobey Keith became central to those authors who wrote about Nelson after the First World War. In pursuing a psychological approach, twentieth-century authors found the explanation for Nelson's insubordination in the appeal to Nelson of 'asserting his own opinion against that of his superior officer'.[30] These authors looked for the reasons for Nelson's acts of disobedience within Nelson's psychology and mostly outside the actual circumstances in which Nelson found himself at Naples.

Few have bothered to investigate Nelson's disobedience against Keith as an admiral's decision taken in very difficult circumstances. Biographers in the early nineteenth century, who still mostly defended Nelson, approached the matter either by pointing out that Keith did not know the real situation Nelson was in (Keith assumed he was in Sicily) or by measuring Nelson's disobedience by its final success. Naval historians of the late nineteenth century found it hard to defend Nelson's disobedience against Keith. They were too worried about the 'grave importance' of the example of the 'crime – and from the military point of view it was a crime' – of Nelson's act of disobedience.[31] When assessing the actual matter they agreed that disobedience must not be measured ex post facto by its outcome, but nor did they succeed in developing any feasible ex ante criteria that would describe when disobeying orders might be justified. In discussing matters of disobedience, the influential naval historian A. T. Mahan alluded generally to the 'conditions of the case' and positively allowed for disobedience to be justifiable: 'It seems scarcely necessary to say that . . . an officer in subordinate command should have the moral courage to transcend or override his orders in particular instances'. However, he then went on: 'it would be impossible for military operations to be carried on at all, if the commander-in-chief were liable to be deliberately defied and thwarted in his combinations, as Keith was in this case'. Since it is in the nature of acts of disobedience to 'thwart' the 'combinations' of a superior, Mahan was unable to offer any general criteria for determining when an act of disobedience is justified. In the specific case of Nelson's decision to disobey Keith, Mahan did not consider the fact that Nelson was better informed about the situation in Naples than was Keith, who did not even know that Nelson was at Naples. Instead of analysing Nelson's decision in the actual circumstances he was facing, Mahan resorted to the hierarchical division of responsibility: 'It was not within his [Nelson's] province to decide whether Minorca or Naples was the more important. That was the function of the commander-in-chief.'[32] But Keith, being ignorant of the true situation, could not possibly be in a position to decide between the relative importance of Minorca and Naples.

Ludovic Kennedy attempted another approach when he argued, in 1951, that, in counteracting Keith's order, Nelson was not taking a decision about the relative importance of Minorca or Naples; instead 'the real issue at stake was . . . the British Fleet', which Nelson endangered by not sending his ships to join Keith.[33] Later authors have not attempted to investigate the matter further. They usually agree in condemning Nelson's disobeying of Keith in the Mediterranean as 'intolerable' or 'unacceptable' and they do not make any great effort to substantiate this claim,[34] let alone develop feasible criteria for judging such acts of disobedience.

Nelson's last is also his most famous act of disobedience. At the battle of Copenhagen, on 2 April 1801, Nelson's superior, Sir Hyde Parker, had dispatched him to attack the Danish ships in their harbour. At the height of the battle, apparently fearing a defeat, Sir Hyde gave a general signal of recall which Nelson ignored. As a result Nelson won the battle. Nelson by now was acting independently of his commander, rather than obeying orders. There had been a hint in a newspaper at the time that it was 'confidently mentioned there was some misapprehension about signals on the 2d of April, which proved rather fortunate than otherwise', but open disobedience was not mentioned.[35] James Harrison, however, quoted Nelson as having said to his captain: 'Foley, you know I have lost an eye, and have a right to be blind when I like; and, damn me, if I'll see that signal!'[36] Other biographers offered a variation: 'You know I can see but with one eye, and I must keep that upon the enemy.'[37] In 1809 Clarke and M'Arthur published a more detailed version, which they took from an eye-witness account that Colonel Stewart had given them:

> When the signal, No. 39, was made, the Signal Lieutenant reported it to him. He continued his walk, and did not appear to take notice of it. The Lieutenant meeting his Lordship at the next turn asked, 'whether he should repeat it?' Lord Nelson answered, 'no, acknowledge it'. On the Officer returning to the poop, his Lordship called after him, 'is No. 16 [for 'close action'] still hoisted?' the Lieutenant answering in the affirmative, Lord Nelson said, 'Mind you keep it so'. He now walked the deck considerably agitated, which was always known by his moving the stump of his right arm. After a turn or two, he said to me, in a quick manner, 'Do you know what's shown on board of the Commander-in-Chief, No. 39?' On asking him what that meant, he answered, 'Why, to leave off Action'. 'Leave off Action!' he repeated, and then added, with a shrug, 'now, damn me if I do'. He also observed, I believe, to Captain Foley, 'You know, Foley, I have only one eye – I have a right to be blind sometimes'; and then with an archness peculiar to his character, putting the glass to his blind eye, he exclaimed, 'I really do not see the signal'.[38]

Southey used this account, slightly reworded, in his biography of Nelson, while Nicholas Harris Nicolas copied word for word from the original of Colonel Stewart's narrative into his influential *Dispatches and Letters of Lord Nelson*,[39] so that this version became part of the standard account of Nelson at the battle of Copenhagen. None of the earlier writers on Nelson commented in any way on this act of disobedience, so that the story merely appeared as an amusing joke, reflecting on Nelson's aggressive fighting style.

As with Nelson's disobeying of Keith, it was Ralfe, in 1828, who first felt reluctant to defend Nelson's act of disobedience at Copenhagen. This time he did so by explaining it away. Contradicting Southey, Ralfe claimed that Sir Hyde Parker had been about to send Captain Otway to ask whether Nelson 'saw a probability of success. But before Captain Otway could reach the Elephant [Nelson's flagship], the signal was made. It was however disregarded.'[40] Southey accepted the criticism and included in the edition of 1831 of his *Life of Nelson* a paragraph in which he described how Sir Hyde Parker decided to make the signal of recall 'for Nelson's sake. If he is in a condition to continue the action successfully, he will disregard it; if he is not, it will be an excuse for his retreat, and no blame can be imputed to him.'[41] The *Recollections of the Life of the Rev. A. J. Scott*, who had been Sir Hyde's chaplain at the time, added another twist to the story. The *Recollections*, published by Scott's daughter and son-in-law after his death, explain 'that it had been arranged between the admirals that, should it appear that the ships which were engaged were suffering too severely, the signal for retreat should be made, to give Lord Nelson the option of retiring if he thought fit'.[42] These explanations, which served the dual purpose of avoiding the issue of disobedience and saving the honour of Sir Hyde Parker, were frequently adopted by later biographers, although they fail to explain why Sir Hyde gave a *general* order (and not one addressed only to Nelson), if he had wished to leave the final decision to Nelson.

Omitting any analysis of the battle of Copenhagen, Edinger and Neep, in 1930, used their characteristic leitmotif of the 'neurotic' Nelson. They described his disobedience on that occasion: 'He had flagrantly disobeyed orders in a gambler's fling for Victory and Renown.'[43] For them, Nelson's actions thus became the expression of a histrionic temperament rather than rational actions dictated by the circumstances of the actual situation in which he found himself. It was only in 1972 that the details of Nelson's disobedience at the battle of Copenhagen were again examined. Dudley Pope looked in depth at the log-books of the ships in Nelson's squadron and concluded that no one involved understood Sir Hyde Parker's *general* order as permissive.[44] Nevertheless, biographers have gone on using or referring to those accounts mentioned above, which are designed to show that Sir Hyde Parker wished to give Nelson a choice of whether or not to retreat.

The issue of Nelson's acts of disobedience, important as these are for his career, has hardly ever been thoroughly addressed. Nelson's acts of disobedience in battle (Cape St Vincent and Copenhagen) have been described as feats of daring, criticized as dangerous examples or reinterpreted as being in accordance with the real wishes of his commander-in-chief. The less spectacular, but more complex, disregarding of orders in the West Indies and the Mediterranean has been harder to address. Even the naval historians of the late nineteenth century did not succeed in explaining their criteria for an ex ante assessment that could justify such acts of disobedience. The field therefore has remained open for dramatization, either in the direction of describing Nelson as a heroic genius able to flout the standards expected of ordinary mortals or towards supposed motives of another kind. The latter became particularly popular in the twentieth century as a result of the growing interest in psychological inquiry and the desire to distance oneself from Victorian hero-worship. So far no author has offered clear criteria by which to judge Nelson's acts of disobedience.

2

The commander

Nelson's main claim to fame is based on his successes as a commander winning great naval battles. The naval encounters that won him fame were the battles of Cape St Vincent (1797), the Nile (1798), Copenhagen (1801) and Trafalgar (1805). The battle of Cape St Vincent, which first brought Nelson's name to the attention of the wider British public, has already been mentioned in the previous chapter, where Nelson's independent, if not disobedient, action was discussed. Questions of obedience, however, were not the focal point of public interest. If anything in Nelson's report, which was meant to publicize his part in the battle, caught the public imagination at the time, it was his dash and daring in taking two much larger enemy ships. Not much more about this bold exploit was known except that Nelson himself had led the boarding party. When Nelson became famous after the battle of the Nile, publishers wished to satisfy their readers with more details about the hero's life and achievements. One journal published a first life of Nelson. For its account about the battle of Cape St Vincent it relied on Nelson's own short report and the more elaborate account provided by an eye-witness, who had observed the battle from a distance. Thus, lacking further information about how Nelson had actually boarded the two enemy ships, these earliest biographers added drama by inventing that Nelson exclaimed, 'Westminster Abbey! or glorious Victory!', when he led the attack on the Spanish ship-of-the-line.[1] Although the choice between 'Westminster Abbey' and a 'glorious victory' is somewhat contradictory in itself (the first is rarely achieved without the second), the ejaculation appealed to contemporary taste.

Early biographers not only adopted this supposed quotation for the battle of Cape St Vincent, but extended its use when interest in Nelson exploded after his victory and death at the battle of Trafalgar. Now it was recorded that Nelson shouted his battle-cry before the battle of the Nile and before the battle of Trafalgar. In some biographies the exclamation became a general battle-cry of Nelson's or even a kind of motto for his life. In their substantial biography Clarke and M'Arthur produced a variation and gave it a more sedate setting, just before the battle of the Nile: 'On his officers rising from table and repairing to their separate stations, he exclaimed, *Before this time tomorrow, I shall have gained a Peerage, or Westminster Abbey.*'[2] This version has been copied and is still to be found in recent biographies, while the earlier version for the battle of Cape St Vincent has been retold so often that it appears to be regarded as established fact.

It is very likely that what Nelson did at the battle of Cape St Vincent would never have attracted as much public interest had Nelson not won the battle of the Nile less than eighteen months later. It was this victory which made Nelson famous, because in modern naval history it was unequalled in its decisiveness and because it was sorely needed at the time it was fought. The victory was of such vital political importance because it finally broke a long chain of uninterrupted conquests by Napoleon Bonaparte. This time he had aimed for India, via Egypt. The French fleet of thirteen ships-of-the-line that transported him and his troops had escaped a small British squadron of four ships-of-the-line under Admiral Nelson and reached Egypt, where General Bonaparte set out on his terrestrial conquest. Nelson, reinforced by ten more ships-of-the-line after a long search throughout the Mediterranean finally found the French fleet on 1 August 1798, in Aboukir Bay at the mouth of the Nile, where it had anchored in a supposedly secure position.

One of the reasons why the French fleet was apparently at an important advantage was because it was at anchor. In order to attack this fleet Nelson's own ships would have to manoeuvre into a position that would give his guns a good angle from which to fire. To achieve that position the ships would have to anchor. The anchoring itself would be a most dangerous act, because the ships would first have to sail at some speed in order to be able to manoeuvre into their chosen positions. In order to stop a sailing ship the anchor would have to be let down at the stern of the ship. Alone the positioning of the anchor for such a manoeuvre was complicated enough, because the very heavy anchor would have to be moved from the bow to the stern of the ship and its cable would have to be manoeuvred through the inside of the ship and out through its rearmost gunport. Another cable would have to be fastened to it (coming through the rearmost gunport of the other side of the ship) in order to ensure that the anchor would not make the ship move sideways when it reached the bottom. Apart from the danger of moving the ship uncontrollably sideways, anchoring with a stern anchor had the unavoidable consequence of pulling the stern of the ship down and raising the bow with a sudden jerk the moment the anchor hit the bottom of the sea. This effect would be aggravated the faster the ship was still sailing, and Nelson's ships would have to sail at about three knots in order to be manoeuvrable. Any crew expected to execute such an intricate manoeuvre would have to be very well trained indeed. In fact, the ship itself needed to be prepared, since the sudden jerk that was to be expected could do serious damage, particularly if it loosened a heavy gun that could hurt many members of the crew and do immense damage to the inside of the ship. Any attack against a fleet at anchor was therefore dangerous enough under any circumstances. In addition to the advantage of a fleet at anchor, the French fleet had anchored in a very favourable position. The bay of Aboukir was surrounded by shoals, so that it was possible to enter it only through a narrow opening. Under ordinary sailing conditions that meant that the incoming fleet would head for the centre of the French fleet, where the French admiral had concentrated his most powerful ships, including his own flagship. In short, an intruder would have to expect the most unpleasant reception. On top of these technical advantages, the timing of Nelson's arrival was unfortunate for the British, since it was just getting dark when they reached the bay. Nelson's ships would have to manoeuvre and fight in the gloom and in waters unknown to them.[3]

Notwithstanding all these disadvantages for the British, Nelson decided to attack immediately. Why? The difficult anchoring manoeuvre did not deter him, because he had experienced crews on board his ships, whom he believed to be able to execute the necessary manoeuvre. He had also prepared everything necessary for such a risky step. During the weeks before he eventually found the French fleet, he had conferred with his captains about different possible situations in which they might find their enemy, and he had 'decreed that if the battle was fought inshore the ships should have an anchor ready at the stern'.[4] Nelson risked the dangers of an attack at night-time for two reasons. First, he could hope to achieve a surprise if he attacked immediately, an advantage which would have been lost if he waited until the following day. Indeed, part of the French crews were ashore and they did not manage to get back to their ships in time for the battle. The speed of Nelson's attack also took the French so much by surprise that they found it difficult to get their ships ready for action in time to receive Nelson. Second, and probably more decisively, the direction of the wind was favourable to the British. It blew from an unusual northerly direction. This meant that Nelson could start his attack not at the centre of the French fleet (for which the French had prepared themselves), but at its relatively weak rear. It was more than doubtful that Nelson would find the same advantageous weather conditions the next day and he knew that his former superior, Admiral Hood, had once waited for three days for the wind to change to another direction, by which time his enemies had prepared their defence so well that he had to give up the thought of an attack.[5] Nelson, therefore, seized his opportunity and attacked at once.

Nelson's attack did not start promisingly. On approaching the French line the *Culloden* ran aground on the tip of a shoal at the entrance to the bay, thus reducing Nelson's fighting force from fourteen to thirteen ships. With this involuntary beacon provided, however, the rest of the fleet entered the bay without problems. The line in which the French fleet had anchored corresponded nearly exactly with the direction in which the British sailed into the bay. That made it easy to choose on which side to attack the French. Since the French ships had anchored only with their bow anchors, it was obvious that there would be no shoals within the radius that the ships could describe round their anchors in case of a change of wind. The captain of the first ship in Nelson's line, Foley of the *Goliath*, decided to sail between the French ships and the shore, the side from which they would least expect an attack. When nearly half of Nelson's squadron had successfully performed the difficult manoeuvre of anchoring with their anchors at the stern of their ships, Nelson himself with the *Vanguard* opened the attack from the sea side, thus exposing the rear of the French fleet to fire from both sides. He then advanced towards the French flagship at the centre of the line. The French ships that had been overwhelmed by the British attack at the beginning of the battle soon started striking their flags, while the British were intensifying their efforts on the mighty French flagship, *L'Orient*, with its 120 guns (no British ship taking part in the battle had more than seventy-four guns). At that crucial phase of the battle a lieutenant of the British ship *Alexander*, without the knowledge of his captain (Ball), decided to accelerate the defeat of the French by throwing a 'combustible matter' into the wooden ship. *L'Orient* caught fire and the flames soon spread to its powder magazine, which exploded and blew up the whole ship. Captain Ball mentioned the cause of this fire years later to his secretary, Samuel Taylor Coleridge.[6] It is impossible to say who else was informed about this act that cost the lives of a great many of the crew of the French flagship and accelerated the defeat of the French fleet. All in all, Nelson captured or sank nearly all of the thirteen French ships-of-the-line, allowing only two to escape.

The news of the dramatic and decisive victory came as a great relief to Britain as well as to many other countries in Europe. Accounts of the battle filled newspapers in Britain for days. The victory also inspired diverse forms of public reaction, ranging from theatrical performances, through poetry and songs, graphic prints, an outpouring of mass-produced commemorative pottery and enamelled boxes, to oil portraits and engravings.[7] The only available oil portrait of Nelson that could be used as a pattern for a fairly authentic portrayal was that by Lemuel Francis Abbott. With the dramatic growth in demand for anything representing Nelson, the painter now used the opportunity to produce more oil portraits. Comparing them with his earlier pieces provides an instructive lesson in the creation of a hero's image. Abbott's very first sketch was painted when Nelson had only just returned from his failed attack on Tenerife, in the Canary Islands, with his arm freshly amputated. The oil sketch, taken from life, not surprisingly shows a pale, emaciated face. Abbott gave fresh life to his portrayal in its final version in 1797 by rounding Nelson's cheeks and adding some pink colouration to the otherwise rather white face (see plate 2). In 1799, when Nelson had become very famous, Abbott, still using his original oil sketch, not only added a hat and colourful decorations to the uniform, but also gave Nelson's face a very fresh brown colour. The image of the bright hero in his shiny uniform was further enhanced by an exotic element: Abbott added the so-called chelengk, an ornament traditionally meant to embellish a turban, but here worn on the hat (see plate 3). Nelson had received the piece, made of diamonds, from the Ottoman sultan for having defeated the French, who had invaded his territories. The enthusiastic British public learned that the foreign reaction was not limited to monarchs. Newspapers were full of how Nelson was honoured everywhere, and prints as well as commemorative artefacts flooded the market so that few bothered to enquire further into how Nelson had actually achieved his famous victory.

When details about Nelson's death were published in newspapers after the battle of Trafalgar,[8] biographers wished to explore more fully what Nelson had achieved during the battle of the Nile, which had first made him a national hero. While it was reported of Nelson's last hours that he had insisted on taking his turn to be treated by the surgeons and that he had spoken to Captain Hardy, there was not much known about what Nelson had done or said at the battle of the Nile. There were only two sources: a doubtful account that claimed that Nelson had written 'the celebrated official letter that appeared in the Gazette' immediately after his head wound had been dressed 'that very night'[9] (this 'celebrated letter' was in fact written two days after the battle) and an anonymously published *Narrative* of Nelson's then flag captain, Edward Berry. In this account Berry simply mentioned how he had to keep Nelson informed about the course of the battle, because Nelson was 'below in consequence of the severe wound which he had received in the head during the heat of the attack', and that, on informing Nelson that the French flagship *L'Orient* was on fire, he 'though suffering severely from his wound, came up upon deck, where the first consideration that struck his mind was concern for the danger of so many lives, to save as many as possible of whom he ordered Captain Berry to make every practicable exertion'.[10] A wounded admiral, 'suffering severely' below decks, could not easily be regarded as acting particularly heroically. A threepenny biography of thirty-six pages that promised *Heroic Actions* in its title offered a remedy in the form of the following account:

> The severe wound which Sir Horatio Nelson received, was supposed to have proceeded from langridge shot, or a piece of iron; the skin of his forehead being cut with it at right angles, hung down over his face. Captain Berry, who happened to stand near, caught the admiral in his arms. It was Sir Horatio's first idea, and that of every one, that he was shot through the head. On being carried into the cock-pit, where several of his gallant crew were stretched with their shattered limbs, and mangled wounds, the surgeon, with great anxiety, immediately came to attend on the Admiral. 'No!' (replied the hero,) [']I will take my turn with my brave followers.' The agony of his wound increasing, he became convinced, that the idea he had long indulged of dying in battle, was now about to be accomplished. He immediately, therefore, sent for his chaplain, the Rev. Mr. Comyns, and

begged him to remember him to Lady Nelson; and having signed a commission, appointed his friend, the brave Hardy, Commander of the Mutine brig, to the rank of Post-Captain in the Vanguard, Admiral Nelson took an affectionate leave of captain Louis, who had come by his desire on board, and then with the utmost composure, resigned himself to death: When the surgeon came to examine the wound, it evidently appeared that it was not mortal: this joyful intelligence quickly circulated through the ship. As soon as the painful operation of dressing was over, Admiral Nelson immediately sat down, and that very night wrote the celebrated official letter that appeared in the Gazette. He came on deck just time enough to observe the conflagration of L'Orient.[11]

Not only the source, but also the contents of the account give reasons to doubt its authenticity. In its first part it looks suspiciously like the death accounts that were so very popular at the time. Apart from Nelson's wish to take his turn (which was a common element of the death accounts), even Hardy (of 'Kiss me, Hardy' fame) is included in the story. Nelson makes him 'Post-Captain in the Vanguard' without bothering about Captain Berry, who at that very moment was busily engaged in that role. It also appears highly unlikely that Captain Louis would have managed to come on board at the height of the battle, let alone before the surgeon had had a close look at Nelson's wound.[12] Finally, the account of the writing of 'the celebrated official letter that appeared in the Gazette' was obviously copied from the equally doubtful earlier source and also contradicted the facts (the letter was dated 3 August — that is, two days after the battle). Notwithstanding these doubts about the accuracy of this account, all elements of it were copied in the following years and most of them survive in accounts even to this day. The only two components that do not seem to have survived into accounts written in the twentieth century were Hardy's commission and the joy spreading through the ship following the news that Nelson's wound was not mortal. Both elements were copied into the influential biography of Nelson by Robert Southey, however, and thereafter gained currency throughout the nineteenth century.[13]

Some components of the story subsequently underwent further elaboration.[14] The biographers Clarke and M'Arthur combined the claim that 'the skin of his forehead . . . hung down over his face' with another biographer's fanciful assertion: 'the wound on that occasion received in his forehead, by rendering him almost wholly blind, had proved the sole cause of a single French ship's escape'.[15] As a consequence, it was now reported that a 'large piece of the skin of his forehead' hung over Nelson's seeing eye, thus blinding him. This version has found its way into recent biographies, although it contradicts first-hand evidence about the character of the wound itself.[16] The supposed blinding of Nelson also formed part of Clarke and M'Arthur's account of Nelson's report writing. Still regarding Nelson as blinded (now probably because of his bandaged head?), they varied the original story by claiming that Nelson needed help from his secretary in writing his report. The secretary was also said to have been wounded[17] and he supposedly failed in his task because he was too shocked at seeing Nelson's 'blind and suffering state'. When the chaplain was called to help with the writing, the impatient Nelson supposedly took the pen himself and wrote his report.[18] How he could do that without being able to see is not explained.

Around the middle of the nineteenth century, the editor of Nelson's letters combined two separate elements of the story into one new sub-story, based on the memory of Captain Berry's widow, some forty years after the event. Now, it was only Nelson (and not 'every one' around him) who thought that the wound was fatal and, instead of waiting for the chaplain on the orlop deck to send his remembrances to his wife, it was Nelson's first reaction (while still in Berry's arms) to wish to be remembered to his wife.[19] This version, again, has been copied by later biographers and one of them interprets it as an example of Nelson's 'typical morbidity'.[20] Also around the middle of the nineteenth century a biographer of Nelson quoted an eye-witness of the battle of the Nile who had been on Captain Louis' ship (the *Minotaur*) and who now added another detail to the story:

> Lord Nelson during the action sent a boat to the *Minotaur* to require the presence of Captain Louis on board the *Vanguard*. He said, 'Louis, I am wounded and know not to what extent, but your support has prevented me from being obliged to haul out of the line, and I thank you from my soul.[21]

Did Nelson say this in his message or aboard the *Vanguard*? How could the (unnamed) witness know what was 'said'? The evidence is quite flimsy, it appears to be a variation of the familiar story of Nelson and Louis at the Nile, and the eye-witness is not very trustworthy, considering that he is obviously trying to stress the importance of his ship in the success achieved at the battle of the Nile. Nevertheless, even the famous naval historian Mahan used this account in his *Life of Nelson*.[22]

Another early biographer developed part of Berry's *Narrative*. He dramatized Nelson's decision to send out *Vanguard*'s last boat to save survivors from the burning *L'Orient*, by claiming that 'the enemy, on the lower deck, either insensible of the danger that threatened them, or impelled by the last paroxysms of despair and vengeance, continued to fire'.[23] If this had been true, it would have been irresponsible of Nelson to send his men, defenceless in a boat, to aid the French flagship. The dramatization of the story obviously defeats its purpose here. The interest in detailed accounts of Nelson's actions during his battles thus created fanciful stories that have been handed down over the generations by Nelson's biographers and that only serve to distort his image. Instead of attributing certain stories to the theatrical imagination of some of Nelson's early biographers, these same stories have been used to make a theatrical and even histrionic figure of Nelson himself.

Nelson's actions at the battle of Copenhagen did not undergo such dramatization. This can be explained by the uneasiness felt about the battle happening at all. On the one hand, it appeared unnecessary. The news of the battle was followed, one day later, by the news of the death of Tsar Paul I who had been – unlike his son and successor – hostile to Britain. *The Times* remarked: 'Had the news of the Emperor Paul's death reached this place a few days sooner, it is highly probable that the bloody action fought near Copenhagen, would not have taken place.'[24] On the other hand, there was probably also a feeling of uneasiness at fighting Denmark (rather than republican France) at all. Apart from these feelings of unease at the battle having taken place, some commentators doubted whether the British fleet had even been victorious.[25] The reason for such doubts was that Nelson had ended the battle with his letter to 'The brothers of Englishmen', offering negotiations about a truce, instead of delivering a crushing defeat of the Danes (like that of the French at the Nile). It was only years later, when Nelson's disobedience discussed in the previous chapter became known, that some interest in his actions at Copenhagen developed.

The last and most famous of Nelson's victories was at Trafalgar. It was at the same time the only battle that Nelson fought as commander-in-chief; at the Nile he had merely been dispatched by Admiral Earl St Vincent. The extensive powers granted to him in 1805 gave him the greatest possible freedom to plan the battle as he liked – and Nelson made use of this freedom by developing his tactical ideas in unconventional directions. So, how did Nelson win the battle of Trafalgar? His tactics consisted of four major elements: an attack in two separate divisions instead of in a single line; a concentration on the rear of the enemy; the concealment of the nature and exact point of the attack until the last moment; and keeping the enemy's van out of action as long as possible.[26] Each of these four elements needs to be explored in more detail.[27]

Nelson himself gives his reason against forming one single line of battle most clearly in a memorandum that he sent to all his captains:

> Thinking it almost impossible to bring a fleet of forty Sail of Line [in the event he disposed of only twenty-seven ships] into a Line of Battle in variable winds, thick weather and other circumstances which must occur, without such a loss of time that the opportunity would probably be lost of bringing the Enemy to Battle in such a manner as to make the business decisive, I have therefore made up my mind to keep the Fleet in that position of sailing (with the exception of the First and Second in Command) that the Order of Sailing is to be the Order of Battle.[28]

Nelson's anxiety to get his ships into battle as quickly as possible is further apparent in his command to the ships in Collingwood's line 'to set all their sails, even steering [= studding] sails, in order to get as quickly as possible to the Enemy's Line'. Apart from advising the necessity of speed, this passage also shows how Nelson wanted the divisions themselves to be organized. He wanted to retain the order of sailing in the actual battle to avoid a time-consuming rearrangement of the formation of his fleet. Only Nelson's and Collingwood's flagships were to change their positions for the actual battle in order to lead their respective divisions. The two divisions into which Nelson formed his fleet were not only meant to sail fast, but also to be spearheaded by his biggest ships. Nelson had arranged the order of the divisions with a striking concentration of three-deckers at their heads, particularly at the head of his own weather column.

As soon as daylight would permit on the memorable 21 October 1805 (about 6 a.m.) Nelson gave two general signals: one to 'form the order of sailing in two columns', and the other to sail on the course 'E.N.E'.[29] The two signals were immediately followed by the signal to prepare for battle and at 6.45 a.m. Nelson ordered a change of course to the east. Without assuming any specific order, the two divisions now headed for the enemy. At that time Nelson's and Collingwood's flagships (the *Victory* and the *Royal Sovereign*) had already set their studding (or steering) sails and were beginning to lead their respective lines. The other ships followed the example set by the two flagships, setting their studding sails about 8 a.m.[30] At about the same time that the *Victory* and the *Royal Sovereign* were starting to head their respective divisions, the French and Spanish ships began to wear, changing in the process their course from south to north. Thus, Collingwood's division was now heading for the enemy's rear, while Nelson's line was sailing in the general direction of the centre or van of the enemy. As the British ships advanced from the west, their two divisions formed up in a more regular fashion.[31]

The second main feature of Nelson's tactics, the concentration of part of the British forces on the rear of the enemy fleet, was the task of Collingwood's squadron. Nelson decided that in case of an attack from windward, which was the one the British actually executed at Trafalgar, his second-in-command was to 'bear up together . . . and to cut through [the enemy's line], beginning from the 12th ship from the Enemy's Rear'. All subsequent ships would then try to head for 'their exact place' in the enemy's line. This required that the ships, instead of sailing in a line-ahead formation (one ship behind the other), would to some extent have to sail next to each other in order that each ship should be able to attack the enemy almost simultaneously. This manoeuvre Nelson also prepared for with a signal. This signal provided for the manoeuvre to 'Cut through the Enemy's line and engage them on the other side'. In an accompanying note Nelson explained:

> The Ships being prepared are to make all possible sail (keeping their relative Bearings and close order) so that the whole may pass thro' the Enemy's line as quick as possible and at the same time it is recom-

mended to cut away the studding sails if set, to prevent confusion and fire. Each ship will of course pass under the Stern of the one she is to engage if circumstances permit.[32]

This signal indicates not only the plan to pass through the enemy's line at different places from the windward in order to engage the enemy from the leeward, but also the importance of doing so at speed. To set all sails, including even the studding sails, was regarded as extremely risky in an attack, because the canvas was easily inflammable, so that in action a greater number of sails increased the danger of fire. Consequently, no previous battle had ever been started with all possible sails set. Nelson, however, seemed to be prepared to take this risk and he provided against its worst consequences with the instruction to cut away the studding sails when actually engaging with the enemy. In order to get his lee line engaged as quickly as possible with the ships in the enemy's rear, Nelson introduced an element into his memorandum that was new to naval tactics: the independent operational role of the second-in-command. The freedom of action given to Collingwood within Nelson's overall plan would help to ensure that the attack on the enemy's rear could be executed without any dependence on signals from Nelson, who might not be in a position to judge the situation facing his second-in-command and whose signals might in any case not be seen clearly by Collingwood's division.

As a consequence of the independent command given to Collingwood, Nelson did not even have to signal what he wanted in the actual battle. At 8.46 a.m. Collingwood himself signalled to his line to 'form the larboard line of bearing, steering the course indicated'. He was now setting out to fulfil Nelson's plan, expressed in the memorandum, 'for the Lee line to bear up together', without waiting for Nelson to make his specially prepared signal.[33] In view of the relative speed with which Collingwood was heading for the enemy, it was only reasonable to make the signal to form a line of bearing as early as possible, so that the ships following could execute the planned formation during the advance on the enemy. In the event, Collingwood 'changed the formation of his division from an irregular line ahead to an irregular line of bearing'.[34] The irregularity was unavoidable when ships, sailing at different speeds, were trying to get as quickly as possible at enemy ships to whose gunfire they would be exposed for some time without being able to respond. The fact that the ships in the rear of Collingwood's line were lagging behind was not of such consequence, because the Franco-Spanish line was not straight, but curving inwards at the rear, towards the approaching British ships. This irregular formation naturally diminished the distance some ships of Collingwood's line had to sail in order to get to their respective positions in the enemy's line. The French and Spanish ships at the rear of their line were not only in irregular order, but also crowded, because they were joined by the reserve squadron under the command of the Spanish Admiral Gravina, to whom Villeneuve had not given any specific role when he ordered his fleet to wear.[35] This created a problem for Collingwood's approaching lee division. According to Nelson's memorandum, Collingwood was supposed to use his force of fifteen ships to attack the last twelve ships in the enemy's line. Since all the enemy ships were not in a distinct and well-formed line, with some enemy ships obscured by others, Collingwood attacked the fifteenth, instead of the twelfth, ship from the end of the enemy's line. This decision may also have been influenced by the fact that the fifteenth ship from the rear was a three-decker, bearing a Spanish admiral's flag. What all this meant was that Collingwood's division did not have the marked superiority over the force he was attacking that Nelson had intended him to have.

While Collingwood's line engaged the rear portion of the enemy's line, the rest of the Franco-Spanish fleet had to be kept busy or at least distracted. This was to be achieved by concealing until the last possible moment the nature and precise point of attack to be made by Nelson's own division – this was the third major element in Nelson's plan. Nelson, as he put it in his memorandum, would 'endeavour to take care that the movements of the Second in Command are as little interrupted as is possible'. In another passage of the memorandum Nelson also made it clear that one of his aims was to get 'at their Commander-in-Chief [Villeneuve]', whom he expected to be in the centre of the enemy line.[36] How were these two aims, the protection of Collingwood's line against interference from the enemy's centre and van, and the defeat of the enemy's commander-in-chief, to be achieved? In a private conversation with Captain Keats, who had commanded a ship in Nelson's fleet until as late as August 1805, but who was not present at the battle of Trafalgar, Nelson had described what he hoped to achieve: 'I think it will surprise and confound the enemy. They won't know what I am about.'[37] In the text of the signal mentioned above, Nelson was even more explicit about how he would attempt to confound the enemy. In it Nelson went so far as to predict his manoeuvre: 'The Admiral will probably advance his Fleet to the van of theirs before he makes the Signal in order to deceive the Enemy by inducing them to suppose it is his intention to attack their Van.'[38] To make it appear as if he would attack the enemy's van and yet, at the same time, retain the possibility of attacking their centre (where he suspected the enemy commander-in-chief to be positioned), Nelson would have to sail for a point clearly ahead of the centre of the enemy's line, in line-ahead formation. If he adopted a formation that would be better suited for attacking the centre, the enemy would know immediately which part of their line he wanted to attack and they could react accordingly. The disadvantage of sailing down onto the enemy's line in line-ahead formation, however, was that it exposed Nelson's leading ships not only to the enemy's fire during their advance, but also to superior firepower at the moment each of his ships reached the enemy's line. Nelson's ships, meanwhile, could not do much damage to the enemy until they were almost upon their ships, because their guns could not bear upon the enemy as they approached. An additional risk lay in a possible change of direction or abatement of the wind, which could isolate a ship that had thus entered into the enemy's line. Nelson tried to provide against these dangers as well as possible by a means 'without precedent', according to Corbett:

> His highly original and scientific idea was a combination of two principles – high speed, and massing guns to the utmost at the point of shock. For the first time on record the attack was to be made not under 'fighting sails' as usual, but under every stitch the spars would carry. He would gather the highest attainable speed and so bring his momentum to the maximum, and the danger period to the minimum. The second expedient was still more remarkable. It was obtained . . . by massing his three-deckers in the van of his line . . . [This manoeuvre had been suggested by Morogues in his *Tactique Navale* in 1763 and by Admiral Rodney], but it had never been used till Nelson now set his seal upon it . . . He would arm the head of his line for the fatal shock with a mass of fire that nothing could resist, and would overpower the time-honoured defensive formation by sheer weight of metal and momentum.[39]

It appears, therefore, that Nelson was preparing his division for a head-on attack, in line-ahead formation, at some ships close to the enemy's van, so that the enemy would have to be prepared for an attack on its van until the last moment. He still hoped, however, that he might be in a position to attack the centre of the enemy line instead, where the flagship of the commander-in-chief was likely to be located.

On the day of the battle of Trafalgar Nelson maintained his irregularly formed line-ahead formation, as planned. This flexible formation enabled him to approach the centre of the enemy's fleet with his own line and yet, at the same time, let it appear to the enemy that he was heading for their van.[40] He was seeking to obscure his real intentions and he went further by making a feint on the enemy's van. He did this by bearing 'a little to port', as the report of the Admiralty Committee of 1913 states.[41] When the ships of the enemy's rear began firing on Collingwood in the *Royal Sovereign*, Admiral Villeneuve, the enemy's commander-in-chief, ran up his flag. This disclosed the fact that his flagship was the *Bucentaure*, in the centre of the Franco-Spanish line. When, soon afterwards, the *Victory* herself, still steering towards the van, had got within range of the enemy's fire, Nelson's flagship 'bore up to starboard', thus changing course towards the centre of the enemy's line, and started firing, while passing 'down the [enemy's] line' heading for the *Bucentaure*.[42] Nelson had now fulfilled the two main aims he had set his own line: to attack the enemy's commander-in-chief and to keep the enemy in some uncertainty about which part of their fleet he was heading for until he actually delivered his attack. The actual attack was sustained thanks to the 'sheer weight of metal and momentum', as Corbett put it in his discussion of Nelson's plan of attack. The *Victory* (one hundred guns) was only slightly ahead of the *Temeraire* (ninety-eight guns) and the *Neptune* (ninety-eight guns), so that these three-deckers appeared to the Franco-Spanish line as if they were almost abreast of each other; they were closely followed by the *Conqueror* and the *Leviathan* (seventy-four guns each). The *Temeraire* and the *Neptune* had been approaching so dangerously close to the *Victory* that Nelson had to order them to keep their distance.[43] According to the log of the *Temeraire*, that ship had to 'immediately put our helm aport to steer clear of the Victory' when the 'Victory opened her fire'.[44] Several other ships followed Nelson in line-ahead formation, but the research done for the Admiralty Committee report of 1913 revealed that the eighth ship was 'apparently the first vessel in Nelson's line that did not follow immediately after him'.[45]

The last of the four main ideas in Nelson's memorandum was just this tactic of trying to keep the enemy's van out of action for as long as possible. By concealing his actual point of attack, Nelson would force the enemy's van to await a possible attack until the moment he had switched the point of his attack in order to engage the enemy's centre. In his memorandum he stated:

> I look with confidence to a Victory before the Van of the Enemy can succour their Rear, and then that the British fleet would most of them be ready to receive their twenty Sail of the Line, or to pursue them, should they endeavour to make off.

Within Nelson's optimistic statement there is another important message, which was that the British victory over the rear and centre must be accomplished before the enemy's van was able to manoeuvre successfully in order to join the battle. If he could achieve this, the morale of the enemy's van would be low, while a considerable number of the British ships would still be in good enough condition to receive the enemy's attack should they attempt to make it.

As with the other three major elements of Nelson's plan for the battle, the last, too, was fulfilled as he had wished. While the van of the line-ahead formation adopted by Nelson's division had fulfilled its task, the rear was still free to repel any attempt by the enemy's van to recover from this blow. By the time the ships in the van of the Franco-Spanish fleet managed to close in on those ships already engaged, Villeneuve's flagship, the *Bucentaure*, had already struck. This undoubtedly had a devastating impact on the enemy's morale. When the French and Spanish ships of the van later joined the fight, they were met by the ships from the rear of Nelson's division, which had not yet engaged the enemy and which were well positioned to attack these enemy ships. The British ships engaged these ships from the enemy van with such spirit that they succeeded in repelling this superior force. Most ships of the Franco-Spanish van sailed down to support the rear of their whole line when they saw that Collingwood's line was still struggling with some of their own ships. This manoeuvre was too late and also failed to bring any

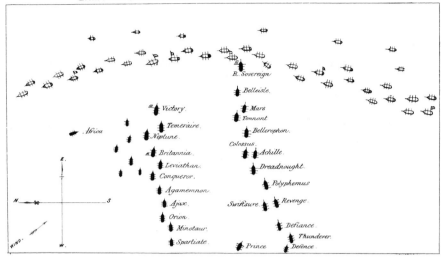

British and Combined Fleets at Noon on the 21st October 1805.

3 Diagram of the battle of Trafalgar, opening stage, from *The Dispatches and Letters of Vice Admiral Lord Viscount Nelson*, ed. Nicholas Harris Nicolas (7 vols., London: Chatham Publishing, 1997, reprint of first edition 1844–6)

material success.[46] The result was a transcendent victory, the greatest in the age of sail.

When the news of the victory at Trafalgar and the death of Nelson reached Britain, no author bothered to enquire seriously into what Nelson's tactics had been. The desire to interpret Nelson's death in battle as an act of martyrdom performed to save his country, as discussed in the prologue, prevented any serious discussion of the tactics he had adopted. Only illustrations of battle plans gave the British public some idea of how the British fleet had approached its Franco-Spanish enemy. These diagrams were based on basic information about the battle: that the Franco-Spanish fleet had formed a long, slightly bent and irregular line which the British attacked from the windward in two 'columns', headed by Nelson's and his second-in-command's (Collingwood's) flagships, the *Victory* and the *Royal Sovereign*. These two columns are shown as sailing parallel to each other and in formation of line-ahead (that is, one ship behind the other) at something like a right angle down onto two points of the centre of the elongated Franco-Spanish line. The emerging pattern of a rectangular approach onto the enemy's centre was not even challenged by the fact that professionals could not make sense of Nelson's tactics when they tried unsuccessfully to include a signal for the *Naval Signal Book* of 1816 copying Nelson's manoeuvre at Trafalgar.[47]

Over the course of most of the nineteenth century the idea that Admiral Nelson had sailed down in two parallel columns onto the enemy at the battle of Trafalgar remained virtually undisputed. Most authors ignored Charles Ekins' suggestion, of 1824, that Nelson planned to attack in line abreast, that is with all ships more or less simultaneously and able to support each other, instead of line-ahead.[48] The contention that Nelson had deviated from his well-calculated plan was brusquely rejected by William James in his influential *Naval History of Great Britain*.[49] Since admirers of Nelson did not analyse Nelson's tactics closely, there remained room to claim that his victories were due more to dash than to thoughtful planning. A widely read author even claimed that Nelson himself had summarized his tactics with the simple rule, 'Never mind manoeuvres, always go at them.'[50]

With the growing interest in naval tactics towards the end of the nineteenth century, the tactics that Nelson employed at the battle of Trafalgar became the most disputed aspect of the battle. In 1899, Admiral Philip Colomb took up Ekins' idea and claimed that Nelson had not only planned to attack in line abreast, but that the British fleet actually fought the battle of Trafalgar in this formation.[51] This challenging new view prompted a vivid controversy of what had happened at Trafalgar. This was fuelled in the first decade of the twentieth century by a variety of publications offering different interpretations, and also by published editions of the log-books of the British ships which had taken part in the battle and of the fighting instructions issued by the Admiralty which advised on tactics at sea in the age of sail.[52] While these publications discarded Colomb's view, they did not offer a clear idea of how Nelson had planned and fought the battle. In his edition of the Admiralty's *Fighting Instructions*, of 1905, Julian S. Corbett agreed that an attack in line-ahead was extremely risky and he therefore termed it 'mad'. He came to the conclusion that, supposedly against Nelson's plan, the British had attacked in the 'mad' line-ahead formation.[53] The contention that Nelson had attacked in a 'mad' formation challenged the journalist, James R. Thursfield, to contradict Corbett and offer his own suggestions. Thursfield claimed that Nelson had intended his two divisions to fulfil different tasks and that each of them was meant to attack in a different formation.[54] Corbett insisted on his standpoint in the most thorough examination of the whole campaign of Trafalgar ever to have been published.[55] Since Thursfield's journalistic efforts did not suffice to counter such a powerful scholarly work, he persuaded the Admiralty to set up a committee to investigate the matter.[56] The result of these thorough and scholarly investigations, published in a report in 1913, contradicted Corbett's views in several aspects. One of its most important conclusions was that Nelson's division had executed a feint against the van of the enemy by sailing in line-ahead formation.[57] These findings have not had their due impact on subsequent discussions of the battle of Trafalgar, mainly because of the inaccessibility of the report and because Corbett's son-in-law, the naval historian Brian Tunstall, as well as Corbett's biographer, Donald M. Schurman, wrongly asserted that the report confirmed Corbett's views.[58] Subsequent popular descriptions of the tactics employed at Trafalgar did not examine their subject as thoroughly as had been done at the beginning of the twentieth century and they neglected the Admiralty report.[59] Interestingly, the findings of the Admiralty report have been confirmed by the signal that Nelson had prepared for the battle to 'Cut through the Enemy's line and engage them on the other side' (discussed above) and that Tunstall himself discovered later in the twentieth century – a discovery that is only beginning to be assessed appropriately.

In conclusion it can be said that Nelson's complex and sophisticated tactics, at the Nile as well as at Trafalgar, have tended to be neglected as less appealing than stories of dash and daring. These, however, can only superficially satisfy the interested reader, intent on exploring at least the outstanding events of Nelson's life.

3

Neapolitan imbroglio

The most criticized and, at the same time, probably the most complex phase in Nelson's public career was his involvement in Naples. His actions in Naples aroused fierce disputes at the time and they have been used frequently to taint Nelson's reputation ever since, or at least to make him out to be a very flawed hero. It is difficult to get to the truth of Nelson's involvement in the death of numerous Neapolitan rebels and the execution of Admiral Caracciolo because the events were very complicated, the sources are inadequate or unreliable, and too many of those involved at the time or writing about these events long afterwards had an axe to grind.

When Nelson arrived at Naples on 22 September 1798 as the triumphant hero of the battle of the Nile, he entered a political and military quagmire into which he was drawn ever deeper as the months passed. At first he had wished merely to get his ships replenished and repaired. Naples was the most suitable place for this purpose since it disposed of the necessary facilities. It was also politically the natural choice, because it was the capital of one of the most influential countries in the Mediterranean and one of the few possible allies of Britain. The country's politics were vehemently opposed to the French republic, not only because the Kingdoms of the Two Sicilies (that is, Naples and Sicily) themselves were monarchies, but also because their queen was a sister of Marie Antoinette, the former queen of France, who had been beheaded by the French republicans. The fact that Naples was not actually an ally of Britain was due to the fact that it had lost a war against the French republic in 1796 and as a consequence of this defeat had accepted a status of neutrality favourable to French interests. The French, meanwhile, had extended their sphere of influence to the Neapolitan borders and had demanded the nominal replacement of Sir John Acton, the Neapolitan 'prime minister', who was of English descent.[1]

In this testing situation for the Neapolitan monarchy, the news of Nelson's victory at the Nile, which was received with public jubilation, gave the weakened state new confidence. Nelson believed that the consequences of his success at sea could lead to a defeat of the French in Italy and he urged the king of Naples, Ferdinand IV, to cross the border and attack the French. Humiliated by French demands for his dismissal, the Neapolitan 'prime minister', Acton, also pressed for the adoption of the same policy. Both Nelson and Acton were carried away by the current mood in Naples and did not consider well the wider implications of an attack on the French. Neither seems to have been aware that a renewed war would force Austria to take sides at a time when it would have preferred not to do so,[2] nor did they accurately calculate the strength of the Neapolitan army in comparison with the opposing French forces. Nevertheless, they managed to convince Ferdinand IV of the wisdom of advancing against the French. After initial successes (the Neapolitans even captured Rome), the Neapolitan troops were eventually defeated and put to flight. Since Nelson had so wrongly advised the royal couple, the queen managed to make him 'promise not to quit her and her family till brighter prospects appear than do at present'.[3] In the face of the approaching French troops the royal family decided to flee Naples and Nelson kept his promise and took them across the sea to their second capital, Palermo, in Sicily.

Nelson stayed at Palermo for the next five months. He may have felt personally obliged to do so, but remaining involved in Neapolitan affairs was also in keeping with his new instructions, which the Admiralty had issued in response to the new situation in the Mediterranean after the battle of the Nile. According to these instructions Nelson's principal duty was 'the protection of the coasts of Sicily, Naples, and the Adriatic, and in the event of war being renewed in Italy, an active co-operation with the Austrian and Neapolitan armies'. There were also minor tasks to be fulfilled, such as 'cutting off all communications between France and Egypt', 'the blocking up of Malta' and 'co-operating with the Turkish and Russian squadrons'.[4] One day after these new instructions were issued, and long before they actually reached him, Nelson dispatched four ships to blockade Malta; he sent two more ships later in October. Obeying orders from his immediate superior, Earl St Vincent, Nelson also sent out ships to destroy French transport ships off the coast of Egypt. Other ships were carrying dispatches, staying at Naples or watching events at Leghorn, so that on 1 January 1799 Nelson had only his own flagship at his disposal in Palermo.

Confirmed by the Admiralty's orders in his choice of focus on the co-operation with the Kingdoms of the Two Sicilies, Nelson tried to control the situation in Naples from a distance. He found it difficult to keep a force constantly employed off the Bay of Naples and he decided not to sail himself, as long as an attack on French-occupied Naples could not be supported from the land.[5] A few weeks later another reason kept him from sailing to Naples. On 12 May 1799 Nelson learned that the French fleet from Brest was on its way to the Mediterranean. Because he assumed (correctly, as it turned out) that the French would 'have formed their junction with the Spanish fleet', he had to reassemble his forces in order to face the enemy's fleet.[6] In the event not all his ships left the Bay of Naples and in the end Captain Foote was left in charge of the tiny squadron left behind. While Foote had to fend for himself at Naples, the French fleet entered Toulon, the Spanish ships sailed to Cartagena and the British, under Nelson, returned to Palermo. By now Nelson's chance to contribute decisively to the reconquest of Naples was increasing for two reasons: one was the internal weakness of the pro-French government in Naples, the other was the fact that an alliance in favour of the Neapolitan monarchy was slowly forming.

The position of French-occupied Naples had been weak from the start. After Nelson had taken the royal family of Naples to Palermo, their capital was not left entirely defenceless. The 'Neapolitan Bourbon state' has been described as 'a partnership of the crown, the church, and the mob, for the exploitation of the intellectual and commercial sections of the community'.[7] The French therefore found the majority of the population opposed to them. The Parthenopean Republic proclaimed by local revolutionaries was supported only by parts of the upper and middle classes, was resented in the countryside and was not even recognized by the French. In pursuing the conquest of the rest of the Kingdom of Naples the French, and some rapidly assembled Neapolitan troops, proceeded ruthlessly, plundering and burning several towns on their way south, thus alienating many local people. The occupying forces were not only in a weak position within the country, but were also soon threatened by external developments when war between France and Austria (allied with Russia) broke out again in March 1799. Initial successes for the allies made necessary the retreat of the French from Naples. By mid-May the French had left the country, leaving only a garrison in the powerful Castle St Elmo situated in Naples itself and other garrisons in the northern towns of Capua and Gaeta. It has been claimed that only now, after the retreat of the oppressive French, did the Parthenopean Republic have a chance to develop; but the Neapolitan republicans did not have much time to put their ideas into practice, because other forces were forming against them. The royalist cardinal Fabrizio Ruffo began to raise an 'army of the Holy Faith' in the south of the country. This army resorted to the rather unholy means of plundering in its efforts to reconquer the Neapolitan kingdom. Even less disciplined royalist forces terrorized their compatriots north of Naples. The only well-organized bodies of troops were those of the Russians and the Turks, which were on their way towards Naples from the east. Their help had been solicited by Antonio Micheroux, a Neapolitan diplomat of Belgian descent, who was now accompanying them without any specific role of his own to perform. Early in June these forces joined Cardinal Ruffo's army of the Holy Faith near Naples.

In the weeks before Nelson appeared on the scene, matters ran out of control. Within Naples it proved to be impossible to maintain order when Ruffo's army of the Holy Faith arrived on the outskirts of the city in mid-June. The Neapolitan republicans took royalist hostages and positioned themselves in several strongholds in the city, mainly in the castles of Nuovo and dell'Uovo, which were situated near the harbour. Their desire to take refuge with the French in the Castle St Elmo was rejected by the French commanding officer, J. Mejan. In the meantime the city witnessed scenes of horror. Ruffo lost control of his troops, which engaged in street fighting, joining the mob in the city in its murderous activities, and exploiting the situation for private vendettas and looting. A few days later, during which time Captain Foote's little squadron seized two towns in the Bay of Naples, Cardinal Ruffo started to restore order. As the royalists were gaining control of Naples, they also brought heavy guns to bear against the republican strongholds. The republicans, scattered over the city as they were, might have given up at this stage if they had not heard rumours that the French fleet had left Toulon. Hoping to be relieved by the French they tried to gain time by negotiating with the royalist forces. Captain Foote issued a declaration that threatened the rebels with the full severity of the law if they did not 'have recourse to' the king's 'clemency'.[8] Ruffo, however, grew increasingly impatient and unwilling to negotiate with the rebels, fearing that the arrival of the French fleet might allow his enemies to take Naples again. The French troops meanwhile stood aloof from the situation, safely marooned in Castle St Elmo, overlooking the city of Naples. At this stage the Neapolitan diplomat Micheroux, whose cousin was a hostage of the republicans, started independent negotiations. He first arranged an armistice (against Ruffo's will) and eventually negotiated a capitulation which would guarantee the rebels the freedom to leave for Toulon. Having prepared the capitulation, Micheroux left Ruffo to sign it. Ruffo was now confronted with either risking a renewal of hostilities or signing something that he had not negotiated, and indeed that he had no authority to accept[9] and that was disadvantageous to his king, because it included only the rebel-held castles (which many rebels had already left) and not the powerfully situated Castle St Elmo, which commanded the city and was still held by the French. The capitulation granted the rebels not only free leave, but also the guarantee of leaving the castles with the honours of war, as if they were foreign military enemies and not domestic insurgents. Despite these difficulties, Ruffo signed the capitulation because he recognized that he had less control of his own troops than he had of the rebels in their castles. Shortly before he put his signature to the capitulation he had reported:

> The duty of governing, or rather of suppressing, a large mob accustomed to anarchy of the worst kind; the duty of controlling a score of uneducated and insubordinate chiefs of light infantry corps, who are all bent on plunder, murder and violence is so terrible and complicated a matter, that it is absolutely beyond my powers. They have just brought to me 1,300 Jacobins whom I cannot place in security . . . They have dragged here and shot at least 50 in my presence, without my being able to stop them. They have also wounded at least 200, whom they also brought here naked.[10]

Ruffo asked the representatives of the foreign forces at Naples (Turkish, Russian and British; with Captain Foote representing the last) to sign their names below his. The French commandant of Castle St Elmo, whose signature was needed for the full acceptance of the capitulation, had to delay until he received the approval of his superior in Capua, and he therefore signed last, on 23 June. Before the rebels managed to make use of these favourable terms, however, Nelson intervened.[11]

The king of Naples had asked Nelson, in a letter of 10 June, to retake Naples. Thus empowered by the king of Naples, Nelson had just sailed from Palermo, on 13 June, when he received intelligence from Lord Keith, his superior, that the French fleet had left Toulon. Nelson now sailed, as he had been ordered by Keith, to the west of Sicily, where he spent several days of fruitless and uneventful waiting for his superior. On his return to Palermo, he discovered that the court had, in the meantime, heard about a 'truce' having been agreed in Naples but later broken by the republicans.[12] To avoid the French fleet reaching Naples before the British, the king, as Nelson put it, 'requested my immediate presence in the bay of Naples',[13] and Nelson left for Naples on 21 June, having taken Sir William and Lady Hamilton on board as interpreters.[14] Approaching Naples, but still at sea, Nelson heard of a 'treaty of armistice' which was said to have been concluded between Ruffo on the one hand and the rebels, as well as the French, on the other, allowing the rebels and the French an armistice of twenty-one days in order to wait to be 'relieved by their friends' before they would surrender. Nelson immediately penned some 'observations' on this agreement in which he remarked: 'All armistices signify that either party may renew hostilities, giving a certain notice fixed upon by the contracting parties.'[15] Nelson was thus thinking only of an armistice, not of an as yet unexecuted capitulation, when he arrived at the Bay of Naples on 24 June 1799.

On his arrival, Nelson found flags of truce flying on board Captain Foote's ship as well as on the castles of Nuovo and dell'Uovo. These informed him that agreement had been reached with the rebels, not with the French. Having heard only rumours about the agreed armistice and capitulation, he 'instantly made the signal to annul the truce'.[16] This signal was only understood by and only meant for the vessels under Nelson's own command. The French and rebel forces ashore had to be informed by intelligible means (not the British naval signalling code) that Nelson did not accept the armistice – let alone the capitulation. Nelson spoke to Captain Foote on the evening of 24 June. Making a clear distinction between military enemies and rebels, he then wrote 'a Summons to surrender' for the French-occupied Castle St Elmo and a 'Declaration . . . to . . . the Rebellious Subjects of His Sicilian Majesty in the Castles of Uovo and Nuovo, that he [Nelson] will not permit them to embark or quit those places. They must surrender themselves to His Majesty's Royal mercy.'[17] After having anchored his fleet in the Bay of Naples, on 25 June Nelson sent captains Troubridge and Ball ashore with his notes to inform

Cardinal Ruffo about their contents. Nelson reported on the events that followed to Lord Keith:

> His Eminence said he would send no papers [to the French and rebels], that if I pleased I might break the Armistice, for that he was tired of his situation. Captain Troubridge then asked his Eminence this plain question: 'If Lord Nelson breaks the Armistice, will your Eminence assist him in his attack on the Castles?' His answer was clear, 'I will neither assist him with men or guns.' After much communication, his Eminence desired to come on board to speak with me on his situation. I used every argument in my power to convince him that the Treaty and Armistice was at an end by the arrival of the Fleet; but an Admiral is no match in talking with a Cardinal. I therefore gave him my opinion in writing – viz., 'Rear Admiral Lord Nelson, who arrived in the Bay of Naples on the 24th June with the British Fleet, found a treaty entered into with the Rebels, which he is of opinion ought not to be carried into execution without the approbation of His Sicilian Majesty,
> Earl St Vincent, – Lord Keith.[18]

While Ruffo accepted Nelson's authority to annul the terms of the capitulation and disregard the armistice,[19] he was unwilling to support him. Since the two representatives of the king of Naples, Ruffo and Nelson, could not agree on how to co-operate, the occupants of the castles and the people in the city were left in an uncertain position. The French commandant of Castle St Elmo, Mejan, neither supported the republican cause in Naples nor followed through on the capitulation which he had just signed. On 25 June, the day after Nelson's arrival, the French dismantled the barracks below St Elmo that had been sheltering some of the rebels. When Mejan learned that Nelson would not accept the armistice and he received a summons to surrender from Micheroux, he reopened hostilities for a short time on the evening of 25 June. The armistice with the French in St Elmo was now obviously at an end. In this tense situation the rebels in the castles Nuovo and dell'Uovo learned from Ruffo that Nelson would not accept the terms of the capitulation. Since they had to fear for their own safety outside the castles, they did not accept Ruffo's offer to leave the castles by land.

How the crisis in Naples could be resolved depended on how Nelson and Ruffo handled their differences. In their conversation on 25 June Nelson had offered Ruffo 'to send 1,200 marines on shore' to prepare for the attack on the French in St Elmo, but Ruffo avoided accepting this offer and claimed 'difficulties . . . as to providing them with quarters'. Back ashore, Ruffo had to face the fact that the French had opened fire from St Elmo in reaction to the summons to surrender which Micheroux had sent in, following Nelson's view that the armistice had ended. This put Ruffo in a very uncomfortable position:

the man who had arranged the capitulation (Micheroux) did not feel bound by it; the man who had the force to hinder the execution of the capitulation (Nelson) did not accept it; those who should profit from it (the rebels in the castles) did not trust in it any more and had not accepted Ruffo's offer to leave by land; and those who were meant to guarantee the fulfilment of the capitulation (the French in St Elmo) had opened fire. Faced with these problems, Ruffo changed his mind and wrote a letter to Nelson on the same evening: 'I implore . . . your Excellency to land 1,200 men, whom it would be well to place within striking distance of St Elmo. I therefore offer for their quarters my house, which is large and empty.'[20] Ruffo was now obviously willing to follow the course previously suggested by Nelson and to regard the armistice as broken and the capitulation as impossible to execute.[21]

Nelson had now three choices before him. First, he could decide not to fulfil the mission he had been sent to fulfil, disobey his instructions and accept the terms of the capitulation, even though there were neither military nor legal reasons to do so, and even though its most important signatory on the royalist side, Cardinal Ruffo, no longer wished to see it executed. Second, he could try to complete his mission and fight both the rebels and the French, causing chaos in Naples. His third choice was a compromise in which he would agree to recognize the armistice, while he would leave the decision about the terms of the capitulation to the king of Naples. Taking this last course of action Nelson could avert damage to the city as well as a threat to its inhabitants; at the same time he would make a concession to Ruffo's viewpoint, without seriously endangering the position of the king of Naples.

Nelson decided to accept the armistice, but to disregard the precise terms of the capitulation. On the morning of 26 June, Sir William Hamilton wrote to Ruffo: 'Lord Nelson begs me to assure your Eminence that he is resolved to do nothing which might break the armistice which your Eminence has granted to the castles of Naples.'[22] In response to a letter from Ruffo on that same morning, asking for troops to be sent to repel French attacks north of Naples, Nelson referred to Hamilton's letter and reassured Ruffo: 'I will not on any consideration break the armistice entered into by you.'[23] It seems to be clear enough that Nelson was now willing to keep the armistice with the rebel-held castles without going so far as to recognize the terms of the capitulation,[24] while Ruffo was busy attacking the French who had been the guarantors of this same capitulation.

These co-ordinated efforts by Nelson and Ruffo had a strong effect on the rebels in the castles. Their situation had become desperate and they could not hope for any improvement. They eventually decided to leave the castles. According to Micheroux, who had negotiated the terms of the capitulation, he himself now achieved the actual surrender, because the rebels 'relied on my word alone'. Whatever Micheroux may have promised the rebels on this occasion is not known. What is known is that they left the castles without the honours of war that had been agreed upon in the terms of the capitulation. It appears that they were aware that their fate now depended on the mercy that might or might not be extended to them by the king. Some of the people who had been involved with the republic, but who had chosen to remain in Naples rather than try to leave for France, wrote letters to Nelson in which they appealed to the king's 'clemency'.[25] Others embarked on little boats during the evening of 26 June, and stayed near the city of Naples for the next two days, hoping to get a chance to go into exile as one of the terms of the capitulation had stipulated. None of the petitions that reached Nelson claimed that the petitioners had trusted in the fulfilment of the terms of the capitulation. A direct reference to faith in the capitulation was, however, made in a petition that was addressed to Ruffo and Micheroux. If this text, printed in an unreliable source, is to be trusted, it would appear that, if anybody did, Ruffo and Micheroux gave misleading assurances that the terms of the capitulation were now to be fulfilled. Nelson still insisted, years after the event, that 'when the rebels surrendered, they came out of the castles as they ought, without any honours of war and trusting to the judgement of their sovereign'.[26]

Over the following days Nelson and Ruffo went on co-operating and the situation in Naples calmed down. Much now depended on a decision from the king of Naples. Instead of sailing to Naples himself, the king simply sent some letters which only arrived in the Bay of Naples on 28 June. These letters confirmed that Nelson had acted according to the will of the king when he annulled the capitulation. Thus powerfully supported in his views, Nelson, after informing Ruffo about his plans, sent out boats from his ships to bring the boats with the rebels on board close to his ships. Since only the king could decide the fate of the rebels, his presence in Naples was urgently required. On 28 June Hamilton and Nelson both wrote letters to Acton, the de facto prime minister, to press the king and queen to come to Naples. The presence of the monarch proved to be necessary for another reason. Ruffo again caused difficulties and did not wish to get involved in the attack on Castle St Elmo, which was still held by the French. To clarify the situation, Nelson himself issued a proclamation, published in Italian and English, in which he set out an ultimatum for 'all those who have served as officers, civil or military, in the infamous Neapolitan republic' to 'give themselves up to the clemency of the king', because they would otherwise be considered 'as still in rebellion'.[27]

On 29 June Ruffo handed over several republicans to Nelson, among them the Neapolitan Admiral Caracciolo. Caracciolo was probably the most respected Neapolitan naval officer of his time. Early in 1799 he had received special permission from the king of Naples to return from Sicily to the mainland in order to save his property from being confiscated by the Parthenopean Republic. Back in Naples he became head of the republican navy. His flotilla of gunboats was meant to act against British ships and had actually damaged a Neapolitan frigate. It is not quite clear whether he was forced into the service of the republic or whether he had acted out of genuine republican sympathies. Whatever the reason for his co-operation with the republicans, instead of giving himself 'up to the clemency of the king',[28] he had gone into hiding. Nelson appears to have concluded, therefore, that Caracciolo did not deserve the clemency of the king, while his attack on a Neapolitan frigate was open treason. Nelson believed that Caracciolo's trial would set a clear precedent in a situation that was still unstable, and so he decided to have Caracciolo tried by a Neapolitan court martial on board his own flagship.[29] The judgement passed was 'death' and Nelson did not hesitate to have it executed the same day.

In the following days and weeks Nelson received increasing marks of approval for his actions in these decisive days in Naples. The king of Naples asked Nelson to carry on against the opposition of Ruffo, and even to seize the cardinal, if he would not obey orders to come back to Palermo. Instead of making use of these powers, Nelson showed what one historian has described as 'generosity towards his opponents which was one of Nelson's most conspicuous virtues'.[30] He not only refrained from sending Ruffo to Palermo, but even defended him in a letter to the king of Naples: 'I really do not believe that his Eminence has a disloyal thought.' Ruffo accepted Nelson's hospitality on board his flagship and both seem to have co-operated without further friction.[31] Shortly after the king arrived at Naples (on 10 July), the French in Castle St Elmo surrendered and Nelson sent his marines ashore to besiege the French in Capua. Only this last action, combined with Nelson's disobedience towards his superior's order to support him at sea before 'the safety of His Sicilian Majesty's Kingdoms is secured',[32] was criticized by the Admiralty. No other part of Nelson's conduct in the summer of 1799 met with the disapproval of the Admiralty. On the contrary, their lordships approved

> of his determination to go to the Bay of Naples to endeavour to bring the affair of H.[is] S.[icilian] M.[ajesty] in that City to a happy conclusion; and of his having ordered Captains Troubridge and Ball to land with so large a body of men from the Squadron to reduce the Castle of St Elmo.[33]

This supports the view that what Nelson did at Naples was covered by his original orders from the Admiralty.

Public opinion did not agree with this positive assessment of the Admiralty. The leader of the parliamentary opposition, Charles James Fox, in a speech in parliament on 3 February 1800, connected 'the horrors and murders perpetrated at Naples' with the breach of the 'Treaty . . . which promised safety and the security of property'. He went on to declare that:

> as this treaty is said to have been signed and guaranteed by a British officer [Captain Foote], he hoped . . . that this foul stain should be washed away from the British name; a stain that in blackness could rival any that resulted from the atrocities of the French Revolution.[34]

In her book about the French Revolution, published in 1801, Helen Maria Williams described the Neapolitan affair in much greater detail. She did not attack Nelson directly, but instead attached much more blame to Lady Hamilton, whom she likened to Lady Macbeth.[35] It seems that Nelson was at that time so widely acknowledged as a hero of his country that it was difficult to attack him seriously, especially from a position of opposition to the government. This was to change after his death, when his involvement in the defeat of the Neapolitan revolution in 1799 became one of the main stains on his reputation.

A few years after Nelson's death Edward James Foote, the captain who had co-operated with Ruffo before Nelson's arrival at Naples, initiated the critical discussion of Nelson's actions with two editions of his *Vindication of His Conduct . . . in the Bay of Naples* (published in 1807 and 1810). Foote claimed that he did not want to speak up at the time, because the criticism of the British involvement came from supporters of the Whig party and he did not want to be attached to a party. Now, however, he felt personally offended because he had learned that Nelson had referred to the capitulation which Foote had signed as 'infamous'.[36] Foote launched his criticism of Nelson because either he himself was going to be blamed for signing the capitulation or Nelson would have to be blamed for annulling it.[37] As a matter of fact, Foote had signed the capitulation, as he himself pointed out, as a powerless spectator of events, whereas Nelson annulled it with the power of a fleet of eighteen ships-of-the-line at his disposal. The decisions of Nelson and Foote, though very different, can be justified when seen in their respective contexts. This was not the conclusion reached by Foote, who declared emphatically: 'it is unreasonable to require me to sacrifice myself at the shrine of Lord Nelson!'[38]

In his *Vindication*, Foote developed two lines of argument. On the one hand, he excused his own involvement by explaining why he could not avoid signing the capitulation.[39] At the time, since he was in no position to receive advice from his admiral, Foote had signed this capitulation below the Russian and Turkish allies' signatures under a 'protest against everything that can in any way be contrary to the rights of his Britannic Majesty, or those of the English nation'.[40] On the other hand, he now justified his signature by defending the capitulation as useful and appropriate.[41] Foote now regarded himself as entitled to act directly for the king of Great Britain,[42] while he also maintained that Nelson had no right to annul the capitulation, because he had not consulted his superiors.[43] Foote's *Vindication of His Conduct* conveniently ignores the fact that he had sent out his ship's barge, on the afternoon of 28 June, in order to seize the boats with the rebels on board.[44] Instead, he now maintained that Nelson had sent him away before 'the garrisons of Uovo and Nuovo [consisting of rebels] were taken out of those castles under the *pretence* of putting the Capitulation I had signed, into execution'.[45] Foote thus created a hypothesis (about Nelson's deceit) based on assumptions (about how the rebels left the castles) that he felt free to make on the basis of his forgetting aspects of his own involvement.

Foote's account of Nelson's actions in the Bay of Naples appealed to Southey in 1813. In describing the surrender of the rebels, Southey used the distorted version presented by Foote and concluded:

> A deplorable transaction! A stain upon the memory of Nelson, and the honour of England! To palliate would be in vain; to justify it would be wicked; there is no alternative, for one who will not make himself a participator in guilt, but to record the disgraceful story with sorrow and with shame.[46]

To this strong view Southey added an account of the trial, sentence and execution of Caracciolo. In the following twenty years Foote's version of events, popularized by Southey, whose biography was to become the most widely read life of Nelson, remained unopposed. It found its way into serious works of naval history and even into popular literature. Some Whigs went so far as to speak of 'treachery and murder' in referring to Nelson's involvement in the events at Naples.[47]

In the mid-nineteenth century expert naval men, who were reviving interest in Nelson, attempted to defend him against these attacks. They did not altogether succeed, and at the end of the century Captain Foote's grandson, Francis Pritchett Badham, revived the dispute. He can be credited with having alerted British historians to the existence of Italian sources on the topic. These sources, however, should be handled with caution, since the Neapolitan revolution is a highly charged issue in Neapolitan history. The suppression of the Neapolitan revolution is remembered as a bloody and terrible event in the history of Naples, not only because of the events before Nelson's arrival and because of the execution of Caracciolo, who appeared as a true gentleman, but also because of the final defeat of the rebels. When the king finally arrived in Naples he did not show any of the mercy for which the rebels might have hoped. Instead, he let his courts condemn to death more than a hundred of the rebels from the castles, among them some leading intellectuals of the city. It appears only natural to ask who was to blame for this disaster. Early sources, mostly written by exiles from Naples, in part blamed the French commandant at Naples for not supporting the Neapolitan rebels. Cardinal Ruffo was also a natural candidate for criticism. In order to avert such condemnation, Ruffo's former sub-secretary, Domenico Sacchinelli, some thirty years after the event, set out to defend his former superior. Trying not to offend the king, the queen or the rebels, whom he called 'patriots',[48] Sacchinelli followed a precarious course. In order not to offend any of the Neapolitan parties involved, he shifted all responsibility on to Nelson, by claiming that Nelson deceived the rebels into believing that he would accept the terms of the capitulation. This was a new contention emanating from a Neapolitan source. Others, if they had shown Nelson in a negative light, did so by describing the supposed detrimental influence on him exerted by Lady Hamilton.

In his efforts to support his claim that Nelson had cheated the rebels, Sacchinelli advanced dubious evidence. Lacking original source material, he appears to have reconstructed letters from memory. He provided only one supposed original document as a facsimile in an appendix to his book. This document is an unsigned Italian text which Sacchinelli did not even manage to quote correctly in the main body of his book, and which he claimed was written by the British Captain Troubridge. Troubridge, however, did not know enough Italian to communicate effectively in this language and his very large handwriting differs notably from the writing in this Italian text. The other supposed letters that Sacchinelli relies upon are paraphrased into his text and their contents contradict reliable documentary sources that have survived.[49] Apart from offering doubtful documents, Sacchinelli's work also contains errors in several details of its narrative. An opportunity for a more balanced account was later missed by the French novelist, Alexandre Dumas, when he edited a collection of letters about the Bourbon monarchs of Naples in the aftermath of Garibaldi's conquest of the kingdom in 1860. Dumas, or his assistant, left out passages that did not suit his case, mistranslated English letters into Italian, quoted as taken from 'original documents' the paraphrased letters of Sacchinelli, and finally left the Neapolitan archives in such a mess that some of the letters from which he copied can no longer be found and therefore cannot be verified. Towards the end of the nineteenth century the German historian Hermann Hüffer and the Neapolitan historian Benedetto Maresca based their accounts of the event on primary sources, instead of the biased accounts by the exiles from Naples and by Sacchinelli. Hüffer as well as Maresca, though critical of Nelson, contradicted Sacchinelli's contention that Nelson cheated the rebels.

When Badham himself approached the subject in order to prove that his grandfather was right and Nelson ought to be censured, he chose to use only those sources which confirmed his view – and he found an abundance of material, mainly in the work of Sacchinelli, whom he called 'the chief Italian authority'.[50] Blissfully unaware of Hüffer's work and not bothering much about Maresca's, he attempted to dismantle A. T. Mahan's account in his substantial biography of Nelson that portrayed its subject as an honest man who had done the right thing in a difficult situation. In his controversy with Mahan – pursued in various articles, letters to the editors of journals and pamphlets – Badham not only used unreliable sources uncritically, but also distorted sources so as to change their original meaning. In one case he left out a passage of a letter of Nelson's that was essential to the argument that Nelson was making but which did not fit Badham's line of attack against him. In another case, Badham simply changed a word in one of Nelson's letters and built an argument on this change. He also quoted Sir William Hamilton as having written what was in fact only Dumas' comment on a letter in his combined edition and narrative about the Neapolitan Bourbons. Badham's uncritical use of unreliable sources, his readiness to change sources and his arbitrary choice of material cleared the way for him to reach his desired conclusions. He then went on to fill the gaps that remained in his narrative, not by dealing with evidence that might disprove his point, but by sheer guesswork.[51]

The discussion of the Naples affair was further revived by Maresca's discovery of a document, first published in 1899, drawn up shortly after the events of 1799 by Micheroux, in which the royalist who had negotiated the capitulation now condemned its 'reprehensible' contents and blamed Ruffo for signing it, yet attacked Nelson for not keeping it. In this vindication of his own conduct Micheroux claimed that Nelson had 'suddenly alter[ed] his mind' and that according to Ruffo's information at the time 'Lord Nelson had consented to carry the capitulation into effect'. According to Micheroux himself, Nelson's supposed change of mind, for which there exists no supporting documentary evidence, was of no consequence. Micheroux claimed in the same document: 'the garrisons . . . relied on my word alone [so that] I was not under the necessity of making use of' any supposed written assurances by Nelson. [52] Although Micheroux's vindication of his conduct did not explain matters clearly, and although he had to account for his own rather dubious involvement in the events, Badham took it as a confirmation of his view that Nelson had cheated the rebels.

In order to 'bring together the mass of evidence' on the Neapolitan affair, H. C. Gutteridge edited a collection of *Documents Relating to the Suppression of the Jacobin Revolution at Naples. June 1799* in 1903. In the introduction to this edition Gutteridge concluded that 'there is not the slightest proof at present of any foul play on Nelson's part'; as to the trial and execution of Caracciolo he conceded that it is 'a question on which opinions will always differ'.[53] Opinions went on to differ on more than that, however, even though Gutteridge had indeed made 'the mass of evidence . . . accessible', and no vital source material has been discovered since. Not even the bare facts have been agreed, in part simply because they are immensely complex in themselves. Moreover, too many authors are inclined to follow the majority of their predecessors and criticize Nelson, because they want to avoid being suspected of hero-worship. Criticising Nelson's involvement at Naples is an easy way of establishing one's reputation as a critical biographer, because the matter is too complex to make it easy to refute the criticism. Biographers have developed the habit of introducing their treatment of the events with a kind of dramatization of Nelson's state of mind, such as 'Nelson was in a tense, fierce mood' or 'Nelson's temper flamed'.[54] As a result the final judgements about the events in Naples are not better founded than before. Biographers have frequently been unaware of what Nelson's orders relating to Naples were. They have often replaced them by fanciful assumptions about the influence of Lady Hamilton, and, more recently, they have sometimes (wrongly) assumed that the French were included in the terms of the capitulation. Worst of all, biographers keep confusing the terms that are at the centre of the whole issue: armistice and capitulation.

4

The love of his life

The most controversial aspect of Horatio Nelson's life is undoubtedly his relationship with Emma, Lady Hamilton. Nelson had first met the wife of the British ambassador to Naples, Sir William Hamilton, on a short visit to that city in 1793, but it was to be their second encounter, five years later, that changed his life for ever. Then he returned to Naples as the hero of the Nile and he received not only a stunning welcome from the city of Naples, but an impetuous embrace from Lady Hamilton, which he described in a letter to his wife: 'the scene . . . was terribly affecting; up flew her Ladyship, and exclaiming, "O God, is it possible?" she fell into my arm more dead than alive. Tears, however, soon set matters to rights'.[1]

The emotional start to an enduring relationship was followed by a period of close political co-operation. Together with her husband, Lady Hamilton formed an important line of communication between Nelson and the king and queen of Naples, as well as informing him about what happened at court and translating for him. Her support became even more essential when French troops approached the city and it was necessary to organize the evacuation of the royal family from Naples. As Nelson assumed that his own and Sir William Hamilton's 'movements were watched', Lady Hamilton became the vital link to the queen of Naples in organizing the embarkation of the court on Nelson's ships. During the very stormy crossing to Palermo, Lady Hamilton made herself useful and, in the admiring words of Nelson, did not 'enter a bed the whole time they [the royal family] were on board'.[2] Nelson was clearly impressed by Lady Hamilton's dedication to her various tasks, and by her energy and drive. It is impossible to say when his appreciation extended to physical attraction, but soon after Lady Hamilton and Nelson had settled in Palermo they developed their sexual relationship.

While the exact nature of their relationship remained obscure to observers, it became ever more obvious that Nelson was not easily separated from the ambassador and his wife. As was noted in the previous chapter, Nelson made Palermo something like his headquarters, while he sent out his ships to fulfil the manifold tasks he had to perform in the Mediterranean. Apart from two cruises to the west of Sicily in vain efforts to meet up with his commander-in-chief, Nelson spent half a year in the company of the Hamiltons in Palermo. And when he left for Naples in June 1799 he took them with him. Even in the British press, Lady Hamilton became thus linked with Nelson's political and naval actions in the Bay of Naples because of her role as his interpreter.[3] The *Morning Chronicle* then suggested that she was also a distraction for Nelson. It reported that 'the English fleet has been ordered to . . . Minorca', but 'his Grace the Admiral [remained at Palermo, where he had] his flag hoisted at a balcony at the house of the British Minister' and took part in a 'Fete Champétre' with Lady Hamilton.[4] This information was not quite correct, since Nelson was still at Naples when he disobeyed his superior's order to join him at Minorca (discussed in Chapter 1), but suspicions about the undue influence that Lady Hamilton was exerting on Nelson were soon published in several newspapers. Her influence on his decisions as admiral in the Mediterranean after the battle of the Nile (from 1798 to 1800) was also recognized throughout the fleet. Even among sailors on the lower decks it was said that Lady Hamilton interfered in political matters as well as in securing favours for ordinary seamen.

Lady Hamilton began participating in all aspects of Nelson's life, both public and private. After the defeat of the Neapolitan revolution in August 1799, he again settled with the Hamiltons in Palermo. After several naval missions to different parts of the Mediterranean, Nelson even took the ambassador and his wife to join the blockade of Malta. On this trip it appears that Nelson made Lady Hamilton pregnant.[5] The cruise was no mere pleasure trip, however. One day Nelson's ship came into gunshot range of a Maltese fort. An eye-witness remembered that 'Lord Nelson was in a towering passion, and Lady Hamilton's refusal to quit the quarter-deck did not tend to tranquillize him'. It is not known whether Nelson successfully 'insisted upon Lady Hamilton's retiring', because the eye-witness had to leave the scene of the disputation, while the two were still 'in high altercation'.[6] Anxious for Lady Hamilton's safety as Nelson undoubtedly was at the time, he also admired her boldness. A year later, when she was worrying about his safety, he reminded her of her own attitude as a fighter: 'How often have I heard *you* say, that you would not quit the deck if you came near a Frenchman. Would you have your attached friend do less than you purpose for yourself?'[7] Nelson clearly regarded Lady Hamilton as a companion even in his naval sphere of action.

Equality, rather than male dominance, was Nelson's ideal of a heterosexual relationship on the most intimate level. This becomes apparent in an early love letter that Nelson, at that time at sea, wrote to Lady Hamilton in Palermo on Friday, 31 January 1800, about a dream he had had:

> last night I did nothing but dream of you altho' I woke 20 times in the night, in one of my dreams I thought I was at a large table [where]

you was not present, sitting between a Princess who I detest and another, they both tried to seduce me and the first wanted to take those liberties with me which no Woman in this World but yourself ever did, the consequence was I knocked her down and in the moment of bustle you came in and taking me in your embrace whispered I love nothing but you my Nelson, I kissed you fervently and we enjoy'd the height of love, Ah Emma I pour out my soul to you.[8]

This passage is telling in three ways. First, Nelson obviously attributed physical power and activity to women; the threat the two princesses posed reminds one of a rape. Second, by describing what the princesses tried to do, Nelson revealed how he enjoyed sexual activity with women, since his would-be female seducer tried to take 'liberties': that is, she tried to take the active part in sex. Third, Nelson's escape from this very active attempt to 'seduce' him was only through Lady Hamilton's 'embrace', that is her initiative, thanks to which he enjoyed 'the height of love'; this again indicates how he delighted in female sexual activity. In short, this account of his dream indicates that Nelson enjoyed an active partner and that his concept of pleasurable and natural sexuality did not demand from him a dominant role. On the contrary, in the same letter he assured his lover: 'You are my guide I submit to you.'

Even to observers, Nelson now appeared inseparable from, if not subservient to, Lady Hamilton. When Sir William Hamilton and Nelson were recalled from their posts in the Mediterranean, Nelson did not take the frigate that had been offered to him, and both men followed Lady Hamilton's proposal to travel overland back to Britain. On this journey Nelson not only encountered the admiration of numerous central Europeans,[9] but he was also exposed to the sharp observations of his countrywomen. In diaries and letters they remarked: 'Lady Hamilton takes possession of him, and he is a willing captive, the most submissive and devoted I have seen' and 'she leads him about like a keeper with a bear'.[10] Whether erotic or not, to some observers the whole relationship made Nelson appear undignified, if not unmanly.

On his triumphant return to Britain, the press there got an opportunity to report on Nelson's public appearances with Lady Hamilton. Lady Hamilton – according to the *Naval Chronicle* – 'looked charmingly, and is a very fine woman'. It was observed that 'These distinguished personages travelled very easily, only two stages a day' and that Nelson had only 'ten minutes' to spare for his wife after his arrival in London.[11] The press recorded his steps meticulously and thus could not fail to notice that he remained constantly in the company of Lady Hamilton. This led to some comments on their scandalous relationship. A caricature, published ten days after Nelson's arrival in London, was entitled 'Smoking Attitudes!', alluding to Lady Hamilton's famous 'attitudes' which she struck for the benefit of her circle. Full of sexual innuendo, it depicts Nelson and Lady Hamilton detached from a greater party of smokers. Lady Hamilton is shown admiring Nelson's pipe and comparing

4 Detail of caricature 'A Mansion House Treat. Or Smoking Attitudes', by Cruikshank, published 18 November 1800 © The Trustees of the British Museum.

him with her husband: 'Pho, the Old man's pipe is always out, but yours burns with full Vigour', to which Nelson replies: 'Yes, yes. I'll give you such a Smoke! I'll pour a whole broad side into you.' Even the *Morning Chronicle*, which prided itself on its 'high standard of propriety',[12] poked fun at the notorious couple. It remarked ironically that 'The heroes of the *sock* and *buskin* [symbols of comedy and tragedy] are great admirers of the gallant Lord Nelson.' Suggesting that Lady Hamilton was pregnant, the text went on:

Without underrating his *past* services to the nation, they are of opinion he may yet confer great *benefits*! The phrase of '*being* in the *straw*' [a reference to a woman in childbirth] may now be applied in a double sense to our literary females, and the '*straw* will be *laid*' whether the object be a *boy* or a *book in sheets*!

Finally, the *Morning Chronicle* concluded, 'The new *Adultery Bill*' could not be expected soon.[13] In this gossipy mood the famous opposition newspaper even forgot to remind the public of Nelson's actions in the Bay of Naples eighteen months earlier. The press also tracked the couple on their way to the south-west of England – with the patient husband. The *Gentleman's Magazine* printed a detailed report of how Nelson and the Hamiltons had spent their Christmas holiday as guests of William Beckford at Fonthill.

When Nelson went back to sea again in mid-January 1801, the flow of gossip dried up. Although the public was denied any new information about the adulterous couple, the relationship went through its most decisive phase. After a last meeting with his wife, on 13 January 1801, Nelson settled half his income on her and started a painful series of letters in which the initially conciliatory gestures were eventually superseded by harsh expressions of rejection.[14] At the end of January, Nelson's and Lady Hamilton's daughter Horatia was born (most probably as the survivor of twins). What might have been discarded as a temporary if passionate affair, begun and continued in exotic places far from home, now had to demonstrate whether it could last in more difficult circumstances. Separated from his lover, Nelson struggled with bouts of intense jealousy, directed against the Prince of Wales. It appears that in order to secure herself in Nelson's affection, Lady Hamilton fed this jealousy. Nelson, on the other hand, was not necessarily a reassuring partner either. He repeatedly complained about his various afflictions, from sea-sickness to spasms and rheumatic fever. While Lady Hamilton had to worry about how best to hide their new-born child and while she did not yet have even the prospect of a common home, Nelson – ill and waiting to be superseded – finished a letter to her not very comfortingly: 'I expect to find a new Admiral when I return off Bornholm, or most probably you will never see again Your affectionate. . .'.[15] Considering that 'fright' about Nelson's health gave his fragile wife 'a cold',[16] and that Nelson therefore avoided as far as possible writing to his wife about his illnesses and wounds, he appears to have found in Lady Hamilton a reliable support. Compared with his letters to his wife, whom he always had to comfort, his letters to Lady Hamilton show that Nelson was the one who needed to be comforted. He wrote on various occasions that he was 'in tears'[17] and he described himself as a 'miserable fellow shut up in wood' or 'a forlorn outcast, except in your generous soul'.[18]

Nelson thus relied on Lady Hamilton's strong personality even in their new and more difficult personal situation. In the flow of letters that he wrote to her (hers to him are not preserved), he kept praising her personal qualities.

Among these are some that remind us of a warrior, such as determined courage and firmness.[19] In his eyes, she also possessed intelligence, judgement and sense,[20] which were not normally in the accepted catalogue of praiseworthy womanly qualities of the day. Moreover, he also perceived her as a political being, keeping her informed about naval and political matters during their whole correspondence, right up to his death.[21] And he saw her as more than a silent partner in the discussion of naval and political subjects; for him she was a politically active person, whose abilities were not adequately recognized by others. He wrote to her about his conviction that she could 'thunder forth such a torrent of eloquence that corruption and infamy would sink before your voice in however *exalted* situation it might be placed'.[22] Among the classical female characteristics that Nelson did discover in Lady Hamilton were those of virtue, a good heart and beauty.[23] Nelson's choice of qualities that he valued in Lady Hamilton confirms his preference for a woman who would be his equal and who would share his professional concerns as well as his private worries. Considering her his equal, it was far from his wish to dominate her in any way. On the contrary, he willingly described himself as 'the Conquered' and he confessed to his mistress: 'You command me. I obey you with the greatest pleasure.'[24] This voluntary subservience also extended to the carnal aspect of Nelson's relationship with her. Years later he expressed it in a letter: 'My soul is God's, let him dispose of it as it seemeth fit to his infinite wisdom, my body is Emma's.'[25]

When peace with France was agreed in October 1801, Nelson finally settled down with Lady Hamilton and her husband. She had in the meantime chosen a house at Merton south of London for them, which Nelson had purchased without having seen it. When she prepared it for his first arrival, he assured her: 'Your management of my affairs at Merton are, like whatever else you undertake, excellent.'[26] He even enjoyed the thought of Lady Hamilton as a proprietor: 'I fancy you setting forth to take possession of your little estate', where she should be the 'whole and sole commander'.[27] When he had desired his wife to choose a house for them, she had complained: 'I wish you would say something more positive about it [the house].'[28] Whereas Lady Nelson had clearly believed that financial matters were the responsibility of men, Lady Hamilton did not hesitate in spending her lover's money. This induced Nelson to complain some years later: 'if you have a fault it is that you give away much more than you can afford'.[29] Though he was the person who now mostly had to pay Lady Hamilton's bills, he had no desire to restrict her financial liberty. Instead, he was rather in favour of the financial independence of women. He wrote to his mistress: 'to the last moment of my breath they [my thoughts] will be occupied in leaving you independent of the world'.[30] After Sir William's death, just before war broke out again and Nelson had to go to sea once more, he sought to make his mistress financially independent by securing a pension for her in her own right. This he did by claiming that Lady Hamilton had achieved much by influencing the queen of Naples, including the victualling of the British fleet before the battle of the Nile. Although he most probably erred here,[31] his efforts again reflect how much he admired Lady Hamilton's political activity – an admiration that was not shared, however, by those in a position to decide whether she should receive a pension. He went on pursuing this aim, nevertheless, over several years with different administrations and he finally laid it down in the last codicil to his will on the morning of the battle of Trafalgar. He summarized her all-encompassing qualities: 'in every point of view, from Ambassatrice to the duties of domestic life, I never saw your equal'.[32] He had to choose the Italian title to describe her political position. The English title of 'Ambassadress of Great Britain' had been denied her, when George III agreed to her marriage to his ambassador to Naples, Sir William Hamilton.[33]

Nelson did not regard Lady Hamilton simply as an economically and politically active person, but also saw her in the position of a decision-maker in family affairs. He himself seems not to have felt any 'manly' constraints when dealing with children, of whom he was very fond, and his daughter's nurse later said: 'Lord Nelson was frequently her [Lady Hamilton's] companion in her visits to her [daughter], and often came alone, and played for hours with the infant on the floor.'[34] In his 'motherly' care of his daughter Nelson feared he might spoil her and so he desired Lady Hamilton to 'be a kind and affectionate *father* to my *dear* . . . daughter Horatia'.[35] What strikes one about Nelson's relationship with Lady Hamilton is the remarkable degree to which traditional gender roles are challenged. It is hard, if not impossible, to find traces in Nelson's relations with Lady Hamilton of the traditional concept of male/female behaviour and it is even possible to speak of them reversing gender roles.

A deep insight into Nelson's relationship with Lady Hamilton was prevented for a long time by the lack of detailed information about it, by doubts about the reliability of those sources that did appear in books, by moral inhibitions about dealing with such a scandalous relationship at all, and last, but not least, by fixed ideas about gender roles. Those early nineteenth-century authors who dealt with Lady Hamilton's role in Nelson's life shared a common interpretation of the roles of men and women. They regarded men primarily according to their position in society, as politicians, warriors, writers, builders, etc., whereas they defined women first of all through their relationship with men. This attitude to gender roles had a double significance for the treatment of Nelson's relations with Lady Hamilton. First, the role expected of Nelson was one of dominance over Lady Hamilton, whereas the role expected of Lady Hamilton was one of subservience to Nelson. Second, instead of dealing with his relationship to her, authors concentrated on hers to him. Since a relationship between a man and a woman was regarded as the defining aspect in a woman's life, the relationships between Nelson and the different women in his life were seen as female affairs that mattered to Nelson much less than to the women in his life. His relations with women were their responsibility.

For his early biographers, Nelson was defined primarily as a warrior, and the question of why Nelson felt attracted to a certain kind of woman or how he treated her did not matter much to these writers. Consequently, his relationship with Lady Hamilton is dealt with as an excursion into her life, if it is mentioned at all.

The first book to pay much attention to Lady Hamilton's role in Nelson's life was James Harrison's biography of Nelson. It appears that Lady Hamilton commissioned the author to write this life of Nelson in order to support her claim to a pension. Harrison stressed repeatedly throughout the text the importance of her support for British interests in Naples, particularly her supposed influence in getting the British squadron under Nelson victualled before the battle of the Nile. The suggestion that Lady Hamilton deserved a state pension was forcibly underlined by the fact that Nelson had included the claim in the last codicil to his will and that Sir William Hamilton was supposed to have made the same claim on his deathbed. In order to ensure that Lady Hamilton would be presented in a very positive light and Lady Nelson would appear in a less favourable one, Harrison portrayed the former as subservient to Nelson and the wife as demanding. Harrison offered some instances to illustrate how Lady Nelson estranged herself from her husband. Among her faults that he listed were her welcoming Nelson back in England with 'obvious coldness' and doing nothing to acknowledge Nelson's 'transcendent worth'.[36] Harrison alluded to there being other reasons for discontent on Nelson's part, but he chose to leave these 'behind the sacred veil of the connubial curtain'.[37] According to Harrison, Lady Hamilton, rather than Nelson's wife, represented the pattern of a good wife: 'the amiable demeanour of Lady Hamilton, whose tender regard for Sir William could not fail to excite the admiration of every virtuous visitor' also appealed to Nelson.[38] Lady Hamilton remained in the role of the faithful wife of Sir William Hamilton in matters concerning Nelson's relationship with his own wife. It was her husband to whom Nelson flew in his despair[39] and it was again Sir William who suggested that Nelson should in future live with the Hamiltons:

> Lord Nelson opposed this arrangement, on account of the slanders of the world: but Sir William Hamilton, with a noble disdain of malevolence, felt sufficiently satisfied of the virtue in which he confided; and Lady Hamilton, who never opposed Sir William in anything, without affecting to raise squeamish objections, readily signified her acquiescence. Lord Nelson then dropped on his knee, and piously appealed to Heaven, as witness of the purity of his attachment; and, with similar solemnity, they each, reciprocally, vowed an equally disinterested and indissoluble friendship.[40]

Though supportive of the proposal, Lady Hamilton is here portrayed as the obedient wife who does not develop an opinion of her own, but follows her husband's wishes, even if they may be construed as being to her own disadvantage.

Harrison's claim that Lady Hamilton was subservient to Nelson's wishes and never interfered in his affairs is difficult to reconcile with Nelson's claim that she had used her political influence to ensure that his fleet was victualled before the battle of the Nile. Since it was Harrison's task to justify this claim in order to help Lady Hamilton to obtain a pension, he described her as helping without positively acting. According to Harrison, Lady Hamilton procured 'from some being of a superior order, sylph, fairy, magician, or other person skilled in the occult sciences' a 'mystic charm' that made any 'Sicilian or Neapolitan governor' obey the wishes of the bearer, which Nelson then applied to the advantage of the British fleet.[41] Instead of portraying his patroness as a politically active person, Harrison preferred to attribute her power to witchcraft. Harrison portrayed Lady Hamilton as a woman who always remained subservient to the wishes of men. In his biography of Nelson, she never actively determines the course of events herself, but rather helps men, Nelson in particular, to do important things. How Lady Hamilton's obedience and unobtrusive encouragement could appeal to Nelson, who had stressed her political abilities so strongly in his last codicil to his will, remains unexplained.

Other biographers followed Harrison in claiming that it was through Lady Hamilton's influence that Nelson's squadron was victualled before the battle of the Nile, and they even went beyond Harrison in attributing an active part to her in the evacuation of the royal family from Naples. They showed, however, a tendency to reverse the ways in which they described Nelson's relations with his wife, Fanny, and with his mistress, Emma. In doing so they also reversed the judgement made on these two women. For them, Fanny Nelson is her husband's 'respected counsellor', who follows his wishes even against her own inclinations,[42] whereas Lady Hamilton does not show such subservience. Even though Nelson's most famous early biographer, Robert Southey, claimed that Nelson had 'forfeited [domestic happiness] for ever',[43] he did not regard the relationship as 'criminal' and he acknowledged positive traits in Lady Hamilton. He even accepted Harrison's claim that Nelson's squadron was victualled before the battle of the Nile thanks to the influence of Lady Hamilton (though this was achieved through 'secret orders to the Sicilian governors', not by means of a 'magic charm').[44]

An opportunity presented itself to examine more closely Nelson's attitude to Lady Hamilton, when the two volumes of *Letters of Lord Nelson to Lady Hamilton* were published anonymously in 1814. Two letters, in particular, contained explicit passages as to the carnal nature of their relationship. In one of them, written a few weeks after the birth of their daughter, Nelson wrote:

> You cannot think how my feelings are alive towards you: probably more than ever; and they never can be diminished. My hearty endeavours shall not be wanting, to improve and to give US NEW ties of

regard and affection . . . a finer child never was produced by any two persons. It was in truth a love-begotten child! . . . Recollect, I am, for ever, your's; aye, for ever, while life remains, your's, your's faithfully.[45]

The other letter (with an enclosure) was written on August 1803 and is equally explicit:

from the first moment of our happy, dear, enchanting, blessed meeting. The thought of such happiness, my dearest only beloved, makes the blood fly into my head . . . My heart is with you, cherish it . . . my wife in the eye of God . . . Ever, for ever, I am your's, only your's, even beyond this world . . . I only desire, my dearest Emma, that you will always believe, that Nelson's your own; Nelson's *Alpha* and *Omega* is *Emma*! I cannot alter; my affection and love is beyond even this world! . . . I feel, that you are the real friend of my bosom, and dearer to me than life; and, that I am the same to you . . . I rejoice that you have had so pleasant a trip into Norfolk; and I hope, one day, to carry you there by a nearer *tie* in law . . . than at present . . . time will pass away, till I have the inexpressible happiness of arriving at Merton [the house Nelson shared with Lady Hamilton]. Even the thought of it vibrates through my nerves; for, my love for you is as unbounded as the ocean![46]

The carnal nature of this relationship and the idea that it did indeed matter very much to Nelson, however, appears to have been too unattractive to develop. There was no investigation of what in Lady Hamilton had so attracted Nelson. When a much-read biography, the *Memoirs of Lady Hamilton*, was published anonymously in 1815, it presented the most scathing criticism of the relationship between her and Nelson, taking the easy course of blaming the scandalous relationship on her, rather than on Nelson. In this work, Lady Hamilton became as far removed from Harrison's subservient supporter of men as possible. She was now presented as the active manipulator of events: 'instead of fainting on the arm of Nelson [as Nelson had described their encounter], she clasped him in her own, and carried him into the cabin, followed by Sir William Hamilton, and the rest of the company'.[47] Lady Hamilton is portrayed as having treated Nelson's wife with similar resolution, 'swinging poor Lady Nelson by the arm round the room', when Nelson seemed tempted to return to his wife.[48] Such acts of aggression show Lady Hamilton seeking to influence matters in her own interest. She is shown controlling Nelson not only by physical action, but also, and mainly, by deluding him. According to this anonymous biographer, Lady Hamilton had frequently practised this method before and it had helped her to rise above her rank in society. She was described as cheating her lover, Charles Greville, and his uncle, later her husband, Sir William Hamilton.[49] The author assumed that otherwise these gentlemen could never have fallen for the blacksmith's daughter. In his judgement, the key to her success with men was her ability as an actress who knew how to perform a histrionic role in real life. She did not use her influence to any good purpose, however. This first biographer explicitly rejected Harrison's claim that Lady Hamilton's influence helped to ensure that Nelson's squadron was victualled at a critical time. Before welcoming Nelson after the battle of the Nile, 'Lady Hamilton began to rehearse some of her theatrical airs, and to put on all the appearance of a tragic queen'. As a result of her theatrical performances, Nelson 'was now so completely under the influence of an artful woman, as to have forgotten the respect that was due to the dignity of his character'.[50] Because of her dominance over Nelson, his involvement in the defeat of the Neapolitan revolution and even his separation from his wife are attributed entirely to her machinations. When physical force and mental domination threatened not to suffice, Lady Hamilton is shown keeping her hold over Nelson by allowing herself to become pregnant. In arguing thus, the *Memoirs of Lady Hamilton* was the first work to claim that the relationship between Nelson and Lady Hamilton had been of a carnal nature and that at least one child had resulted from the affair.[51] Taken together, Lady Hamilton's various attempts to gain influence over Nelson led to a reversal of gender roles. Instead of the female partner being obedient and dutiful towards the male partner, as Lady Hamilton had been described by Harrison and Lady Nelson had been depicted by other biographers, it was now Nelson who ended up being 'dutiful and attentive to the commands of this artful and rapacious woman'.[52]

This biography made it abundantly clear that the responsibility for the immoral attachment between Nelson and Lady Hamilton rested entirely with her. It offered two major and in part contradictory reasons to explain the supposed moral degradation of Lady Hamilton. On the one hand, it blamed her 'pristine meanness', which 'continued through life', on her lowly social origins; in this context it was maintained that there is a 'Scoundrelism about persons of low birth'.[53] On the other hand, she was also portrayed as a victim of circumstances; she was shown as a girl who was drawn into 'intrigue and duplicity' by her unfortunate situation and by malign influences.[54] Far from blaming the limited opportunities available to daughters of poor parents in eighteenth-century Britain, it was suggested that to prevent such women following the immoral path taken by Lady Hamilton they should remain within their humble sphere. According to this anonymous work it was the fact that a poor woman was allowed to break out of her social sphere that led to the ensnaring of Nelson.

The publication of some of Nelson's letters to Lady Hamilton, which was attributed to her, and this book about her, which was more of a diatribe than a biography, strongly influenced what was written about Nelson's relations with his mistress in the following decades. The publications of 1814 and 1815 had the effect of driving serious biographers away from the subject of Nelson, and no author devoted any space to exploring any further the scandalous details of his relations with Lady Hamilton. Those who for some reason touched on the subject (authors of naval histories, for example) mainly adopted the view that Nelson had been 'possessed by a demon'.[55] Some writers increased Lady Hamilton's vileness to monstrous proportions. Even before Nelson had received the dukedom of Bronte from the king of Naples, Lady Hamilton was depicted as inciting Nelson to be ruthless with the Neapolitan rebels: 'Haul down the flag of truce Bronte . . . No truce with the rebels.'[56] Among the new descriptions of Lady Hamilton's influence over Nelson the *Personal Memoirs or Reminiscences* by Pryse Lockhart Gordon has the greatest claim to authenticity. Gordon, after all, had met the two in Palermo in 1799. Thirty years later this upper-class and outspoken Whig, who sympathized with the Neapolitan revolution, remembered the royalist scene at Palermo. He concluded his slighting judgement of Lady Hamilton with the comment: 'what could be expected from such a *parvenue*?' This social prejudice against the 'vulgar' Lady Hamilton recurs throughout his whole account. Not surprisingly, Gordon detected severe character faults in the social upstart: 'ambition and intrigue were her ruling passions'.[57] Like her earlier, anonymous, biographer, Gordon saw her as crossing gender boundaries and empowering herself by dominating Nelson. She was not only unladylike, but even lacking in any womanly traits: 'There was nothing feminine about her.'[58] Nelson hardly appears as anything else but her prey. Although Gordon believed that Nelson was originally 'amiable' and possessed of 'noble qualities', he concluded that 'his heart was corrupted, and his mind paralysed', his 'qualities were paralysed by the syren into whose hands he unfortunately fell', and he ended up 'in her chains'.[59] When it actually came to narrating accounts of the activities of Nelson and Lady Hamilton, Gordon relied on the Bronte story mentioned above. Sensibly leaving out the impossible address of 'Bronte', Lady Hamilton was now reported as simply exclaiming: 'This will never do – we must have blood!' Gordon also, somewhat contradictorily, reported that Lady Hamilton fainted, when still in the Bay of Naples, at seeing a pig being carved up to be eaten, because it reminded her of Caracciolo. Nevertheless, she did 'eat heartily of it – aye!'[60] Lady Hamilton was not the only woman to faint conveniently when something dramatic was occurring. 'Mrs C[harle]s L[ock]e, the beautiful and amiable wife of our consul general', fainted, according to Gordon, when Lady Hamilton kissed 'the encrusted Jacobin blood' on a sword that a Turk passed to her, claiming that he had cut off the heads of twenty French prisoners with it.[61] Although the story suspiciously fits the taste of the day for denigrating Lady Hamilton and clearly supports Gordon's blatant prejudice against her, it has been repeated frequently ever since.

When Nelson's reputation began to recover in the early 1840s, Lieutenant G. S. Parsons, who had served under Nelson as a midshipman in the Mediterranean in 1799, published his *Nelsonian Reminiscences. Leaves from Memory's*

Log. In these memoirs he also dealt with Lady Hamilton, 'this unjustly treated and wonderful woman'.[62] In the few passages in which Parsons mentioned her, he praised her 'kindness'.[63] Feeling personally indebted to her, he commented: 'May it be made up to thee in another and a better world, sweet lady! for man's injustice in this — *where thou hast been most foully calumniated.*' In assessing the criticism levelled at Lady Hamilton, Parsons was aware of the importance that her social background had played in fuelling these attacks. He attributed any weakness she may have had to her 'low birth', but pointed out: 'Had that well-proportioned head been encircled by a diadem, thy memory would have been held up for the adoration, instead of the execration, of mankind.'[64] Parson's *Nelsonian Reminiscences* give an insight into how Nelson and Lady Hamilton interacted that confirms the way they challenged gender stereotypes. Nelson was reported to have 'blushed like a fair maiden', when Lady Hamilton '[b]ending her graceful form over her superb harp . . . sang the praises of Nelson'.[65] In contrast to such shyness, Parsons described Lady Hamilton as a very determined person. Half-jokingly she is said to have 'declared, "His lordship must serve me"'. She indeed made Nelson support young Parsons, 'dictating a strong certificate, which, under her direction, he wrote'. She went on arranging matters: '"Now, my young friend", said her ladyship, with that irresistible smile which gave such expression of sweetness to her lovely countenance, "obey my directions minutely; send this to Lord St Vincent, at Brentwood, so as to reach him on Sunday morning".'[66] In this very sympathetic account, Nelson hardly appears to make any decision for himself.

As the surviving eye-witnesses to this relationship died, writers had to rely increasingly on Nelson's letters in assessing the nature of his attachment to Lady Hamilton. In this context, Nicholas Harris Nicolas's edition of *The Dispatches and Letters of Lord Nelson* was of particular importance, because it was used as a work of reference by later biographers. In matters regarding Lady Hamilton, however, it was unreliable. Nicolas not only omitted many of Nelson's letters to Lady Hamilton in his work, but also doubted the authenticity of the two most telling letters from the collection that were published anonymously in 1814, and which were quoted above.[67] Having discarded these passages as not being authentic, Nicolas argued that there was 'great doubt . . . whether the intimacy between Lord Nelson and Lady Hamilton was ever, in the usual sense of the word, of a criminal nature'.[68] Nicolas clearly struggled to convince, because he also stated that 'during a long separation from his wife on the Public service in the Mediterranean, he [Nelson] so far yielded to temptation as to become the father of a child'.[69] Nicolas had also to explain why Nelson had actually separated from his wife if his relationship with Lady Hamilton was of a purely platonic nature. Here Nicolas referred to a letter which he had received from Nelson's solicitor, Haslewood, who blamed Nelson's wife Fanny for the separation. Haslewood remembered that when Nelson had mentioned Lady Hamilton at a dinner, his wife protested and left the party, 'muttering something about her mind being made up . . . to the day of her husband's glorious death, she never made any apology for her abrupt and ungentle conduct above related, or any overture towards a reconciliation'.[70] As a result, Nelson merely appeared as the victim of female 'temptation' and of his wife's lack of consideration, instead of being acknowledged as a committed lover.

Nicolas's assessment of the relationship between Nelson and Lady Hamilton as platonic was forcibly challenged by Thomas Joseph Pettigrew's two-volume *Memoirs of the Life of Vice-Admiral Lord Viscount Nelson*. The justification for Pettigrew's revelations was his claim that Nelson himself had made his relationship with Lady Hamilton 'a subject of history by naming her and his child Horatia in a Codicil to his Will on the day of his death, and leaving them as a testamentary bequest to his country'.[71] This biography of Nelson, making use of a near complete collection of Nelson's letters to Lady Hamilton, advanced two main arguments: one about Lady Hamilton and the other about her relationship with Nelson, each in a separate chapter at the end of the second volume. The claim, that Nelson and Lady Hamilton were the parents of Horatia, was only a secondary consideration and the argument was not well developed. Pettigrew wrote much more about Lady Hamilton being an intelligent woman, who firmly supported Nelson. He acknowledged that some aspects of her youth had previously been the subject of criticism. In her praise, however, he quoted George Romney, whose model she had been. He also described how she had assisted Nelson to victual his squadron before the battle of the Nile and how, later, she had helped the Neapolitan royal family to flee Naples. Having thus praised Lady Hamilton, Pettigrew went on to describe her unsuccessful attempts to obtain a pension, which were partly thwarted because Nelson's brother failed to make public Nelson's last codicil to his will. Pettigrew's claim that Lady Hamilton had been let down by her native country roused the interest of his contemporaries. In reaction to a review of his biography in *The Times*, which had treated the issue only in passing,[72] letters to the editor focused on nothing but the neglect of Lady Hamilton. If it was not referred to as a shameful act by an 'ungrateful nation', it was blamed on Nelson's brother. No one seems to have doubted Lady Hamilton's claim to the nation's gratitude and, in two letters, published on the same day, it was suggested that Nelson's daughter, at least, should belatedly benefit from her father's sacrifice.[73] A Nelson Memorial Fund was created, to which Prince Albert among many others subscribed.[74] In the following years the public was keen to fulfil 'the last request of the illustrious Nelson' by patronizing and supporting Horatia's sons.[75] Subsequent biographers did not react in the same way as public opinion had done. Only a few insignificant accounts took up Pettigrew's view of the carnal relationship between Nelson and Lady Hamilton. This was partly due to the fact that biographers still neglected the subject of Nelson in general and his relationship with Lady Hamilton in particular. In the 1880s, John Knox Laughton went further and rejected 'Pettigrew's bulky work' as 'mainly filled with the story of Nelson's supposed amour with Lady Hamilton, and . . . better suited for the society of the "School for Scandal" than for the student of naval history'. With some difficulty Laughton denounced the most telling letter printed by Pettigrew as 'fictitious'.[76]

The treatment of Nelson's relationship with Lady Hamilton did undergo lasting change in the late 1880s. At a time of rising interest in Nelson parts of the letters that Pettigrew had used, but which had not been published in the anonymous edition of 1814, as well as letters that had never been published before, became available to the public. The wealthy collector Alfred Morrison made the original letters accessible, first to authors on a private basis and then, more widely, by publishing them himself in 1893. The disclosure of these letters wrought two major changes in the image of Nelson. First, they initiated a serious discussion of his relationship with Lady Hamilton, mainly whether it was of an erotic and carnal nature, but also whether Lady Hamilton had indeed helped him to get his squadron victualled before the battle of the Nile. Second, the sheer mass of letters that Nelson was now known to have written to Lady Hamilton during long spells of separation forced biographers to acknowledge at last the obvious importance that this relationship had for Nelson.

Those who bothered to read these letters could hardly fail to notice the carnal nature of the relationship. Passages that Pettigrew had suppressed or that had not been at his disposal included: 'My longing for you, both person and conversation you may readily imagine. What must be my sensations at the idea of sleeping with you! it setts [sic] me on fire, even the thoughts, much more would the reality' (written on 1 March 1801);[77] and 'I shall soon return, and then we will take our fill of love. No, we never can be satiated till death divides us' (written on 9 March 1801).[78] In an elaborate two-volume study about *Lady Hamilton and Lord Nelson*, based on the Morrison collection, John Cordy Jeaffreson was the first to deal with the erotic nature of the relationship and with Lady Hamilton's practical support for Nelson. The author cautiously argued in support of Pettigrew's view that Horatia was the daughter of Nelson *and* Lady Hamilton. But, unlike Pettigrew, he denied Lady Hamilton's part in the victualling of the British fleet. Jeaffreson's view of the erotic nature of Nelson's relationship with Lady Hamilton was soon generally accepted. The discovery that many of the letters that Pettigrew had printed were actually authentic was often difficult to accept, however. Laughton, who had before so vehemently defended Nelson's morality, focused now just on the claim that Lady Hamilton had not helped to get Nelson's squadron victualled and it took several more years before he openly acknowledged that Nelson and Lady Hamilton had had a daughter together.

With the erotic nature of the relationship now accepted, biographers of Nelson had to endeavour to analyse and interpret the affair. Jeaffreson, however, still minimized Nelson's guilt, mainly by suggesting that the intercourse that had led to the birth of Horatia had merely been a 'momentary submission to an overpowering impulse of passion'.[79] He did not acknowledge that Nelson loved Lady Hamilton; against the evidence, he even wrote of a 'platonic attachment' and 'brotherly liking'.[80] He also insisted that Nelson's judgement was never affected by Lady Hamilton. Even so, Nelson's 'lamentable misadventure' needed some explanation, and here Jeaffreson stuck to the image of Lady Hamilton as an actress in real life.[81] What had drawn Nelson towards Lady Hamilton was, according to Jeaffreson, his 'shyness', 'rusticity' and his 'disposition to regard women worshipfully'.[82] Once he was drawn in, his wife committed the mistake of confronting him with 'sudden anger' so that he felt compelled to stay with his mistress.[83] From then on, Jeaffreson calculated, Nelson and Lady Hamilton were not that much together and, if together, mostly in the company of others. Jeafferson even assumed that Nelson's marriage would have been restored over time 'by force of their never-uprooted love'.[84] He drew his conviction of the superior attraction of Lady Nelson from her letters, which he described as 'more nervous and eloquent of womanly devotedness than the epistles he received from Lady Hamilton'.[85] Jeaffreson, like so many of his predecessors, was influenced by the nineteenth-century ideal that women should devote their lives to men. He ignored the indications that Nelson might not have shared this notion of the gendered roles in an ideal partnership.

Later biographers had even more difficulty in dealing with Nelson's affair with Lady Hamilton, because they did not follow Jeaffreson's assumption that Nelson's attraction to Lady Hamilton had only been a rather short-lived and unimportant affair. Nevertheless, Nelson's deep and enduring love for Lady Hamilton was still particularly hard for them to understand, because they hero-worshipped him and regarded her as a 'vain, low-born, unprincipled woman'.[86] Over the next decades Lady Hamilton remained a decidedly unpleasant person in any account of Nelson: she was a 'wicked', intemperate, 'vulgar', 'empty-headed' and 'silly' 'liar', and a manipulating actress with a 'love of notoriety', who could not even boast an attractive appearance, since she was 'decidedly over-plump'.[87] Biographers of Nelson agreed that she never loved Nelson as he loved her. In one biography of Nelson, published in 1919, her name is replaced by disparaging epithets referring to her as a 'female nightmare' and a 'noxious creature'.[88] The more positive image of Lady Hamilton that developed at that time in biographies about her[89] did not affect the low opinion of her that appeared in biographies of Nelson.

The very negative image that biographers of Nelson had of Lady Hamilton compelled them to examine how Nelson could enter into a relationship with her and long maintain it. Mahan helped to spread Jeaffreson's opinion that the explanation lay in Nelson's character. He asserted that Nelson had a 'tendency to idealize' and that he had an 'impressionable fancy', which led to 'extravagance of admiration'.[90] According to Mahan, Nelson also showed these characteristics in his professional life – in his relationship with his friends and subordinates, for example. Thus, Mahan saw Nelson the lover and Nelson the warrior as related. Philip H. Colomb, too, recognized the connection between

Nelson's character and his love for Lady Hamilton. He pointed out: 'The earlier biographers of Nelson, especially Southey, altogether failed to realize his passionate, impulsive character, and to them, therefore, the lamentable relations with Lady Hamilton were incongruous.'[91] Later authors extended the analysis of what it was in Nelson's character that made him fall in love with Lady Hamilton. They observed an emotional side to Nelson that they regarded as 'feminine' and which was expressed by a need for approbation, if not downright flattery.[92] Nelson's emotional needs and his particular circumstances combined to conspire to make him a slave to Lady Hamilton. The affair was even threatening to his masculinity. Mahan saw Nelson as relinquishing his masculinity to a masculine woman, who 'dragged a man of Nelson's masculine renown about England and the Continent, till he was the mock of all beholders'.[93] The view that Nelson was degraded by his relationship with Lady Hamilton was not new, but what was original was that biographers of Nelson now saw him actually submitting to Lady Hamilton. Nelson's decision to enter into a full relationship with Lady Hamilton is sometimes referred to in terms of a naval defeat, such as: 'he struck his colours to Lady Hamilton'.[94] The result of this surrender to an artful woman was seen to have had serious effects on Nelson's mental stability: 'everything was unhinged with him'.[95]

As authors developed their arguments about the feminine aspects in Nelson's character and about his loss of masculinity, they constructed an image of Nelson that was increasingly removed from their stronger image of Nelson as the successful warrior. While Mahan could still assert that passion and professionalism went together, his followers, resenting Nelson's relations with Lady Hamilton, dropped this connection. Thursfield was the first, in 1909, to reach the conclusion that a biographer needed to divide Nelson into two characters. The letters published by Morrison were so shocking to him that he proclaimed that they showed that: 'the incomparable Nelson of the *Victory*'s quarter-deck and cockpit is as completely degraded into the sensual, erotic, and frantically jealous paramour of Lady Hamilton as the Dr Jekyll of Stevenson's story was ever transformed into Mr. Hyde'.[96] The introduction of the double Nelson – one, the glorious warrior; the other, the besotted and emasculated lover – had a profound effect on the image of Nelson. Instead of investigating the aspects of Nelson's character that had come to light with his letters to Lady Hamilton, and seeking to integrate them into other aspects of the man, biographers split them off from their pre-conceived image of Nelson, which was that of the warrior. Their former image of Nelson could thereby survive untouched, merely accompanied by a subordinate image of the 'weak' side in Nelson.

Some authors built further theories on the pattern of the double Nelson. C. S. Forester claimed in his biography of Nelson that towards the end of his life the warrior side of his personality was again gaining the upper hand:

> Nelson . . . felt a yearning for the ordered routine of shipboard life
> and the unchallenged position of a Commander-in-Chief after the late

hours and melodramatic jealousies of Merton . . . From all the evidence it seems as though he had grown beyond the really wantonly, mad phase of passion.[97]

The last remark was not borne out by contemporary evidence, since Lord Minto, visiting Nelson and Lady Hamilton at Merton during Nelson's short stay in England in 1805, remarked in a letter to his wife at the time: 'the passion is as hot as ever'.[98] Instead of arguing for a breach between Nelson and Lady Hamilton, Edinger and Neep described Nelson's efforts to have the two sides of his personality and the two parts of his life equally acknowledged in public. According to Edinger and Neep, the rest of his life became a doomed struggle for some public recognition of his relationship with Lady Hamilton.[99] They ridiculed Nelson's visitors to Merton:

> Local celebrities such as Mr Stinton the grocer, Mr Halfhide the gentleman farmer, or Mr Abraham Goldsmid 'the financial gentleman', might hang breathlessly upon the favour of his patronage and load him with invitations and hampers of game; but the Court, Officialdom, the Nobility, London and Society were inflexible in their enmity.[100]

Faced with this social ostracism, Nelson was said to have determined on a form of suicide in a decisive naval action: 'his world had not accepted his Emma. They would not do it, even for his sake while he lived; but it would be hard for England to deny his wishes if he died victorious.'[101] The assumption that Nelson desired to be acknowledged as a member of the upper classes is contradicted, however, by Nelson's taste in company, expressed in letters to Lady Hamilton: 'None of the great shall enter our peaceful abode.'[102]

Much more enduring than ideas of tension between Nelson and Lady Hamilton or notions of a breach between Nelson and British society was the suggestion of a conflict within Nelson himself. C. J. Britton, though very favourably inclined towards Lady Hamilton, unknowingly gave this inner conflict an outward expression by distinguishing between Nelson at sea and Nelson on land.[103] This difference between the shore-based Nelson and the Nelson on and in his natural element was taken up by Admiral W. M. James as the key to Nelson's love for Lady Hamilton. He contrasted 'the Nelson of St. Vincent and the Nile' with 'another Nelson who was seen very occasionally — never on board ship'.[104] Admiral James even hinted at a possible explanation for this duality, by stressing the importance of an all-male society: 'whenever he was alone with other men, and free from the influence of Emma, he was always the same simple, rather boyish, fellow'.[105] With such powerful backing from an ideology of masculinity, the supposed split in Nelson's character that was offered as an explanation for his relations with Lady Hamilton survived throughout the second half of the twentieth century. Clemence Dane's interesting remark in her preface to an edition of Nelson's letters was not followed up by later biographers of Nelson:

One has to realize that, until he met his 'guardian angel' as he calls her, a side of Nelson's nature was undeveloped. It was through Emma that he found himself a human being. His love-letters are the raw material of his nature, and will, I suppose, some day serve a dramatist as the stuff of the Cleopatra story in Plutarch served Shakespeare, even though a classic distance of time must elapse before the greatest of all English love-stories can come into its own.[106]

With Nelson's passionate relationship with Lady Hamilton relegated to a subordinate aspect of his life and character, many other facets of his personality went unexplored and the judgement on their relationship that had been developed in reaction to the publication of Morrison's collection of letters remained unchallenged. Biographers went on describing the woman whom Nelson loved passionately as simply 'vulgar' and they have not much explored her personal traits, which they have preferred to regard as the mere poses of a 'consummate actress'.[107] Instead of analysing the relationship itself and how Nelson himself saw it, biographers went on using the same explanations as to why Nelson fell in love with this seemingly unattractive person: his ill health, partly caused by his head wound; the 'feminine streak in his character'; the early death of his mother; and the striking contrast between his modest home and the splendour of Naples.[108] As to Nelson's wife, Frances, there remained, throughout the second half of the twentieth century, a strong tendency to regard her as 'ill-suited' to him.[109] Since the late 1960s authors have also made clear the time when Nelson's 'love affair with Emma became a physical relationship'.[110]

In his biography of 1958 Oliver Warner attempted a new assessment of why Nelson felt so attracted to Lady Hamilton. He pointed out that, in contrast to Frances Nelson, Lady Hamilton was an active, energetic woman and that this was exactly what Nelson liked in her. He was also the first to conclude that Nelson was actually happy with Lady Hamilton.[111] This tentative effort to understand Nelson's love for Lady Hamilton has not been followed up by subsequent biographers, however. Even Warner himself did not build upon it in his later works. This may be explained by the fact that he never challenged the traditional characterization of Lady Hamilton and therefore he still found it difficult to offer a fuller explanation of Nelson's love for her. Other authors have merely underlined the predominant view of Nelson's relationship with Lady Hamilton as that of a weak man dominated by an indecently strong woman. Only in the mid-1990s did a biographer follow Warner's early lead. Roger Morriss judged that Nelson and Lady Hamilton felt 'mutual passion' for each other and that they were 'at a personal level . . . clearly highly compatible'.[112] Edgar Vincent's biography of Nelson supported this view. He saw Nelson 'cooperating politically' with Lady Hamilton and he maintained that the 'relationship . . . gave him everything he had been looking for'.[113] Observing some 'important similarities' between the lovers which help to explain their mutual attraction, Vincent insisted that the relationship was based on equality and that Nelson was *not* simply seduced by an 'enchantress'.[114] It remains to be seen whether these ideas will be developed more fully by future biographers.

A number of factors have conspired to prevent authors changing the established perception of the relationship between Nelson and Lady Hamilton, notwithstanding the evidence about it provided in the explicit letters from Nelson to his mistress. One reason lies in the scattering of these letters over various printed primary sources (and over a much greater number of manuscript sources), which makes it difficult to assess the significance of this correspondence as a whole. Few biographers have explored this unwieldy mass of evidence. Another reason is that biographers wished to distance themselves from any form of hero-worship. What most late Victorian hero-worshippers had found impossible to defend, later biographers could still not show in a positive light decades later. Moreover, there remains an enduring class bias against Lady Hamilton which has obstructed a balanced interpretation of Nelson's relationship with her. Even her accent has been made the subject of amusement: Jack Russell told how a nun compared Lady Hamilton's 'classic features' to those of a 'marble statue she saw when she was in the world. '"I think she flatered me up", said Emma, who had only to open her mouth to ruin the whole impression.'[115] Last, but not least, some stereotypical attitudes about gender roles have led authors to resent the whole affair because it appears to be such a serious challenge to traditional ideas about masculinity and femininity. Biographers of Nelson should seek to understand this complex emotional, passionate and sexual relationship that was clearly so important to Nelson. Only then will they understand the whole man and his multifaceted personality.

5

A hero's death

In his book about *Nelson and the Hamiltons* Jack Russell claimed: 'Nelson had been great in his life, but in his death he was sublime.'[1] Indeed, a dramatist could hardly have created a more heroic death. The part of the battle of Trafalgar that Nelson could influence, the approach and attack, had just been finished and the battle was at its height when Nelson was hit by the fatal musket ball. He was conscious to the end, leaving messages and receiving the news of his victory. He eventually fell silent when the battle was decided and he died when the last distant shots were fired. This apparently perfect heroic death was nevertheless as arbitrary and painful as any death in war can be.

Dressed in his usual frock-coat,[2] Nelson was walking the *Victory*'s quarter deck, surrounded by smoke and the deafening noise of battle, when he was shot. His flagship was at that moment engaged in intense fighting with the French two-decker, *Redoutable*. Musketmen, posted in the *Redoutable*'s rigging, filled their outdated weapons with pieces of metal, among them old bullets that would not fit into slim modern gun-barrels, and fired randomly down onto the *Victory*'s deck. One of the old, outsized bullets hit Nelson in the left shoulder,[3] taking a piece of his epaulette through his left lung, 'dividing in its passage a large branch of the pulmonary artery' and breaking two dorsal vertebrae, where it finally came to lodge.[4] Hurled onto *Victory*'s deck by the impact, Nelson was assisted by two seamen, who carried him below.[5]

On the orlop deck, below the water-line, where the wounded were being cared for, Nelson was received by the surgeon William Beatty and the purser Mr Burke, who carried him to a bed. There the ship's chaplain Dr Scott joined Nelson and was not to leave him again. Nelson immediately told all about him that he knew he was dying, adding 'in a hurried, agitated manner': 'Remember me to Lady Hamilton! remember me to Horatia! remember me to all my friends. Doctor, remember me to Mr Rose: tell him I have made a will, and left Lady Hamilton and Horatia to my Country.' Scott wrote two months later, on his voyage home with Nelson's body, to the said Mr Rose that Nelson 'repeated his remembrances to Lady Hamilton and Horatia, and told me to mind what he said, several times'.[6] Nelson calmed down eventually. The severe pain he was suffering prevented him from connecting more than a few uninterrupted words and it permitted him to speak only in a low voice. Although communication was both difficult and painful, Nelson made great efforts to express himself. Whereas Nelson had addressed the nature of his wound openly, those around him denied the fact that he was dying. Beatty, the surgeon, examined Nelson's back, but concealed 'the true nature of his wound' to Nelson himself, though not to Scott, the chaplain, Burke, the purser, and Captain Hardy. Burke tried to cheer Nelson up by telling him that he himself would be 'the bearer of the joyful tidings' of his victory, but Nelson – in the words of Beatty's elegant account – cut him short: 'It is nonsense, Mr Burke, to suppose I can live: my sufferings are great, but they will all be soon over.' When Scott, the chaplain, insisted that Nelson should not 'despair of living' and should trust 'that Divine Providence would restore him', Nelson had just energy left to say: 'it is all over; it is all over'. When the desperately awaited Hardy arrived, he tried to encourage Nelson by speaking of 'some prospect of life', but Nelson remained unconvinced. Having received news of the battle and having ascertained that 'none of *our* ships have struck', he asked Hardy to make sure that Lady Hamilton would receive all his belongings.

Nelson had now very little time, and even less energy to live. Well aware of his situation, he sent the surgeon away to care for those wounded whom he could assist, 'for you can do nothing for me'. Nelson now repeatedly asked for something to drink, for air to be fanned towards his face, for his face to be wiped, and later for his breast to be rubbed. Every now and then pain seized him so vehemently that 'he suddenly and loudly expressed a wish to die'. So far, no one had yet admitted to Nelson that he was indeed dying. Knowing that a broken backbone was mortal, Nelson told Burke and Scott: 'The lower part of me is dead.' When Burke lifted Nelson's legs, Nelson insisted that he could not feel anything.[7] It remained for the dying Nelson to make Beatty, the surgeon, acknowledge his situation. He sent for him and in order to make it easier for Beatty to stop claiming that he would live, Nelson began: 'I forgot to tell you before that all motion and feeling below my breast are gone; and *you* very well *know* I can live but a short time.' When Beatty, in response, started to examine his legs, Nelson merely remarked: 'I am too certain of it, Scott and Burke have tried it already.' Only now did Beatty admit to Nelson that he was indeed dying. While Beatty was so affected by his own declaration that he had to withdraw 'a few steps to conceal his emotions', Nelson merely declared: 'I know it. I feel something rising in my breast which tells me I am gone.' Beatty's final admission enabled Nelson to make his peace with the world. He soliloquized: 'God be praised, I have done my duty', and he asked Scott to pray for him. Although he wished to die because of the pain he was suffering, he still whispered 'one would like to live a little longer, too', he worried what would become of Lady Hamilton, and he desired that she should be given the ring on his finger, of which she had the corresponding one.[8]

Captain Hardy came to visit Nelson a second time. Although he could not yet be certain of the exact number of enemy ships that had surrendered, he was already in a situation to congratulate Nelson on a 'complete' victory. Nelson now started to think about what might happen after the battle, and since it was obvious that a storm was coming, he emphatically requested Hardy to anchor the ships. When Hardy cautiously referred to Admiral Collingwood, Nelson's second-in-command, Nelson unsuccessfully tried to raise himself up and vehemently insisted that Hardy should anchor. His mortal wound, however, soon forced him to calm down. Nelson spoke again of Lady Hamilton and then addressed the matter directly: 'I shall die, Hardy.' Hardy, too, was more open now: 'Is your pain great, Sir?' To this, Nelson answered: 'Yes, but I shall live half an hour yet. – Hardy, kiss me!' Hardy met this request and after a while knelt down to kiss Nelson again. It appears he wanted to show Nelson that he too had understood this was the final goodbye and that he wished to express this with an appropriate gesture. Nelson acknowledged this: 'God bless you, Hardy.' When Hardy left, 'Nelson exclaimed very earnestly more than once, "Hardy, if I live I'll bring the Fleet to an anchor; if I live I'll anchor; if I live I'll anchor;" and this was earnestly repeated even when the Captain was out of hearing.'

In order to relieve his pain, Nelson asked to be turned on his right side. This made the blood flow even more into his lungs and thus accelerated the process of suffocation. Nelson confessed to Scott, 'I have *not* been a great sinner', and he asked him to '*Remember* that I leave Lady Hamilton and my daughter Horatia as a legacy to my country: and never forget Horatia.' He spoke less now, mostly demanding 'drink', 'fan', 'rub'. He also stated again, 'Thank God, I have done my duty'; these appear to have been his last words. After uttering them, Nelson became much calmer and 'went off, as if asleep'. Half an hour after he had become speechless, Beatty ascertained that Nelson was indeed dead.

When news of the battle of Trafalgar reached Britain, there was great public curiosity about how Nelson had died. The very first accounts of Nelson's death were not based on any direct information from eye-witnesses; instead, they reflected more those ideals which their authors expected to find in a perfect heroic death. Several authors felt free to furnish their readers with a mixture of vague second-hand accounts about how Nelson had died and some romantic additions of their own. Some elements of these early accounts were corrected, but others survived into later descriptions. The accounts of Nelson's death centre around two main narratives: the scene on deck, where Nelson was shot, and the scene below deck, where Nelson finally died.

One of the questions that naturally demanded an answer was: how was Nelson hit? An account published in *The Times* only one day after the news of Nelson's death asserted: 'the gallant Nelson received a musket ball in his breast. What was very remarkable, it absolutely penetrated through the star which he wore.' The allegation that the ball had passed through Nelson's 'star' was never explicitly denied and the point of impact was only corrected over time as being at the shoulder. One biographer concluded, still in 1805:

> There can be no doubt that a deliberate aim had been taken at his lordship. He had on the insignia of the different orders conferred on him . . . He received the musket ball below his left shoulder through the centre of one of his decorations.[9]

This doubtful claim, that the orders on Nelson's uniform had attracted the attention of sharpshooters supposedly positioned in the rigging of the French ship, raised the question of whether Nelson could have avoided exposing himself in this way. Most authors who repeated this claim were unaware that Nelson had embroidered versions of his orders stitched on each of his uniform coats and that at the battle of Trafalgar he was simply wearing an ordinary undress uniform coat, not a dress coat with all of his decorations pinned to it. They assumed that Nelson could have laid aside his orders (as if they had not been sewn to his uniform), that he was dressed in 'full uniform', that he 'unfortunately, was dressed in a coat which was decorated with the Stars of the various Orders with which he had been honoured' (as if he had had any uniform coat without orders), or even that he had 'in the morning put on the stars of his different orders'.[10] The supposition that Nelson had had a choice as to whether to wear his orders on the day of battle led to different explanations as to why he actually wore these orders. It was asserted that he had been alerted to the possible danger of wearing his orders – according to several biographies by 'his secretary and chaplain', but more commonly by Captain Hardy. The reasons that Nelson is supposed to have given for not changing his uniform range from having no time to do so, to a conscious pride in his honours that had been so hard won. The dramatic phrase 'in honour I gained them; in honour I will die in them', became particularly popular in accounts of his death.[11] Accounts of Nelson not wishing to change his uniform have survived until today, although Nelson's surgeon at Trafalgar, Dr Beatty, pointed out as early as 1807 that Nelson wore his usual frock-coat. Beatty even explicitly commented: 'It has been reported, but erroneously, that His Lordship was actually requested by his Officers to change his dress, or to cover his stars.'[12]

Different versions circulated as to how Nelson actually fell when he was shot. Some early accounts did not even accept that he had fallen at all. In their descriptions Nelson had merely 'staggered against the officer who was next him'.[13] Even if an account accepted that Nelson had fallen, this fall was described in a heroic manner. One account stated that Nelson was in the act of giving an order when he was shot; another report described how Captain Hardy tried to warn Nelson just before the fatal shot was fired. Captain Hardy became the favourite figure in Nelson's dying moments on deck. On 7 December 1805 *The Times* published an article from the *Gibraltar Chronicle*:

Nelson 'was immediately sensible of the wound being mortal, and said, with a smile, to Captain Hardy . . .: "They have done for me at last!"' This phrase appealed so much that it was not only copied, but also transferred to another episode in Nelson's life. He was now reported to have said, when he received the wound in his right arm in 1797 which led to its amputation: 'The Dons have me at last!'[14] On receiving his fatal wound at Trafalgar, Nelson was also reported to have asked Hardy to 'Put something over my face', so that none of his crew would notice that he was wounded.[15] The authenticity of all these words that Nelson was supposed to have uttered was questioned when the *Victory* arrived in England – and with it the eye-witnesses of Nelson's death. A 'statement . . . authenticated by Mr Beatty and Mr Bourke', the *Victory's* surgeon and purser, clarified that Nelson 'was not, as has been related, picked up by Captain Hardy'; instead two seamen had found him and carried him below.[16] Not all regarded this plain account as appropriate to the occasion, however. Some authors mentioned the two sailors, but then had Hardy join the scene. When Beatty, the surgeon of the *Victory*, published his *Authentic Narrative of the Death of Lord Nelson* in 1807, he now – contradicting what he had 'authenticated' before – embellished his own narrative: he added 'the Serjeant-Major (Secker) of Marines' to the two seamen, let Hardy join the scene, inserted Nelson's words, 'they have done for me at last', and claimed that Nelson had covered his face with his own handkerchief.[17] Through the authority of Beatty, this version of events has become the accepted account.

On being carried below Nelson was said to have noticed that the tiller ropes were slack or shot through. According to this little story, Nelson had so much presence of mind – even in the arms of death – that he asked Captain Hardy to be informed of the fact. This too was first spread by Beatty and then by the fact that Southey printed it. Later authors, however, rejected the claim that such a story would show presence of mind and doubted its authenticity. The tiller ropes connected the wheel with the tiller, but since the wheel of the *Victory* had been shot away at the beginning of the battle and 'the ship was being steered at the time by the relieving tackles', if it was steered at all at the time when Nelson fell, it would have been useless to replace the tiller ropes.[18] The only aspect of the reported scene on the quarter deck that appears to be true is the account that the man who had shot Nelson was later shot dead himself.[19]

Early descriptions of what happened after Nelson had been carried to the orlop deck were not much more reliable than those accounts of the scenes that passed on the quarter deck. It was reported that Nelson was 'placed on a chair', that he kept giving orders, and that 'although in extreme pain, not a sigh, not a groan escaped him'.[20] In the end, Nelson was merely supposed to have 'laid his head upon the shoulder of Captain Hardy, who remained with him to the last'.[21] As to the details of what Nelson talked about in his dying moments, accounts remained vague until the 'statement . . . authenticated by Mr Beatty and Mr Bourke' was published. Beatty and Burke contributed three major events to the narrative about Nelson's dying moments on the orlop deck: first, that Nelson had told Beatty that 'he had better attend to others'; second, that Nelson requested his flag captain: 'Kiss me, Hardy!' and that Hardy kissed him on the cheek; and third, that Nelson had asked Captain Hardy to tell the second-in-command, Admiral Collingwood, to anchor after the battle, that Hardy had replied that this would be Collingwood's decision, and that Nelson had protested strongly.[22]

The first account that was much more detailed in its description of the scene below decks than these early reports, was also noticeably different in its contents. It was published in the biography of Nelson by Harrison, written for Lady Hamilton. Harrison pointed out that he had been 'honoured by the kindest communications from . . . dear and intimate friends, professional and private, who were united to his Lordship by the closest ties of a tender reciprocal amity'.[23] In his account of Nelson's death, Harrison makes frequent direct references to 'Dr Scott', who had stayed at Nelson's side throughout his dying moments on the orlop deck, so that it appears that he received his information from him.[24] Harrison described how Nelson was 'suffering the most extreme agony'. Although the account also insists that Nelson would be otherwise 'calm and collected', it conveyed much more of the sufferings that Nelson had to endure in his dying moments. According to Harrison, Nelson could only speak 'in low, though broken and unconnected sentences' and he frequently ejaculated short demands, such as 'drink, drink' or 'fan, fan' in order to gain some relief from the pain he was suffering. Apart from these descriptions of Nelson's physical 'agony', Harrison's account also contains more about what Nelson said in his dying moments. In addition to Nelson's conversation with his captain about the course of the battle and his request to Hardy to 'Kiss me, then', which had in a similar form already appeared in the report by Beatty and Burke, Harrison also reported how Nelson had repeatedly referred to his will and that he left Lady Hamilton 'a legacy to my country'. While this could have been stressed to reinforce Lady Hamilton's claims which Harrison was meant to further, the end of his account could be interpreted as reflecting Nelson's doubts as to the morality of his affair with Lady Hamilton. According to Harrison, Nelson put the phrase 'I have not been a great sinner' as a question to Scott. On not getting an immediate answer, he 'eagerly interrogated': 'Have I?' With another 'paroxysm of pain now suddenly seizing him', he did not get a final answer. Though the question of Nelson's morality was thus left open, Harrison's claim that Nelson had left Lady Hamilton and his daughter as a legacy to his country was further supported in the year 1806, when the last codicil to Nelson's will, written just hours before the battle of Trafalgar, was published.

The most thorough account of Nelson's death was published in 1807 by William Beatty, the surgeon who had attended Nelson in his dying hours. Beatty had been sent away by Nelson to attend to other wounded men, so that great parts of his account had to be recounted from Scott and Burke. His narrative differed most notably from that of Harrison in the way in which it described the physical pain Nelson was suffering. Anything relating to Nelson's wound and bodily needs was dealt with in a very sober medical fashion, using words such as: 'He replied that "his breathing was difficult, and attended with very severe pain about that part of the spine where he was confident that the ball had struck"' and 'he now felt an ardent thirst'. Beatty now gave much more detailed information about what Nelson talked about. Most significantly, Beatty confirmed Harrison's claim that Nelson had repeatedly stressed that he left Lady Hamilton and his daughter as a 'legacy to my country'. Now Nelson's concern for his mistress could no longer be easily ignored.

Such detailed examination of Nelson's last moments outraged parts of the public. A letter to the editor of the *Gentleman's Magazine* condemned as 'a breach of Christian charity'

> reports of those who, called in to relieve those agonies [of expiring mortality] . . . [are] occupied in remembering or *noting* down every word that falls from the lips of their dying *friends* or *patients* . . . it would have been indeed the part of a good friend to the great Victim of our cause, to have left untold the concern *he* expressed for Lady Hamilton and her *Ward only*.[25]

In their account of his death, Nelson's otherwise thorough biographers, Clarke and M'Arthur, perhaps reacting to public protests, avoided references to Nelson's sufferings and his comments on Lady Hamilton. An utterance that described Nelson's pain was reformulated into an unrealistically elegant expression: 'My Pain is so severe, that I devoutly wish to be released.'[26] References to Lady Hamilton were omitted altogether. The difficulty of dealing with Lady Hamilton was increased after the publication of some of Nelson's letters to her in 1814. The author of an influential naval history, William James, was not content with simply ignoring Lady Hamilton. In the first edition of his work James referred to Nelson's 'dying, and at time irrational moments which the injudicious part of his friends, to the regret of the others, and certainly not to the honour of this great man's memory, have published to the world'.[27] In the second edition of his work, published just after the third edition of Beatty's account, James felt compelled to extend his treatment of Nelson's death. In order to explain away Nelson's references to Lady Hamilton, he inserted some supposed actions of Nelson on his deathbed that were meant to disqualify Nelson's other remarks as simple 'rhapsodies of a disordered mind':

> stripped of his clothes . . . he kept constantly pushing away the sheet, the sole covering upon him; and one attendant was as constantly employed in drawing it up again over his slender limbs and emaciated body. This recklessness about exposing his person afforded a strong

proof of the injury done to his intellect; and well would it have been for Lord Nelson's memory, had the listeners around his dying couch possessed discernment enough to distinguish, and friendship enough (as writers) to separate, the irrelevant utterings of a mind in a paroxysm of delirium, from the patriotic effusions of the same mind, when lit up, for a moment or so, by a ray of returning reason.[28]

As a consequence of James's treatment of the death of Nelson, later accounts of it now avoided any mention of Lady Hamilton altogether or referred to her only cursorily until anonymous authors in the late 1830s dared to include her again in their accounts.

The public was able to gain a new insight into how Nelson died when a biography of Alexander Scott, who had been with Nelson in his dying hours, was published by his daughter and son-in-law in 1842. This book included a letter that Scott had written to Nelson's friend Mr Rose on 22 December 1805, on board *Victory*, when he was accompanying Nelson's body back to England. Scott did not attempt to provide a full account of Nelson's death in this letter, but he did provide quite a few details about it.[29] A lot of elements of the known death accounts, particularly Beatty's, are confirmed in this account. Most interestingly, perhaps, Scott's account coincided with that of Harrison in several details which do not appear in Beatty's account. Scott, like Harrison, stressed repeatedly 'Nelson's mortal agony' and his 'intense pain', and he remarked, almost in the same words as Harrison, that Nelson was 'compelled to speak in broken sentences, which pain and suffering prevented him always from connecting'. One might now have expected that Harrison's version of the death of Nelson, thus confirmed as being based in great part on Scott's eye-witness account, would have become more widely acknowledged, but the impact of Nicolas's work prevented that. Nicolas included in his influential edition of *The Dispatches and Letters of Lord Nelson* the account of Beatty, to which he added Scott's letter in a footnote.[30] Subsequent generations of biographers completely ignored Harrison's account, mostly based their accounts on that of Beatty, and only rarely used Scott's eye-witness account. Descriptions of Nelson's intense suffering that emanate from Scott's and Harrison's accounts were never included in those accounts based on Beatty's version of events.

With the account of Nelson's death apparently thus settled, future generations who dealt with it focused more on abbreviating and interpreting Beatty's account. In the second half of the nineteenth century not only the passages about Lady Hamilton, but also Nelson's request, 'Kiss me, Hardy' (in Beatty's version), were perceived as awkward parts to be included in accounts of Nelson's heroic death. The easiest solution was simply to omit the latter. The request became so well known over time, however, that towards the end of the nineteenth century the popular explanation developed that Nelson had, in fact, said 'Kismet, Hardy'. People felt so awkward about it that even someone who defended the words 'Kiss me, Hardy' as being authentic, had to resort to attributing the expression to Nelson's supposedly 'sentimental [character], and . . . strong histrionic temperament', instead of simply accepting it as a common request at the time.[31] It was only in 1951 that Ludovic Kennedy reassessed Nelson's request to Hardy to kiss him and came to the conclusion: 'Nothing could have been [more] fitting, nothing in the circumstance more profoundly right.'[32]

In their attempt to dismantle the heroic status of Nelson, Edinger and Neep focused particularly on Nelson's death. In order to make it impossible to interpret Nelson's death as a heroic sacrifice, they described it as one of Nelson's publicity stunts. According to Edinger and Neep, '[s]ociety repulsed' Nelson and Lady Hamilton, so that in 'his dismay he decided to die; and with a superb sense of the dramatic contrived to become the mark for a French bullet in a battle that was to seal the destiny of Europe'.[33] The suggestion that Nelson had wished to commit suicide at the battle of Trafalgar tends to be revived as an idea every now and then, but it has not had a lasting impact on accounts of how Nelson's death is described.[34] Narratives of Nelson's death have generally been based on Beatty's account since the beginning of the twentieth century, leaving Scott's and Harrison's versions virtually unconsidered.

6

Nelson's character

The controversial aspects of Nelson's life that have been discussed so far concern only a small fraction of his life, even though they have influenced the overall image readers have of him. All Nelson's famous battles put together, for example, fill a mere twenty-four hours or so of his life. In order to form an idea of the personality and character behind these deeds, we need to consider Nelson's more normal routine and usual activities. An understanding of his personality needs to be sought in how, during long spells at sea, he acted towards his subordinates, and in what he wrote in the many thousands of letters he sent to his superiors and his friends at home. In order to assess his behaviour, moreover, we need to be aware of the complex personal networks within which he operated. These networks influenced not only his personal aims, but shaped even more the various tasks, responsibilities and personal obligations which determined his actions. The wider context within which Nelson operated needs to be taken into account if we are to understand his character. If we neglect this wider context, it is easy to be misled by a narrow concentration on Nelson's battles and acts of disobedience into thinking that he was a single-minded fighter, and by a focus on his love for Lady Hamilton into concluding that he was soft and emotional. This, in turn, leads to reaching the overall conclusion that he was a 'split personality' – a conclusion reached by too many authors.

Difficult as it is to characterize any person, some major traits can be observed in Nelson. By closely following his career and attentively reading his correspondence, it becomes clear that Nelson was exceptionally driven. His motivating drive pushed him in two directions. Only one of these has so far been generally acknowledged: high achievement in his chosen profession. As was noted in the first chapter, Nelson developed an enormous zeal to fulfil whatever task was set him; this zeal to achieve his goal was so strong that when he was not assigned a specific task he would not hesitate to set one for himself. Nelson's letters abound with a desire for action and an impatience when prevented from doing certain things. This urge to achieve something significant, though it diminished towards the end of his life, was far more characteristic of his psychological makeup than those spells when he longed for rest or dreamed of retiring to a 'cottage'. Such longings were really a product of exhaustion following a bout of intense activity. Nelson's drive to achieve something significant and worthwhile undoubtedly helped him to achieve promotion in his professional career, even though it sometimes made him appear overambitious, even 'pushy'. Nelson's ambition had a fundamental impact on his outlook on life that made him focus always on the future. All his actions were designed to influence what would happen in the future. Nelson rarely pondered over or reflected upon what had happened in the past and there is little indication that he had much sense of history. This approach to life made him an ideal person to serve the state in a career that required drive and decisiveness.

In contrast, Nelson possessed a second driving force that was quite different from his ambition, and that was the desire for social contact. When he was starting to appreciate the consequences of the fame he had gained by his victory at the battle of the Nile, he complained in a letter to Lady Hamilton: 'I am now perfectly the *great man* – not a creature near me. From my heart, I wish myself the little man again!'[1] Nelson was intensely sociable, and if there was no natural opportunity to meet others and to converse with them, he engineered such opportunities. The meetings he had with his captains and other subordinates were not the result of some 'leadership course' which Nelson had been taught so that he could receive important 'feedback' and could motivate his subordinates. Rather they were the outcome of Nelson's natural desire to bring people together. Nelson became accessible to his subordinates through his habit of deliberately creating such encounters. He used different pretexts for such meetings, which were not always strictly professional ones, such as anniversaries of battles or even Lady Hamilton's birthday. In these meetings he sought to create a relaxed atmosphere. The joy Nelson himself felt in such encounters was easily transmitted to the others who were present. His two main driving forces – personal achievement and regular social contact – combined to make him a great leader of men.

In contrast Nelson was *not* driven by two characteristics that tend to drive other people. One of these was fear. His battles and the minor naval engagements in which he was involved give ample evidence that he was not easily afraid. His acts of disobedience as well as his quite public relationship with Lady Hamilton show that he had scarcely any moral fear either. Because Nelson was not distracted by fears for his own safety, or concern about his superior's attitudes or about public ridicule, he could make momentous decisions in very difficult circumstances.

The other force that drives many men who reach outstanding heights and that was strikingly absent in Nelson was the attraction and exercise of power for its own sake. This again can be observed in Nelson's private as well as his public life. As was seen in Chapter 4, Nelson did not show the remotest desire to dominate Lady Hamilton, but on the contrary wrote to her: 'You command me. I obey you with the greatest pleasure.'[2] This lack of interest in power is also reflected in his professional life, most strikingly in his decision to give an independent role to his second-in-command, Admiral Collingwood, at the battle of Trafalgar (as seen in Chapter 2). Nelson's aim was to win the battle and he perceived that this was best achieved by relinquishing part of his command, so that is what he did. Achievement, honour and the admiration of others clearly motivated Nelson, but power was only of indirect interest to him. He desired power only in so far as it could help him to achieve any goal he may have set himself or to fulfil any task which he had been ordered to undertake. Nelson felt no particular desire to demonstrate his power and to exercise his authority merely so that he could dominate others. This is very apparent in details of his professional career. His secretary, who was at the same time the *Victory*'s chaplain, Alexander Scott, remembered later:

> Lord Nelson was constantly studying the characters of those whom he had about him, and would lead them into discussions in which he afterwards took no part, for the mere purpose of drawing out their thoughts and opinions; and even for debating the most important naval business he preferred a turn on the quarter-deck with his cap-tains, whom he led by his own frankness to express themselves freely, to all the stiffness and formality of a council of war.[3]

Such an informal approach, on the one hand, enabled Nelson to get a fairly clear idea of what his subordinates thought and, on the other hand, gave his subordinates the impression that their ideas were being taken seriously, and this motivated them in their professional conduct. As Captain Duff put it: 'He is so good and pleasant a man, that we all wish to do what he likes, without any kind of orders.'[4] Nelson motivated his subordinates, too, by his generous praise when they had done well. Examples abound, not only from the period when Nelson was already famous. As an aspiring captain in the Mediterranean, Nelson reported to the influential viceroy of Corsica, Sir Gilbert Elliot: 'Lieutenant Andrews has a principal share in the merit, for a more proper opinion was never given by an Officer than the one he gave me on the 13th, in a situation of great difficulty.'[5] In the event, as at Trafalgar, Nelson's readiness to delegate actually gave him greater control and more influence than he might otherwise have achieved by seeking to dominate his subordinates. It needs to be stressed that this is not to say that Nelson disliked power or shrank from using it – quite the opposite. What needs to be emphasized, however, is that power was not an aim in itself for Nelson. His lack of fear as a driving force and his lack of interest in power for its own sake contributed to making him both a brisk and effective decision-maker and a natural leader of men. He was therefore ideally suited for the hard tasks of a fighting admiral facing desper-ately challenging situations.

The characterization of Nelson presented so far – as sociable, as possessing a strong desire to achieve something, and as not being motivated in his actions by fear or a desire to dominate others – is an attempt to reconstruct how he would have appeared to his contemporaries. Such a reconstruction must necessarily fall short in its attempt to recapture his charismatic personality, which appears to have been a major factor in the influence he had over his men and in his professional success. One of his minor subordinates, then only a midshipman, G. S. Parsons, provides a good example of how difficult it is to recapture Nelson's personal charm. In his memoir, Parsons recollected particularly Nelson's 'inimitable', 'sunny', 'good-natured' and 'fascinating smile', which he mentioned nearly every time he wrote about an encounter with Nelson.[6] Since it is impossible to recover Nelson's smile, it is difficult to establish his character or to show how he was perceived by others.

Early characterizations of Nelson tend to be mere enumerations of his virtues. Bravery and loyalty, regarded as natural elements of a warrior's personality, were always attributed to Nelson. These driving forces were, according to the same biographers, accompanied, and one may assume checked, by piety and humanity. Among other positive character traits that early biographers detected in Nelson, his ability to establish good relations with, and to be supportive of, his men stood pre-eminent. The sheer number of different sources that testify to this aspect of Nelson's character clearly demonstrates that these authors were reflecting a commonly perceived image of Nelson, probably spread by word of mouth during his lifetime. Public opinion acknowledged, for example, that Nelson 'was not avaricious of praise', but was always 'ready to bestow commendation on desert'. This view was supported by further evidence in the following years and it has never been challenged seriously since. In addition to his outstanding professional ability, early biographers recognized Nelson's interest in, and care for, his subordinates in combination with other positive personal traits. Among Nelson's endearing characteristics they stressed, with appropriate examples, his modesty and his generosity. Additionally, they observed constancy in his friendships and agreeable personal manners. They could hardly find words and superlatives enough to describe his intelligence and his professional ability. In the application of his abilities Nelson was described as having been driven by zeal and ambition, qualities which helped him to overcome physical weakness. Nelson's energy was sometimes described as bordering on impatience.

Among these generally admirable and, for an admiral, eminently suitable qualities, Southey also detected 'a pardonable pride in the outward and visible signs of honour which he had so fairly won'.[7] Earlier authors had not addressed this trait directly. Clarke and M'Arthur were aware, however, that 'a proper estimate of his own powers' could give 'to a zealous mind the appearance of vanity', but the unanimous admiration for Nelson's modesty kept all earlier biographers from openly describing Nelson as vain.[8] This changed dramatically with the publication of the *Memoirs of Lady Hamilton* in 1815. This work, together with the publication of some of Nelson's letters to Lady Hamilton in 1814, marked the beginning of Nelson's fall from grace in the opinion of his biographers. It was also the first publication to describe Nelson as 'vain'.[9] After 1815, no biographer ever dared to assert again, as early biographers had done, that Nelson was *not* vain. His vanity became so much an accepted truth that Christopher Hibbert could summarize Nelson, in 1992, as 'England's greatest and vainest Admiral'.[10] This fundamental and lasting change in the characterization of Nelson calls for closer examination.

In order to explore what authors meant when they started to describe Nelson as 'vain', it is important to distinguish vanity from arrogance and conceit, because biographers still showed a striking unwillingness to portray Nelson as arrogant or conceited. Indeed, these characteristics do usually exclude that of vanity. While vanity is the ridiculous preoccupation with outward show and symbols, arrogance is the unpleasant display of an actual or believed superiority towards others. When Wellington is described as having felt class conceit towards his intellectual equals and intellectual conceit towards his social equals, he is portrayed as possessing both: high social status and intellectual ability. What was disagreeable was the fact that he made his inferiors feel their inferiority. Nelson has never been reproached with having made others feel inferior. On the contrary, it is claimed instead that he tended to overestimate his subordinates.[11] When Nelson is described as 'vain' the stress does not lie on the unpleasantness of his behaviour towards others, but on the incongruity of his preoccupation with his outward appearance in comparison to his many real and substantial achievements. During Nelson's lifetime some of his contemporaries recognized the vanity they observed in Nelson from the inappropriateness of his preoccupation with the outer form, by which he sought to demonstrate his achievements. After his great success at the battle of the Nile, they described him as 'a gig from ribands, orders, and stars', while at the same time acknowledging that he had maintained 'the same honest simple manners'.[12]

During the period when Nelson was being ignored by respectable biographers (in the twenty years after 1814–15), some upper-class writers of memoirs sought to prove that Nelson was not one of them. His 'vanity' was the perfect vehicle to assert this, since it enabled them to disclose the emptiness behind the glamorous surface of the successful admiral. They did not find fault so much with Nelson's appearance, but they did attribute to Nelson a lack of intellectual endowments and social graces, the presence of which might have allowed him to be placed among the upper classes. This was best expressed by Lord Holland (a nephew of Charles James Fox), whom Nelson had disliked:[13]

> His greatness (For who shall gainsay the greatness of the conqueror of Aboukir, Copenhagen, and Trafalgar?) is a strong instance of the superiority of the heart over the head, and no slight proof that a warm imagination is a more necessary ingredient in the composition of a hero

than a sound understanding. He had . . . acquired . . . great knowledge of the management of a fleet . . . His courage, the natural consequence of a boundless love of glory, and a devotion to his duty bordering on superstition, enabled him in the moment of danger to apply all the knowledge and exercise all the judgment he possessed . . . It is perhaps no ill office to the memory of Nelson to correct any favourable opinion that may be entertained of his understanding . . . his vanity, often ridiculous, was utterly unmixed with pride, arrogance, ill-nature, or jealousy. It was rather a diverting proof of his simplicity than a dangerous or offensive quality in his intercourse with others.[14]

Intellectual shallowness was thus connected with a modest character yet vain appearance. Other authors followed in a similar strain, so that the period after 1815 settled the image of Nelson as the vacuous star of popular opinion, who never rose above the level of ordinariness in intellectual endowments and personal demeanour. Such a view long remained undisturbed because of a lack of research into his actions and behaviour.[15]

The interpretation of Nelson's vanity as a rather ordinary man's inappropriate display of decorations and honours was then transformed into a suggestion that he lacked ability. Two people, describing meetings with Nelson about thirty years earlier, accused him of actually boasting, contradicting the earlier view that Nelson was modest. One of them was Pryse Lockhart Gordon, who had shown such strong prejudices against Lady Hamilton and whose memory about Nelson's boasting is contradicted by contemporary evidence.[16] The other person was the Duke of Wellington. His memory of events some twenty-nine years earlier has only come down to us through a note by John Wilson Croker, describing a conversation with Wellington which had touched on Nelson's 'vanity'. Wellington is said to have described how Nelson entered into a conversation with him at the Colonial Office that was 'almost all on his side and all about himself, and in, really, a style so vain and so silly as to surprise and almost disgust me'. After a break in the conversation which Wellington attributed to Nelson having noticed that he was talking to '*somebody*', Nelson changed and he

> talked of the state of this country and of the aspect and probabilities of affairs on the Continent with a good sense, and a knowledge of subjects both at home and abroad, that surprised me equally and more agreeably than the first part of our interview had done; in fact, he talked like an officer and a statesman . . . I don't know that I ever had a conversation that interested me more.[17]

Nelson's vanity appears to have irritated Wellington because he had not recognized quickly enough that Wellington indeed was '*somebody*'. Interestingly, on one of the two or three days on which Wellington must have met Nelson,

Lady Foster met him too, and had a very different impression of his 'vanity' at the time:

> far from appearing vain and full of himself, as one had always heard, he was perfectly unassuming and natural. Talking of Popular applause and his having been Mobb'd and Huzza'd in the city, Ly. Hamilton wanted him to give an account of it, but he stopp'd her. 'Why', said she, 'you like to be applauded – you cannot deny it'. 'I own it', he answer'd; 'popular applause is very acceptable and grateful to me, but no Man ought to be too much elated by it; it is too precarious to be depended upon, and it may be my turn to feel the tide set as strong against me as ever it did for me'. Every body join'd in saying they did not believe that could happen to him, but he seem'd persuaded it might, but added: 'Whilst I live I shall do what I think right and best; the Country has a right to that from me, but every Man is liable to err in judgement'.[18]

It is impossible to say how accurate Wellington's memory was, but in using his evidence for Nelson's vanity it needs to be kept in mind that at the time he was recollecting his meeting with Nelson the latter was regularly accused by his biographers of being vain.[19]

The first major revival of interest in Nelson, from about 1840 onwards, originally saw a repetition of earlier assessments of his character, focusing on his professional abilities, his modesty and his good relations with his men. Nicolas's edited collection of *The Dispatches and Letters of Lord Nelson* went much further, however. It was a frontal attack on the characterization of Nelson as possessing nothing but vanity and dash. In order to destroy the image of Nelson as vain, Nicolas was particularly intent on clarifying how Nelson had been dressed at the battle of Trafalgar. The notion that Nelson had died because he had been so vain as to wear all his orders[20] could be regarded as clear proof of his vanity. Having discovered the actual coat worn by Nelson and having noticed that it was an undress coat with four orders stitched onto it (all of Nelson's uniform coats had his orders stitched onto them), he dedicated a whole chapter in the last volume of his edition to 'the Coat in which Lord Nelson fell'.[21] In this chapter he concluded that all stories of Nelson deliberately dressing himself in a brilliant uniform were 'ridiculous . . . and . . . inconsistent with Nelson's character'. Nicolas also defended Nelson against 'the insinuation that his vanity caused him to wear his orders more frequently than was then usual'.[22]

In the wake of Nicolas's publications, it became easier once more to regard Nelson's character highly. Pettigrew dedicated a whole chapter to an examination of Nelson's personal traits in which most of the earlier perceived strengths of Nelson reappear, but are now supported by more reliable evidence. Pettigrew also explicitly denied the assumption, propagated particularly by the French politician and historian Thiers, 'that Nelson was in fact only qualified to fight'.[23] It needed a second revival of interest in Nelson, from the 1880s onwards, to produce a more thorough assessment of his personality. With his 1886 edition of the *Letters and Despatches of Horatio, Viscount Nelson* John Knox Laughton opened up a new period of investigation into Nelson's character, inspired, perhaps, by the developing interest in the study of leadership. Laughton started by pointing out that 'Nelson's genius has been misunderstood and undervalued', and he went on to present his character as a kaleidoscope of 'feminine affection . . . childlike vanity . . . masculine courage, honour, and integrity'. In arguing that Nelson's 'innocent and unblushing vanity of a child' led to 'the very general belief that . . . Fortune favoured the brave', Laughton warned against simply labelling Nelson as 'vain' and called for a closer examination of Nelson's strengths and weaknesses.[24] In his subsequent biography of *Nelson*, published in 1895, Laughton was the first to observe a tendency to idealize in Nelson, which in Laughton's view helped to inspire his men: 'it was a marked feature of Nelson's genius to "think all his geese swans", and to believe his ship, as afterwards his fleet, the very best in the navy', even though this was far from true:

> The effect of this was that any officer or man coming under his command presently felt that his chief considered him one of the finest fellows that ever lived, and forthwith endeavoured, so far as lay in his power, to show that this flattering opinion was a true one.[25]

In his *Life of Nelson*, Mahan investigated many aspects of Nelson's professional ability in more depth than any of his predecessors or successors.[26] Instead of simply calling him 'vain', Mahan attempted to explore the nature of Nelson's vanity – for example, by describing how he recorded 'his exploits with naïve self-satisfaction'.[27] Mahan also explored Nelson's emotional side (even in a professional context), while he observed that Nelson at the same time 'feared no responsibility' and was 'insensible to bodily fear'.[28] Though Mahan's *Life of Nelson* regarded him as an outstanding warrior, it was too outspoken about Nelson's softer traits to allow these to escape the notice of one eminent reviewer, Theodore Roosevelt. The future president of the USA observed that Nelson was distinctly lacking what Roosevelt himself regarded as masculine attributes; he described Nelson as 'hating field sports, not fond of country life' and 'distinctly afraid of horses'.[29]

After the Second World War the preoccupation with Nelson's presumed femininity was taken up again and it became common to speak of 'his curiously dual nature': 'At sea he was master of his fate. Ashore he was at the mercy of his emotions.'[30] This analysis, born out of an inability to reconcile Nelson's relationship to Lady Hamilton with the rest of his image,[31] affected the characterization of Nelson as a whole. Admiral W. M. James saw how 'the most human of men, modest and proud of his achievements' turned 'when surrounded by flatterers' into 'a vainglorious Nelson' and he assumed that 'sick of flattery and scent-laden rooms he [Nelson] craved for the company of plain-spoken seamen and the salty tang of a sea breeze'.[32] The habit of separating attractive from unpopular traits in Nelson may have been a way of providing an easily accessible image of Nelson's character. It was clearly inadequate as a means of representing the complexities of his real character.

In 1958 Oliver Warner made a fresh attempt to explore Nelson's vanity by cautiously hinting at the possible element of self-publicity in Nelson's character. Quoting the following note by Nelson in a letter to his wife, 'I find it good to serve near home; there a man's fag and services are easily seen – next to that is writing a famous account of your own actions', Warner remarked: 'This aside is one of the more notable glimpses of a nature which saw in action the material for glowing representation.'[33] The idea that Nelson was motivated to achieve success in action in order to gain personal recognition was further developed at the end of the twentieth century, when Nelson was increasingly seen as a self-publicist. In 1995 Roger Morriss claimed that: 'By the time of Trafalgar, Nelson's reputation was what he had made it.'[34] This assessment ignores the fact that what made Nelson famous, the battle of the Nile, triggered off such a wave of public response that Nelson could hardly have influenced or increased it by any self-publicity of his own. Indeed, he was far from the sources of publicity and he actually did not take the initiative in creating this public response.[35]

Apart from discussions of his vanity and self-publicity, not much was added to the characterization of Nelson during the twentieth century. Most biographers stuck to the usual terms, such as vanity. Some also revived the portrayal of Nelson as 'irritable'. The repeated use of these labels, combined with the failure to penetrate Nelson's character and a lack of interest in the professional aspects of Nelson's career,[36] has led to superficial judgements of his personality. The result is assessments that offer a mixture of generalizations that return to the image established in the 1820s of the vain hero whose only claim to fame was dash, assisted by good luck.[37] In wishing to dismantle the image of Nelson, authors have focused on nothing but the image or self-image of Nelson.[38] With such an obvious disinterest in exploring the professional context of Nelson, such assessments of his character are bound to fail. Only very recently have authors started to explore Nelson's personality in his professional context.[39]

Over the course of the last two hundred years interpretations of Nelson's character, as presented in biographies, have shifted from a focus on his professional abilities (usually supplemented by some references to his piety or humanity) to a focus on his personal demeanour, particularly his 'vanity'. The clearest examples of these extremes can be observed in the first three decades after his death, when the characterization of him shifted from positive-professional to negative-personal. The criticism of Nelson, triggered by a condemnation of his affair with Lady Hamilton, shows elements of upper-class bias against Nelson. Only towards the end of the nineteenth century did naval historians again attempt a serious characterization of Nelson, exploring some of his complexities. During the twentieth century authors have preferred to show their distance from the heroic image of Nelson, focusing more on Nelson's descriptions of his deeds rather than the deeds themselves, thus neglecting traits of his character that enabled him to achieve his successes in the first place. With the support of material from the nineteenth century about dash and vanity, they have set out to dismantle what they perceive to be the false image of Nelson provided by a hero-worshipping nineteenth century. In seeking to show that he was far from perfect, they have ignored his very great achievements which were the product of his personal qualities. He was a more complex character than they have recognized.

LORD NELSON'S FUNERAL PROCESSION BY WATER, FROM GREENWICH HOSPITAL TO WHITE-HALL, JAN.ᵗ 8.ᵀᴴ 1806.

Taken from Bank-side Shewing a View of S.ᵗ Pauls, London Bridge &c.

1 *Lord Nelson's Funeral Procession by Water, from Greenwich Hospital to White-Hall, Jan.ʸ 8ᵗʰ 1806*, painted by Turner, engraved by J. Clark & H. Merke © National Maritime Museum, London

2 *Nelson*, by Lemuel Francis Abbott (1797) © National Maritime Museum, London

3 *Nelson*, by Lemuel Francis Abbott (1799) © National Maritime Museum, London

4 *The Death of Nelson*, Benjamin West (1806) © National Museums Liverpool (The Walker Art Gallery)

5 *The Death of Lord Nelson*, by A. Devis (1807) © National Maritime Museum, London

6 *The Immortality of Nelson,* by Benjamin West (*c.* 1809) © National Maritime Museum, London

7 *The Battle of Trafalgar, as seen from the Mizen Starboard Shrouds of the Victory*, by J. M. W. Turner (1806, reworked 1808) © Tate, London 2005

8 *The Spiritual form of Nelson guiding Leviathan, in whose wreathings are infolded the Nations of the Earth*, by William Blake (1809) © Tate, London 2005

PALERMO PIER   NEWCOME VICTORIOUS.

9 *Palermo Pier. Newcome Victorious*, print from John Mitford, *The Adventures of Johnny Newcome in the Navy*. The portrayal of Sir William Hamilton (behind Nelson) is copied from James Gillray's *A Cognoscenti contemplating ye Beauties of ye Antique*, ridiculing Sir William Hamilton as the betrayed husband © National Maritime Museum, London

10 Oil sketch of *Nelson*, by John Hoppner (1800) © Royal Naval Museum, Portsmouth

11 Oil sketch of *Nelson*, by William Beechey (1800) © National Portrait Gallery, London

Part II

*The uses and abuses of
a controversial hero*

7

Early visual representations of Nelson

The strong emotional reaction to the news of Nelson's death that has been described in the prologue triggered a wave of visual representations of Nelson in the years after the battle of Trafalgar. These representations took various forms, including pictures, material artefacts and monuments. Foremost among the Nelson imagery produced in immediate reaction to the battle of Trafalgar were depictions of the 'Death of Nelson'. Since details about how Nelson had actually died emerged only slowly,[1] the early and often relatively cheap visual representations of the event relied on the vivid imagination of their creators. They usually focused on the scene on deck, portraying Nelson as still standing or merely leaning on (or held by) an officer. The artists appear to have been intent on depicting a still active and conscious commander. In many of their pictures only Nelson's leaning position or his hat and sword in front of his feet indicate that he is no longer in full control of his body. In some cases Nelson is still holding a sword or even pointing with it to the raging battle. A falling speaking trumpet indicates that he retained actual power to give orders until the very last moment.

Some of the early imagery dared to address the reality of Nelson's death more directly. Some prints show Nelson being carried. Such scenes, however, are still carefully arranged. Nelson's body is represented in a kind of sitting posture. The upper part is held by officers, while sailors support the weight of his lower body, often in a kneeling position. Behind such a group can be seen figures on the elevated poop deck in the act of avenging Nelson. Few of the early pictures of Nelson's death show him below decks and never in the cockpit (where Nelson actually died), but in his cabin with a view of the battle unfolding in the background. Instead of showing Nelson's control of and participation in the battle, these images show him stretched out on a sofa; and instead of the surrounding figures supporting him, they have now started mourning him. They react to Nelson's death in different ways: by taking his pulse, by praying or by weeping into handkerchiefs.

Many of the cheaply available glass pictures avoided the gruesome details of

5 *Battle of Trafalgar and Death of Lord Viscount Nelson. To the Memory of the Immortal Nelson, and to the Honour of our Brave Countrymen, who so nobly fought & conquered the combined fleets of France and Spain*, painted by W. M. Craig, engraved by R. Cooper (1806). © National Maritime Museum, London

Nelson's death by resorting to allegorical imagery. Sometimes this imagery is inserted into a recognizable death scene on the deck of the *Victory*, with the battle raging in the background. Instead of falling into the arms of one of his officers, Nelson is shown falling into or lying in the arms of the goddess of Victory, less often those of Neptune or Britannia. Other allegorical glass pictures abandoned any references to the battle whatsoever. Apart from the figure of Nelson himself, in his uniform, the images are allegorical, depicting the dead hero in the arms of Britannia or Neptune. Such presentations were sufficiently detached from the subject of the death of Nelson that they can even be the subject of a caricature. About ten days before Nelson's funeral a *Death of Admiral Lord Nelson* by Gillray was published. It follows a recognizable pattern: Nelson, with his sword still in hand and his hat in front of him on the deck, lies in the arms of a weeping Britannia; Captain Hardy is at his side and a kneeling sailor brings a French flag; above, Fame with her trumpets proclaims: 'Immortality'. For the amusement of his customers Gillray gave Captain Hardy the appearance of George III and the sailor that of the Duke of Clarence (later William IV) with whom Nelson had served as a young captain in the West Indies. As Britannia his contemporaries could recognize Lady Hamilton.[2]

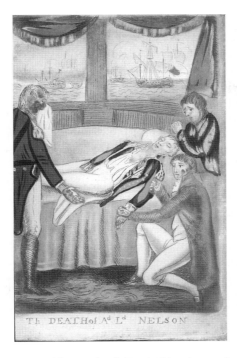

6 *The Death of A^d Ld Nelson* (no publication details given). This print was also used for glass pictures.
© National Maritime Museum, London

More elaborate prints about the death of Nelson took longer to be produced, since they were detailed engravings copied from equally accurate oil paintings. The pattern for such elaborate works of art was Benjamin West's *Death of General Wolfe*, a then widely known and admired death scene. West had set the standard by presenting both the dying hero and those observing the death scene in contemporary costume, instead of imitating the dress of classical antiquity. This example was now applied to the scene of Nelson's death by Arthur William Devis and by West himself. The results of their efforts differed fundamentally, however. Whereas West portrayed Nelson dying on the quarterdeck of his flagship, surrounded by many of his colourfully dressed companions in arms and in front of the dramatic background of a battle (see plate 4), Devis placed the death scene in the dark orlop deck (see plate 5). West's approach was in keeping with contemporary ideas about history painting as having the task to instruct. Reynolds had declared: 'a painter of history shews the man by shewing his action . . . He cannot make his hero talk like a great man; he must make him look like one.'[3] West himself had developed more specific criteria about how to make a hero 'look like one'. He suggested that the painter should 'change the order, time and place of events by fresh inventions and combinations'.[4] Indeed West, who had worked closely with eye-witnesses of the battle, was well aware that Nelson did not die on deck. In order to stress the heroic character of the scene West included many details in the scene on deck, such as 'a swirl of flags', marines and officers on the poop deck in the background, and jubilant members of the *Victory*'s crew.

Devis was developing further what West had started with his painting of *The Death of General Wolfe*: trying to give a convincing idea of the actual scene that would move its viewers. In preparation for his painting he had stayed for three weeks on board the *Victory*, while she was waiting in Portsmouth to sail with Nelson's body to the Nore. He had the opportunity to talk to eye-witnesses and to make sketches of the site where Nelson had actually died and of those present at the event. Although he mentioned to Farington that he had taken care 'in painting the death of that Hero to represent everything faithfully', he also manipulated some details of the scene in order to heighten the dramatic effect. The heightening of the deck and 'Rembrandtesque atmosphere', with the body of Nelson appearing to emit light, contribute to create the effect 'at once of a "Deposition" and a "Nativity"'.[5]

Although West's and Devis's depictions of the death of Nelson are different from each other, they both make use of elements that can be found in the most simple images of Nelson's death that were on sale at the time. West's picture shows Nelson's hat in front of him on deck, Hardy bringing the news of the victory and members of the crew avenging Nelson in the background. Devis depicted Beatty, the surgeon of the *Victory*, taking Nelson's pulse, and a marine mourning in the foreground. All these elements appear on glass pictures that were published in immediate response to the news of Nelson's death. Perhaps it was because of these popular and therefore recognizable elements that both pictures were well received at the time and copied on cheap prints. When West exhibited his painting of the death of Nelson in his own house, in 'a little over a month thirty thousand people went to see it'.[6] Even before Devis's rendering of the famous scene was finished, his publisher, Boydell, had registered '800 Subscribers' for the engraving.[7] Once the finished piece was exhibited, *The Times* enthused that '[a]mong the many pictures which have been painted of the last Moments of Lord Nelson . . . the superiority undoubtedly rests with that which the pencil of Mr. Devis has given with so much effect and appropriate circumstance'. Only West appears to have disagreed. He opined in private that

there was no other way of representing the death of a Hero but by an *Epic* representation of it. It must exhibit the event in a way to excite awe & veneration & that which may be required to give superior interest to the representation must be introduced, all that can shew the importance of the Hero. Wolfe must not die like a common soldier under a Bush, neither should Nelson be represented dying in the gloomy hold of a ship, like a sick man in a Prison Hole. To move the mind there should be a spectacle presented to raise & warm the mind,

& all shd. be proportioned to the highest idea conceived of the Hero. No Boy, sd. West, wd. be animated by a representation of Nelson dying like an ordinary man, His feelings must be roused & His mind inflamed by a scene great & extraordinary. A mere matter of fact will never produce this effect.[8]

West was given the opportunity to heighten even further his view of Nelson as the hero when James Stanier Clarke and John M'Arthur asked him to produce a painting that would be engraved and inserted opposite the title page of their massive biography of Nelson. West created a thoroughly allegorical piece on the death of Nelson. The allegorical image of *The Immortality of Nelson* (see plate 6) is arranged as an apotheosis and described in Clarke and M'Arthur's biography, most probably by West himself:

The leading point in the Picture represents Victory presenting the dead Body of Nelson to Britannia after the Battle of Trafalgar, which is received from the arms of Neptune, with the trident of his dominions and Nelson's triumphant flags. Britannia sits in shaded gloom, as expressive of that deep regret which overwhelmed the united kingdom at the loss of so distinguished a character.

Apart from some drops of blood near Nelson's left shoulder nothing reminds the observer of the violence of battle and the pain of death. The wound itself is covered by a piece of the cloth in which Nelson's body is wrapped. The stump of his right arm is hidden behind one of the 'winged boys round his body [which] are emblematic that the influence of Nelson's genius still exists'.[9] In this apotheosis not only is the body of Nelson lifted in a physical sense; his death is elevated at the same time, in a figurative sense, to sublime significance.

J. M. W. Turner approached the subject of the death of Nelson in a manner that did not owe anything to conventional patterns of death scenes. Instead of focusing on the death itself, he chose to depict the fall of Nelson as part of *The Battle of Trafalgar, as seen from the Mizen Starboard Shrouds of the Victory* (see plate 7). Strictly speaking this perspective was neither a traditional battle scene nor a traditional death scene. The fallen Nelson, though close to the centre of the picture and highlighted by his white clothes and an empty space in front of him, is only a tiny part of the whole scene. Most of the canvas is covered by sails, masts and rigging; by smoke (fiercely yellow near the hulls and grimly grey above); and by the bows of ships as well as the deck of the *Victory*, on which wild fighting scenes unfold. No sea and hardly any sky are to be seen, which strengthens the impression of confusion and intense fighting. Like West and Devis, Turner drew his imagery from first-hand accounts. As soon as the *Victory*, carrying Nelson's body, had arrived off Sheerness, he hurried on board, made sketches of what he saw and notes of his conversations.[10] Consequently, his minuscule depiction of Nelson himself shows him having fallen, with an ordinary sailor standing next to him, taking him by the arm; and there is no indication of Captain Hardy joining them.

There was only one artist who deeply resented Nelson being portrayed in a positive way or even lifted into the regions of the sublime: this was William Blake. In 1809 he produced a couple of tempera paintings, one of *The Spiritual form of Nelson guiding Leviathan, in whose wreathings are infolded the Nations of the Earth* (see plate 8), and the companion piece of *The Spiritual Form of Pitt guiding Behemoth*. The title is as enigmatic as the picture of Nelson itself. In private, Blake wrote of 'Contemptible Idiots who have been call'd Great Men of late Years', and added: 'I wonder who can say Speak no Ill of the dead when it is asserted in the Bible that the name of the Wicked shall Rot'.[11] In public he did not dare to express himself so ruthlessly about recently deceased figures of national importance. As a consequence he painted Nelson and Pitt in what modern scholars call a 'demonic parody'. Paley defines the term: 'A demonic parody caricatures the nature of the celestial world as, for example, the three-headed Satan at the centre of Dante's Hell caricatures the Trinity. The demonic could also be regarded as a grotesque imitation of the sublime'.[12]

In Blake's picture of Nelson the observer first perceives the element of the sublime. Nelson is portrayed as a golden, naked and complete standing figure with two outstretched arms and a halo around his head. In choosing this kind of representation Blake used a pattern of idealized representation that he had developed himself in earlier paintings. The difference that presents the ironic element lies in the surrounding of the figure.[13] Instead of stretching into open space, Nelson is surrounded by a dark monster and a sharply defined halo. Mark Schorer argues that the symbolism of the *Leviathan*, led by Nelson, goes beyond a mere parallel to *Behemoth*, the monster that accompanies Pitt and embodies the land: 'the leviathan is not only the symbol of the sea, with which Nelson would quite properly be coupled, but also of the tyrannical state'.[14] Blake exploits this symbolism, well known from Thomas Hobbes' use of it. The Leviathan on the picture of *The Spiritual form of Nelson* has in his *wreathings . . . infolded the Nations of the Earth*. All nations have the shape of female bodies who struggle to free themselves from the snake-like winding body of Leviathan. The figure that David Erdman identifies as France also has her hair torn by Nelson's right hand. At the bottom of the picture, in front of one of the coils of the monster, on which Nelson stands, lies a black man with hidden face and with manacled hands, a symbol of 'the continuing institution of slavery'. In the jaws of the fierce monster that Nelson leads is Christ himself, so that the shining figure of Nelson is finally turned into the embodiment of the 'heroic Antichrist'. The satanic Nelson of Blake's picture is about to receive his punishment, however. What at first glance may appear as rays from his light figure are in fact flashes of lightning, striking at him. Erdman remarks: 'In Blake's preliminary drawing his purpose is less disguised: a great bolt of lightning is piercing Nelson's right shoulder'.[15] This may have been meant as a reference to the fatal wound which Nelson received in the shoulder (though it was the left one). Paley summarizes the picture as a 'parody of the sublime'.[16] Blake's fiercely critical interpretation was not understood at the time and indeed it only started to be fully appreciated in the twentieth century. Blake's awkward interpretation of Nelson therefore did not have any noticeable impact on the development of the imagery of Nelson in general.

The popular market settled for what it regarded as an authentic representation of the death of Nelson. In 1825 Devis's painting was made part of the Naval Gallery that Edward Hawke Locker (a son of Nelson's mentor, Captain William Locker) had created at Greenwich Hospital. Thus, positioned in the shrine of British naval history, the painting was seen more often than West's heroic interpretation, which to later generations appeared dated. Devis's painting has thus become the standard version of the death of Nelson.

The visual commemoration of Nelson went beyond paintings and engravings and found expression in a variety of material artefacts. Those which attempted to illustrate the grief expressed at Nelson's death have already been mentioned in the prologue. There were even more material artefacts that commemorated Nelson himself, rather than the mourning of his death. The first artefacts that poured onto the market were quickly produced ceramic items, reusing earlier motifs. Some mugs and jugs were transfer-printed with the depiction of a much earlier naval encounter, fought in 1758. This motif had already been used for ceramic items meant to commemorate the victory at the battle of the Nile. Retaining a short poem referring to the battle of the Nile, it was adapted to the new occasion merely by changing an inscription that now referred to the battle of Trafalgar. In general, however, the visual representation of the battle of Trafalgar resulted in artefacts that were less attractive than those produced after the battle of the Nile. They did not contain motifs that could be developed into fanciful decorations. There was no colourful blowing up of a French flagship to be depicted and the grey Atlantic did not conjure up any exotic imagery, such as pyramids or crocodiles. In order to represent the sombre subject of the battle of Trafalgar producers of commemorative ware therefore reverted in part to traditional elements of decoration, such as a plan of the battle, but they mostly focused on the hero of the day.[17]

The most common portraits of Nelson were transfer-printed ceramic items, taken either directly from portrait prints or developed out of them. Nelson, always without a hat, is recognizable by the empty sleeve, his decorations and his white hair. Additional inscriptions give his name, and often a short reference to his achievements, a verse or the words of his famous signal, usually incorrect rendered as 'England expects every man to do his duty.'[18] Nelson's stunning victory at Trafalgar is sometimes summarized by varying the Caesarean quotation (veni – vidi – vici): 'He saw – he faught [sic] – he conquered – and he died.'[19] Most telling, however, are the verses that often accompany the portraits of Nelson. Without exception they express grief at the hero's death. The shortest of them goes:

Dear to his Country,
Shall his Mem'ry live:
But sorrow drown the Joy,
His Deeds should give.[20]

In addition to the different inscriptions, the portraits were surrounded by common maritime and naval imagery, such as anchors, flags and naval trophies. A striking omission on such pottery is the actual death scene that figured so prominently in prints and paintings that were produced in response to the battle of Trafalgar. The reason for this omission may lie in the fact that potters tended to reuse earlier prints in varying combinations and simply adapt the wording of their products to the new occasion. Nelson was also the subject of moulded and hand-painted ceramics. Some elegant pieces applied as a relief a copy of the Medallion which Wedgwood had first produced in response to the battle of the Nile. Cheaper ceramics showed a moulded one-armed admiral with a speaking trumpet in his left hand, resting on a gun behind him. The simplest versions of commemorative ceramics were those that merely bore a hand-painted inscription, such as 'To the Memory of Lord Nelson.'[21]

Although ceramics dominated the commemorative market, the immense interest in Nelson after the battle of Trafalgar also found expression in other media. Medallions of different sizes, medals, glasses, wax pictures, patch boxes, fans and even handkerchiefs bore Nelson's portrait. Patch boxes often included short verses or phrases to commemorate Nelson, such as: 'Trafalgar the Battle was Fought – Nelson's Life the Victory bought.'[22] More elaborate items took longer to produce, but still found a market years after the battle of Trafalgar. Ceramic busts of Nelson, wine coolers with his portrait moulded onto them and a box with pictures of the 'naval victories' (prominently figuring Nelson) were produced towards the end of the Napoleonic Wars.[23]

A more enduring reaction to the death of Nelson than these material artefacts and prints was the building of monuments to his memory. In that respect Nelson's death had happened at a convenient point in time, because public monuments became extremely widespread across Britain at the beginning of the nineteenth century. Before that, monuments had been mainly produced as sepulchral architecture or sculpture. The most common exceptions were a few monuments to monarchs. Other monuments, such as the columns to commemorate the Duke of Marlborough or the fire of London, were extremely rare. This situation changed with the Napoleonic Wars, which created a novel interest in public figures other than the monarch and an interest in warriors in particular. As a response to his spectacular success at Trafalgar, Nelson was among the first to be commemorated.

When news of the battle of Trafalgar reached Britain and Ireland in November 1805 projects to build a monument to Nelson developed immediately in different parts of the kingdom. Only a few monuments were as

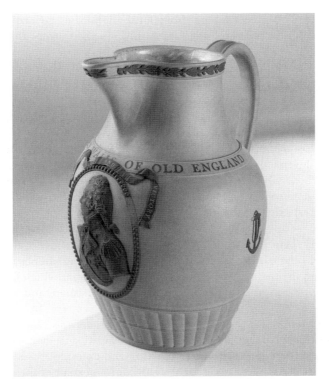

7 Stoneware jug with profile medallion of Nelson after John de Vaere (first produced in 1799, this jug is from before 1820). The inscriptions read: 'Nelson and Victory' and 'The wooden walls of old England' © National Maritime Museum, London

quickly executed as they were conceived; one example was a crude arch erected in Ireland. More common were planned monuments to celebrate the career and achievements of the great admiral. Although most of the projects for erecting a monument to Nelson were started in direct reaction to the news of the battle of Trafalgar, they were usually the product of extensive deliberations. This was necessary because most of the monuments were erected by public subscription. Britain did not adopt the French system of extravagant state patronage and only two monuments were erected directly at the public expense; one, voted for by parliament, was erected in St Paul's Cathedral, while the other was erected by the City of London in the Guildhall. Both monuments were thus indoors, which made them less accessible to the public. St Paul's Cathedral, in particular, was as much a building of art as a church, and it levied an entrance fee. The state's restraint in financing monuments to Nelson was also regarded as a virtue, however: 'The pillars of Trajan and of Antonine were erected to gratify vain-glorious conquerors, while ours will owe its origin to public gratitude and veneration for the best and bravest of our Admirals.'[24] People ranging from local dignitaries to ordinary sailors expressed such gratitude and veneration through their attendance at numerous processions.

There were several reasons for such manifestations of public interest in monuments to Admiral Nelson, the most obvious being the desire to honour the memory of Nelson himself. This motivation was naturally strong in members of the navy. Those who had fought at Trafalgar dedicated a monument of their own on a hill near Portsmouth 'to the memory of Lord Viscount Nelson . . . to perpetuate his triumph and their regret'. Thus, reminding the public of Nelson's achievements could also serve to present him as an example to 'encourage those who are entering on the same career'.[25] The often declared aim 'to stimulate others to emulate his bright example'[26] could also influence the choice of the site for the monument:

> Whatever plan is adopted . . . [the monument] will, no doubt, be
> erected in the most frequented part of the place, the oftener to excite
> emulation in others . . . being reminded of a character which holds out
> so many objects of imitation – as a warrior, a christian, and a man![27]

More common than intricate didactic considerations was the desire of cities and their citizens to hand 'down to the latest posterity a memorial of their gratitude for his unexampled services to his King and Country'.[28] Such monumental gratitude to Nelson had quite a real significance for some of the contributors. Nelson's pursuit of the Franco-Spanish fleet across the Atlantic and back again, prior to the battle of Trafalgar, was widely interpreted as the preservation of the British West Indian Islands. The 'grateful inhabitants of Barbados' consequently inscribed their monument as 'a tribute of esteem, admiration and gratitude to their illustrious Deliverer',[29] while, in less directly concerned Edinburgh, it was recognized that Nelson was 'our great hero, to whom the Country owes such signal obligations'.[30] It was sometimes admitted that these obligations were for material gain. A Glasgow newspaper stressed the economic interests that Nelson had helped to protect:

> *We* have shared largely in the benefits procured to the nation by the
> vigour of his arm, and by the terror of his name. – *We* have had *our* gain-
> ings from the established security of the ocean. The panic-struck inac-
> tion, and subsequent flight, of the combined fleets from Martinique,
> must yet be fresh in the recollection of our merchants; and a tithe of
> what has been saved to the commercial part of the Island, by the exer-
> tions of this man alone, would rear up a more magnificent mausoleum
> than ever rose at the command of eastern pride.[31]

Business organizations, such as London livery companies and the East India Company, contributed money more than thirty years after Nelson's death at the battle of Trafalgar, when subscriptions were collected for the monument to be erected in Trafalgar Square.

The construction of a monument to Nelson had the pleasant consequence of embellishing a particular place, in some cases with the town's first public monument (as in Birmingham and Montreal). A leading member of the subscription committee in Liverpool promised that the monument would 'do honour to the town . . . as an effort of art'.[32] Such hopes must have been shared by those living close to the proposed site for a monument to Nelson in Dublin's Sackville Street, because the 'Sackville-street Club' and the neighbouring 'Kildare-street Club' subscribed to it.[33] In some places the monuments to Nelson, instead of being seen as mere embellishments, formed part of various town-planning projects. In Birmingham the Nelson monument was placed in the market place, which had been 'formerly thronged with mean shops, and butchers' shambles'.[34] In Barbados the subscription committee purchased, with the financial support of the 'Legislature', an area in Bridgetown that was called 'the Green' and renamed it 'Trafalgar Square'. Shamed by the condition of a place with such a proud name the same Legislature was motivated in 1826 to invest some money in the 'purchase and removal' of 'some unsightly houses [which] obstructed the square'.[35]

The much more famous Trafalgar Square in London was also part of a major town-planning project. This time it was not the subscription committee that influenced the outlook of the place, but, on the contrary, the appearance of the existing square, recently named after Nelson's last and most famous battle, had to be considered in the choice of design for a monument. The area which had been occupied until the beginning of the nineteenth century by the royal stables and poor housing had been transformed into an open space, thanks to the ambitious plans of John Nash. His desire had been to make a previously neglected space between Westminster and the City of London into an elegant part of the metropolis, connecting the two cities. Although his specific plans were not adopted, the area was cleared of poor housing, regulations were introduced that excluded 'waggons, carts or other carriage' from remaining in the area, and the passages were cleared of obstructing 'Signs or other Emblems'. In this exquisite setting the proposed monument to Nelson could not be allowed to obscure the new building of the very broad but low National Gallery by William Wilkins.[36] At the same time the monument had to be big enough not to appear minuscule on the huge square. Yet another local problem was posed by the sloping ground of the square.

Such difficulties did not assist the efforts of the subscription committees to raise money. In order to make the investment seem worthwhile, they published subscribers' lists which gave publicity to those who contributed and they sent out circular letters to stimulate further subscriptions. Shortly after the battle of Trafalgar the feeling of triumph engendered by the victory and the deep grief felt over Nelson's death had stimulated many subscriptions, and civic pride was challenged in a kind of competition as newspapers reported the amounts of money that were collected in Liverpool and that were 'hourly increasing'.[37] Some cautious subscription committees either used only the amount they managed to collect in this first enthusiasm for the project of a Nelson monument (in Liverpool and in Birmingham, for example) or stated that the money that would be collected, after the foundation stone had been laid, would 'be applied towards increasing the height and dimensions of the Monument'.[38] In Hereford the committee was forced to refrain from putting a statue of Nelson on top of a column; they had to be content with an urn that proved to be cheaper. A project for a Nelson monument in Bristol had to be abandoned.

How can it be explained, then, that the most famous monument to Nelson was not erected earlier, in direct response to the battle of Trafalgar? It appears that in London, where two monuments, in St Paul's Cathedral and the Guildhall respectively, were being built, people hoped that a monument paid for by nationwide subscriptions would soon be placed in the capital. Such a national subscription failed for three reasons, however. First, local projects for monuments in the provinces appealed more to those living outside London, because they could enjoy the result more directly. Second, subscribing to a national monument did not seem attractive, since a similar project had failed just four years earlier, when the joyful reception of the Peace of Amiens (in 1801) replaced the enthusiasm for the naval victories of the 1790s. When a new subscription was opened after the news of the battle of Trafalgar had reached Britain, several letters to editors of newspapers reflected the dislike of contributing to a new fund for a national monument, without having proof that the earlier subscriptions had been properly used. Third, the fact that parliament voted money for monuments to the victories at Trafalgar and Waterloo in 1816 must have discouraged any project for a subscription for a national monument to Nelson at that time, although this money was never actually spent on any monuments.[39]

At first sight it appears surprising that it took until the late 1830s for a project of a monument to Nelson paid for by national subscription to materialize in London. Perhaps it needed some time for old friends of Nelson or their relatives to get together and start such a project. There is also a noticeable distance of more than twenty years from the scandalous publication of some of Nelson's letters to Lady Hamilton, which had damaged Nelson's reputation so severely. Finally, the late 1830s was a time of rising interest in national heroes, which conveniently suited a project for a monument to the great naval hero of the French wars. Whatever the additional reasons for a Nelson monument were in about 1840, the subscription committee overestimated the amounts of money it could collect. The Office of Woods, Forests and Land Revenues finally had to take over responsibility in 1844 for the cost and production of the monument to Nelson in Trafalgar Square. Although this office introduced minor changes, it could not alter the whole design, since the committee had already started to realize the design for the whole monument by building the column and putting a statue of Nelson on top of it. The changeover in managing the project did not accelerate the completion of the monument (which included bas-reliefs and lions) and it took until 1867 for it to be finished.

Since the subscription committees depended on support from the public for the money raised, they also had to consider public opinion in their choice of the style and design of the monument erected. This could even lead to the proposal for a building, to be used for some charitable purpose, that bore scant resemblance to a monument. Thus, the resentment of the Quakers in Birmingham against a monument, which in their view glorified war, led to the proposal for 'a dispensary and a post-office' as a monument to Nelson in that town.[40] In Edinburgh the subscription committee had decided on erecting a tower, part of which 'should be fitted up into half a dozen of neat cabins, for the gratuitous reception of *deserving wounded Seamen* or *Marines*; the preference to be given to those who have bled with the *Great Nelson*'.[41] This idea was changed into a caretaker's flat in the basement of the monument and this monument to Nelson is the only one that shows any trace of a charitable purpose.

When the subscription committees took purely artistic decisions about the design of their monuments they still had to consider the taste of the day. This was difficult to determine, because public monuments for war heroes did not have a long tradition in Britain. It would have been possible to develop features of sepulchral monuments, especially since Nelson had died so dramatically at the height of his most successful battle. Indeed, the design for the monument in Liverpool bears evidence of such an influence: 'The figures constituting the principal design are Nelson, Victory and Death [in the form of a skeleton] . . . Death lies in ambush for his victim; intimating, that he received the reward of his valour and the stroke of Death at the same moment.'[42] Other sepulchral features are more restrained. William Wilkins added to both of his designs for Nelson columns in Dublin and Yarmouth a sarcophagus, 'which is placed on the Pedestal, over [the inscription] Trafalgar, to indicate that he there terminated his mortal career'.[43] Even sepulchral monuments that had been erected since the second half of the eighteenth century, however, had abandoned the previously common direct references to death, such as skulls and hourglasses. Julie Rugg describes the phenomenon: 'Enlightened theories that removed the terrors from death were in perfect accord with the neoclassical aesthetics that were all-pervasive in the visual arts of the late eighteenth and early nineteenth centuries.'[44] Influenced by the new character of sepulchral architecture, designs for monuments to Nelson tried to follow examples of classical antiquity and sought to avoid Christian symbols of death. Such Christian symbolism was replaced by national and naval emblems, such as lions, representing Britain (in London), in Trafalgar Square and St Paul's Cathedral, for example), or anchors, representing the navy (in St Paul's Cathedral, in Barbados and in Hereford). Whereas a design for the Nelson monument in Trafalgar Square proposed 'piled trophies of Nelson's valour', most other monuments seem to have tried to avoid too many different elements. A competitor simply claimed 'Allegory . . . cannot

8 *Nelson's Pillar, Sackville-Street, Dublin,* by G. Petrie and R. Winkles (1829) © National Maritime Museum, London

be tolerated' and a critic of the Nelson column in Yarmouth praised 'chasteness of decoration'.[45] As to the form of the monument itself, two main types developed: column and statue.

A pattern for a monumental column existed in Trajan's column in Rome, which was probably the most famous surviving monument to a Roman warrior. Its shaft is decorated with bas-reliefs which tell the story of Trajan's campaigns in a series of pictures that are organized in a spiralling series up to

NELSON'S COLUMN.

9 This print shows Nelson's Column near (Great) Yarmouth by Wilkins in its ideal shape (the sarcophagus was never executed) © National Maritime Museum, London

the top, on which a statue of Trajan used to stand. Below the statue is a platform to which visitors were supposed to climb up a winding staircase built into the interior of the column. To imitate the elaborate bas-reliefs that decorated the column was well beyond the means of any subscription committee for a monument to Nelson. They sometimes (in Montreal, for example) placed bas-reliefs on the base of the column, but in the case of the column in London's Trafalgar Square even that proved to be beyond the means of the subscription committee. In any case, this left the question open of how to design the shaft of the column itself. The Roman architect, Vitruvius, whose work was widely known and admired, had divided columns into a 'masculine' and a 'feminine' type. Naturally only the 'masculine' Grecian Doric column and its Roman variant, the plain shafted Tuscan column, were regarded as appropriate for a monument to a warrior. Consequently, the Nelson columns in Hereford and Montreal have plain-shafts, while William Wilkins designed those for Dublin and Yarmouth with Doric flutes and a Doric capital. He had intended a statue of Nelson on top of both of them. This was executed in Dublin, although Wilkins did not oversee the erection of the monument himself, whereas he changed his plan for the later column in Yarmouth.

Wilkins seems to have had doubts about simply copying Trajan's column. He might have agreed with the critic who pointed out at the time that Trajan's column was 'raised by the Romans in degenerate times, when the arts were declining, from a vain emulation to vie in height with the Egyptian obelisks' with 'a round tower in masquerade'.[46] Wilkins, who had travelled for four years through Greece and Italy and was a great admirer of ancient Greek architecture, may well have felt inclined to introduce more Grecian elements. A contemporary observer noticed that he had copied the 'decoration of the lower structure' of his Nelson column from that of the Thrasyllus monument in Athens.[47] The same author admired the platform in Yarmouth with its statue of Britannia, supported by six caryatids on top of the monument, although he was surprised about the number six, which he described as being 'original, and extremely elegant'.[48] Wilkins may here again have been inspired by Greek monuments. A Corinthian column in Delphi is surmounted by three caryatids, who carry a tripod, the trophy in a choragic competition. Another choragic monument – the Lysikrates monument in Athens – is decorated with six Corinthian half-columns. The Corinthian column is obviously chosen deliberately, because the acanthus leaves in its capital represent not only death, but also immortality,[49] an imagery which was known even in Wilkins' day, since the Corinthian column had been used frequently on sepulchral monuments. So Wilkins introduced Corinthian elements of monumental sculpture, symbolizing immortality, while avoiding at the same time the 'feminine' Corinthian column and capital itself.

It has been claimed that the Corinthian order was used for Nelson's Column in Trafalgar Square because the monument had to harmonize with the Corinthian columns on the front of Wilkins' National Gallery which had been built on the northern side of the same square. Here again, William Railton, the artist who had proposed the overall design, might have been aware of the Corinthian symbolism of death and immortality. This had been stressed, even in antiquity, by executing the acanthus leaves in bronze to imitate their naturally green colour. Railton's design was changed several times in several respects and the planned bronze statue of Nelson was finally executed in stone, but the bronze acanthus leaves of the capital were never questioned. The choice of the Corinthian order may here, again, have been made deliberately to use the symbolism of death and immortality. Some criticized the choice and a representative of the Treasury even wondered whether the flutes could be altered 'so as to suit a Doric capital',[50] but the column was also praised for its 'lofty and elegant proportions'.[51]

The great disadvantage of a column to a hero was that the commemorated person could not be easily represented. A statue on top, 'raised so high above the natural point of focus of vision, would lose all distinctness of expression . . . unless they [its features] are colossal, and overcharged with expression beyond nature, even to caricature'.[52] When Nelson's statue was on show, before it was mounted on top of the column in Trafalgar Square, an observer remarked that the face had 'sharp, angular features, the expression of great activity of mind, but of little of mental grandeur'.[53] To solve the problem of a statue so far from ground-level observers, the monument in Hereford, which bears an urn on top, has a portrait-medallion of Nelson on its base. Some proposed designs had included a statue of Nelson in front of the base of a column, but none of them were executed.

The possibility of representing Nelson himself was the great advantage of statues. This, however, posed the question of how the figure of Nelson should be dressed. Only the early monument in Liverpool shows Nelson as a nude with nothing but a piece of cloth over his right shoulder, thus hiding the missing arm, and over the lower part of his body. When the choice for a monument in Trafalgar Square was about to be made, somebody insisted:

> Surely it is not necessary to hand down specimens of the bad taste of a nation – to perpetuate in stone the ephemeral fashions of the times . . . Marble should perpetuate character, not costume – should exhibit the attributes of the mind, not the decorations of the body'[54]

Several designs showed Nelson in 'classical costume'.[55] A sculptor vehemently protested: 'What is the English tar to say when he sees his beloved Nelson in a Roman petticoat!'[56] Other artists and various subscription committees seem to have agreed with this view and so all other monuments that represent Nelson full-length show him in an admiral's uniform.

Realism in the representation of Nelson posed the additional problem of whether to show him idealized with two arms or to portray him with only one arm. Several authors and artists suggested portraying Nelson with two arms. The sculptor John Flaxman wondered how to deal with Nelson's major physical defect: 'in the execution of a statue the loss of his arm might so be indicated yet obscured that it would not injure the general effect of the work, or he might be represented . . . in his perfect figure'.[57] Flaxman actually drew a design for such a monument to Nelson of a figure with two arms. His concern about how to portray Nelson was taken out of Flaxman's hands, since he was commissioned to execute a statue of Nelson for St Paul's Cathedral after the design of Richard Westmacott, who had decided to be truthful in his representation. The

10 Flaxman's sketch for a Nelson Monument shows Nelson 'in his perfect figure', representing Nelson with two arms, *c.* 1806 © National Maritime Museum, London

11 *Statue to the Memory of Admiral Lord Nelson, Birmingham* (Gentleman's Magazine, May 1812)
© National Maritime Museum, London

same Westmacott executed the Liverpool monument (after a design of M. C. Wyatt) and the statues of Nelson in Birmingham and Barbados, and thus contributed to the representation of Nelson with only one arm. This does not mean that this approach was uncontroversial, however. One of the critics of the monument in Birmingham commented indignantly:

> Were a great man, Admiral or General, to have both legs shot off in Battle, should we then put up the mutilated trunk – a statue without legs – in the market place? Can we not imagine ourselves as meeting great men in a future state, whole and perfect?[58]

The subscription committee for a Nelson monument in London's Trafalgar Square, however, would only have accepted a naturalistic representation of Nelson with one arm. His image by the late 1830s seems to have been too settled to allow for a right arm to be added.

If the image of Nelson was settled in its general outlines before the building of his column in Trafalgar Square, it was more widely spread by the erection of this monument. The powerful impact that Nelson's Column in Trafalgar Square had on the revival of the public image of Nelson can be measured particularly in an upsurge of Nelson souvenir items on offer in the wake of the discussion about the monument (from 1839 onwards) and the placing of the statue on top of it (in 1843). As with biographies, monuments and pictures, material artefacts had also neglected the subject of Nelson in the period between 1815 and 1839, when the project to erect a monument to Nelson in Trafalgar Square finally got under way. Only a very few items produced in this period referred to Nelson. Though material artefacts are often difficult to date, there is a noticeable upsurge in the production of Nelson commemoratives from 1840 onwards. Early symptoms of the new interest were stoneware jugs in the form of Nelson busts, produced about 1840. A song even advertised an image of Nelson by referring to his 'grand monument up charing Cross'.[59] Along with the production of memorabilia of the new Nelson monument on Trafalgar Square, Staffordshire figures of Nelson flooded the developing market for interior decorations.[60] The Staffordshire figures were intended more as decorative elements than as accurate representations. Nelson in particular is portrayed in different coloured breeches, patterned vests, and dark hair and hence is generally not very lifelike. Simple as the representation of Nelson is, he remains recognizable through his empty right sleeve, his uniform coat and his cocked hat. The potters gave their imagination free rein in moulding the figures. In about half of their designs they chose to portray Nelson dying. In comparison with the standing figures, often produced as companion pieces to Wellington or Napoleon or both, these death scenes were much more elaborate. They showed a sitting Nelson, usually with his hat still on and accompanied by two men, who can be identified as surgeon Beatty

12 Staffordshire 'Death of Nelson' group with William Beatty, the *Victory*'s surgeon, offering a cup to Nelson and Captain Hardy holding Nelson's hand and supporting him with his right arm. This item was produced in the 1840s © National Maritime Museum, London

(offering Nelson something to drink) and either the Reverend Scott or Captain Hardy.

A much more elaborate depiction of Nelson's death was the influential painting of the *Death of Lord Nelson* by Daniel Maclise, on which the painter worked from 1863 to 1865 in a fresco technique in the House of Lords. The picture, a companion piece to a depiction of the battle of Waterloo, is nearly four times as long as it is high, so that it offered Maclise the opportunity to paint the scene on deck along the length (and not as usual the width) of the *Victory*. The dying Nelson reclines in the centre of the picture, supported by an officer. He rather gives the impression of relaxing in a comfortable pose than of dying. Although the figure of Nelson himself is not very successfully depicted, the surrounding scene is of some interest. In his close-up view Maclise clearly attempted to give an idea of the chaos of battle. He shows marines firing, sailors handling a gun, a powder-monkey supplying the gun-crews, and several wounded men in the foreground. Though many sailors look distinctly Victorian (with side-whiskers), Maclise also tried to represent the variety of people on board by including, for example, in prominent positions a black man (near the dying Nelson) and a woman (in the foreground, caring for a wounded sailor). As late as in the 1860s the British public was still aware that women had been on board battleships, because they were from time to time mentioned in newspapers as veterans of the French wars. Maclise's painting became popularly known in great part through mass-produced silk embroidered pictures, so-called Stephengraphs, that reproduced his *Death of Admiral Nelson* for those admirers of Nelson with only modest means.

Nelson remained popular as a subject for material artefacts throughout the second half of the nineteenth century. These items developed into different forms. Busts of Nelson, some of them made of porcelain, also catered for those with more expensive tastes. Artisans used their imagination and ingenuity to design an ever greater variety of Nelson commemoratives as the century wore on, without, however, creating any noticeable Nelson fashion. That would remain a task for some propagandistic efforts to achieve at the end of the nineteenth century.

8

Transferring the image of Nelson

As has been shown, interest in Nelson was expressed in a great variety of forms during the nineteenth century. This had two main consequences. First, from the mass of imagery available the public developed a growing interest in life-size representations of Nelson and things that used to belong to him or that were closely associated with him. Those who wished to gain a closer experience of Nelson himself might well go to exhibitions that contained this kind of material. Second, the iconic treatment of Nelson made it possible to regard him as the pattern of a variety of stereotypes, such as the admirable hero, the romantic lover or the ruthless aggressor. These stereotypical elements have been so strongly reinforced by different means that it was and is possible to adhere them like stickers to certain products, in order to convey certain characteristics. These characteristics are usually regarded as positive, including reliability, success or patriotism. As a result Nelson's iconic status was used to propagate or promote something not primarily concerned with Nelson himself. This chapter examines how these two developments reached their apogee at the end of the nineteenth and beginning of the twentieth centuries.

Both exhibitions and propagandistic use of Nelson found their early expression as immediate responses to the battle of Trafalgar. At least one opportunistic businessman exploited the commercial value of the revered sailor by advertising 'Nelson's new Patent Sideboard and Dining Table . . . the first of which article ever manufactured was intended for the most brave and ever to be lamented the late Admiral Nelson.'[1] Other private enterprises that profited from the interest in Nelson that was stimulated by news of his death in 1805 offered the very first public exhibitions. One of these businesses was 'Mrs. Salmon's Wax Work', which included a scene of the death of Nelson in its exhibition. Madame Tussaud's waxworks produced their first Nelson figure at about the same time and they carried Nelson's waxen image across the country on travelling exhibitions. Westminster Abbey, too, commissioned a wax figure of Nelson. The abbey took this step in order to compete with St Paul's

Cathedral in attractiveness. The abbey was suffering severe financial losses at this time, whereas St Paul's Cathedral attracted curious visitors, first with its preparations for Nelson's funeral and then with his grave. The work that wax portraitist Catherine Andras produced for the abbey not only pleased Lady Hamilton, but also helped the abbey's 'tourist revenue' to recover.[2]

Another business commemorating Nelson and his deeds in exhibitions was the panorama. The new art form of panorama, developed at the end of the eighteenth century, was particularly suited to representations of battles. These representations, however, sometimes owed more to the excitement of the event than to historical accuracy. While the well-established panorama in Leicester Square offered a depiction of the battle of Trafalgar, a competitor combined in a 'Grand Nautical Moving Spectacle of the Naumachia' the different 'Splendid Victories achieved by Lord Nelson, with the Elements and Ships in Motion . . . depicting the Havock and Destruction which took place, with all the majestic Horrors which characterised those great Events'.[3]

While crowds flocked to waxworks, panoramas and St Paul's Cathedral, a new exhibition was established in Greenwich, when Nelson's funeral car was positioned in the Painted Hall of Greenwich Hospital. It also attracted tourists and was even the subject of an engraved print. Probably because of a decline in interest in Nelson after the publication of some of his letters to Lady Hamilton, the hospital administration did not take care to preserve it and 'having been suffered to go to decay, it was broken up about the year 1826'.[4] Its destruction may also have been ordered because the funeral car did not appear to suit the new use of the Painted Hall as a place for an exhibition of paintings and sculptures. Edward Hawke Locker, the son of Nelson's mentor Captain William Locker, initiated this 'Naval Gallery' at about the time the National Gallery was founded and he managed to win influential backing for the venture so that the collection of naval art was continuously enriched, mainly with portraits of naval officers, but also with battle-paintings and Devis's painting of the death of Nelson. By focusing exclusively on 'high' art, however, the exhibition neglected popular art as well as relics of famous naval men. This left a public need unfulfilled, particularly in relation to Nelson. This need was met by other means. The musket ball that killed Nelson had been the subject of a print, facsimiles of his signatures were inserted into biographies, the purser of the *Victory* made gifts of miniature coffins, produced out of the outer coffins in which Nelson was brought home from Gibraltar, and sailors, too, tried to keep some personal mementoes of their famous chief: 'The leaden coffin, in which he was brought home, was cut in pieces, which were distributed as relics of Saint Nelson, – so the gunner of the *Victory* called them.'[5]

The response to Nelson's death included the use of him for patriotic purposes, mostly by the navy. The Royal Navy endeavoured to keep the spirit of Nelson alive and to conjure it up in the moment of battle. The Admiralty let it be known, in the same month in which they had received the news of Trafalgar, that they had decided to lay 'down a first-rate man of war . . . to be named after' Nelson.[6] Officers who had served under Nelson spurred their men on by reminding them of Nelson, by entering into battle with the song 'Nelson of the Nile' and with a portrait of Nelson hanging on the mizzen stay or with the signal 'Remember Nelson'.[7] The tradition of giving a toast to 'The Immortal Memory' (first drunk in November 1805) on Trafalgar Day in officers' messes appears to have been observed continuously ever since Nelson's death.[8] Ordinary sailors (not only in Britain) are said to commemorate Nelson, most of them unknowingly, in their dress. The three white stripes on their blue collar are supposedly there to commemorate Nelson's victories at the Nile, Copenhagen and Trafalgar. The black silk handkerchief draped round the opening of the sailor's jumper, over his chest, was originally worn around the neck and it is said that the men who attended Nelson's funeral were ordered 'to drape the handkerchief round the V-opening of the jumper, and tie it with a small tape at the bottom, to keep it in its place'. Admiral Kerr commented in 1932: 'The order was never rescinded, and the men continue to mourn Nelson and all that he stood for.'[9] Without a set pattern of Nelson celebrations, the patriotic use of Nelson and his battles was subject to chance, as for example in 1814, when peace with France coincided conveniently with the anniversary of the accession of the Hanoverian dynasty to the British throne and the anniversary of the battle of the Nile. The festivities on 1 August included an elaborate re-enactment of the battle of the Nile on the Serpentine in Hyde Park, London. After sunset, these miniature ships engaged in a 'Grand Sea Fight', which attracted many viewers at the time and later became the subject of several prints.[10]

Since there were no other major naval engagements in the nineteenth century, after 1815 Nelson increasingly became a focal point for the expression of Britain's national and, particularly, her naval identity. At first, however, he was not used for a clear propagandistic message. He started to figure more prominently in the national consciousness only when the revelations about his affair with Lady Hamilton were all but forgotten and as the last participants of his battles began to pass away and members of the rising generation were wondering how to emulate him. J. M. W. Turner sensed the spirit of the times and anticipated a whole movement when he painted his watercolour of 'Yarmouth Sands' in 1830. The painting shows the Nelson monument at Yarmouth towering over a beach, on which sailors arrange improvised ship models into battle formation, while women and boys look on, 'absorbing the Nelson legend'.[11] In Turner's wake a variety of paintings show survivors of Trafalgar, with a portrait of Nelson or Greenwich Pensioners celebrating Nelson's battles and discussing their plans. The participants of Nelson's battles (including women) remained in the news and, in 1847, the Admiralty distributed 'Naval General Service Medals 1793–1840' for the participants of these battles (excluding the women who had taken part).

This patriotic urge to commemorate Nelson and to acknowledge his followers strongly associated Nelson with patriotism and loyalty, but this was exploited for different purposes. One of the most obvious examples is the naming of one of the two settlements founded in New Zealand after Nelson (the other was called Wellington) and filling it with fitting streets, such as 'Trafalgar' and 'Nile'. The settlers of the New Zealand Company, though not on a governmental mission, thereby manifested their allegiance to Britain, an action which helped to convince the government to accept the distant archipelago as a British colony. Back home in Britain a town in Lancashire and innumerable Victorian streets adopted Nelson's name and others chose the names of his captains, ships or victories. By choosing these names, town councils as much as the owners of public houses gave expression to their sense of national identity, an identity strongly linked to British naval supremacy and the man who was seen as its prime representative.

Official institutions did not show such patriotic eagerness to promote the memory of Nelson. Towards the mid-nineteenth century even the statues in St Paul's Cathedral were so far neglected that they had gathered dust on 'every part where dust will lie, even on sloping arms and limbs, it reposes in a thick and offensive appearance'.[12] As a result the flags that had been captured at the battle of Trafalgar were passed on from St Paul's Cathedral to the Naval Gallery of Greenwich Hospital. This collection, that had originally contained only works of art, extended further into the field of relics by another chance. Thanks to the suggestion in 1845 by the editor of *The Dispatches and Letters of Lord Nelson*, Nicholas Harris Nicolas, Prince Albert bought the coat that Nelson had worn at the battle of Trafalgar in order to give this relic to Greenwich Hospital.[13] Interest in relics of the great sailor was rising so much in the 1840s that it even led to a 'manufacture of Nelsonian relics'.[14] Private as well as public collections[15] now started to be grouped around battle paintings and relics. Other items, such as ship models, were regarded simply as a way of illustrating battles and as gaining value through their association with Nelson, rather than as examples of shipbuilding or the social environment of sailors.

The personalized approach in exhibitions was also used for propagandistic effect in 'The Royal Naval Exhibition, 1891', probably the largest ever display of Nelson paintings, prints and relics. Aiming to bring the importance of the Royal Navy before the public, the organizers 'restricted [their display] to purely national objects' and exhibited items that had caught the public interest in the preceding years.[16] Although the exhibition covered several centuries of naval history and included contemporary matters, it had a particular focus on Nelson. Apart from the huge 'Nelson Gallery', it provided a model of the *Victory* and a 'Panorama of the Battle of Trafalgar'. In the full size reproduction of the *Victory* visitors could contemplate a waxen recreation of Nelson's death scene on the orlop deck, produced by Mr Tussaud and largely based on the painting of the death of Nelson by Devis. The Trafalgar panorama, a 'private speculation' by a German, gave its visitors a supposedly historically accurate impression of the battle as seen from the *Victory*'s quarterdeck. Those who entered the 'polygonal building' looked 'straight

13 Nelson's undress uniform coat, worn at the battle of Trafalgar © National Maritime Museum, London

ahead towards the bow, and there, in the middle of the quarterdeck, you observe the great scene on account of which the picture was painted. You look upon Lord Nelson at the moment that he has fallen mortally wounded.'[17] In the Nelson Gallery of the Royal Naval Exhibition, which presented pictures and relics, quantity appears to have counted for more than quality. Though eminent specialists such as John Knox Laughton sat on the 'Arts Committee' and tried to find authentic pieces, they included many duplicates (such as tufts of Nelson's hair) and some items of doubtful authenticity. A sword which Nelson supposedly wore at Trafalgar was on display, whereas, in fact, he did

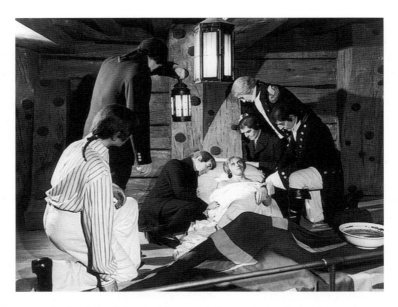

14 The scene of Nelson's death (inspired by Devis's depiction) was displayed at Madame Tussauds from 1967 to 1990 © Madame Tussards Archives, London

not wear a sword on that occasion. Pieces of furniture were so numerous that they prompted a contemporary to comment: 'It is simply a physical impossibility that it [Nelson's cabin on board the *Victory*] should have contained all the "favourite chairs", "arm-chairs", "chairs and beds combined", and "folding bedsteads" here exhibited as having been used by Nelson at sea.'[18] These relics, together with a great number of prints and paintings of Nelson and of scenes from his life, combined to produce a strong visual impression of the admiral. Some visitors were alert enough to notice that 'It is curious among so much that belonged to Nelson that there is no collection of relics of his "beloved Emma", the mistress of his heart, who in spite of all her failings, was one of the inspiring motives of his final heroism.'[19]

At the end of the nineteenth century, political organizations went beyond exhibitions in seeking to exploit the significance of Nelson for the country's national identity. The first of a series of associations that did this was the Primrose League (founded in 1884), which propagated Conservative ideas in a pleasant social setting. It organized evening entertainments, at which 'magic lanterns and *tableaux vivants* . . . displayed a series of images of imperial splendour such as . . . Nelson on the Victory' and where songs were played, such as Braham's 'Death of Nelson'. This had first been performed in 1811, but it revived in popularity during the second half of the nineteenth century. Women, children and all social classes were included on such occasions and their different interests were catered for. A 'Question Paper set for Juveniles' by the Primrose League in 1900 contained questions such as:

'Give a brief account of the great naval battle of Trafalgar, and the death of Lord Nelson.'[20]

Whereas Nelson figured merely as one of many elements of national identity within the patriotic repertoire of the Primrose League, his commemoration took centre stage within the propagandistic efforts of the Navy League. This association, bearing a portrait of Nelson in its crest, was founded at the end of 1894 as a pressure group promoting the interests of the navy. Similar to some other leagues, it attempted to further national strength against a perceived external danger. More specifically it argued for the strengthening of the Royal Navy by a variety of means, such as building dreadnoughts and ensuring the supply of a rising generation of British sailors. Like the Primrose League, the Navy League also tried to attract members from all strata of society, from both sexes (a 'Ladies' branch' was founded as early as 1895) and particularly from the younger generation (whole schools were enlisted as members). Anne Summers observes that the Navy League and other 'Leagues grew continuously in numbers and vigour despite their inability to influence government policy; it is arguable, therefore, that for many of their members they fulfilled functions quite other than those outlined in their official literature.'[21]

One of the greatest non-political attractions of the Navy League was the celebration of Nelson on Trafalgar Day (21 October). In 1895, following the suggestion of the navalist and journalist, Arnold White, the Navy League laid a wreath to the memory of Nelson at the base of Nelson's monument in Trafalgar Square on Trafalgar Day. Supported by Arnold White's letter to the press about this 'national demonstration', the event attracted some attention in the newspapers.[22] This was the beginning of a tradition. Until then, there appears never to have been any regular habit of celebrating Trafalgar Day outside the Royal Navy. When the Navy League celebrated Trafalgar Day more lavishly in the following year, investing £50, instead of £10, for the decoration of Nelson's Column with wreaths and garlands of evergreens, its members were surprised by the impact of their own celebration. In the *Navy League Journal* they called it a 'triumphant success', partly because it was celebrated in different parts of the country, but mostly because of the demonstration in Trafalgar Square itself: 'The hundreds of thousands who for six days from morning till night defiled before the column have shown the unsuspected strength of feeling latent in British hearts.' The executive committee called a 'special meeting' on 22 October 1896 in order to 'consider what steps should be taken to reap the benefits of the demonstration on Trafalgar Day'.[23] They decided to enlarge their League, including its *Journal*. In the meantime private businessmen used the opportunity to make money by selling fake reprints of *The Times* of 7 November 1805 with the news of the battle of Trafalgar and Nelson's death in it.

Stunning as the success of the Trafalgar Day celebrations was, the Navy League did not celebrate Nelson for his own sake, but merely used his memory as a propaganda tool to enlist support for a stronger navy in terms of ships and recruits. The Navy League would readily have dropped any reference to

Nelson, had he not served the League's purpose. The executive committee twice discussed giving up the Trafalgar Day celebrations, in 1900 and in 1906.[24] On the first occasion, they lowered their investment in the decoration of Nelson's Column from £100 in the previous three years to a mere £20,[25] without any impact on the popularity of the event. *The Times* remarked that, though the meagre decoration 'caused some disappointment to many in the large crowds . . . it in no way diminished the interest taken in the celebration'. Since the crowds were 'as large as ever', the report concluded: 'the patriotic endeavours of the Navy League to bring about a national celebration of Trafalgar Day have borne fruit'.[26] By then Trafalgar celebrations were held in a great number of towns and cities across Britain; particularly large ones were held in Liverpool.

The Navy League, however, had reason to feel uneasy about the success of its Trafalgar Day celebrations. The early protests from the 'Increased Armaments Protest Committee' did not greatly disturb the Navy League, which responded with public statements in the press about its aims, so that the success of the Trafalgar Day celebrations was not affected. The Navy League took French sensibilities much more seriously, however. The *Navy League Journal* printed, next to the overwhelmingly positive response recorded in the British press, those hostile responses to the massive Trafalgar Day celebrations of 1896 printed in nine different French newspapers.[27] In 1897 Arthur Conan Doyle suggested that Trafalgar Day should be exchanged for Nelson's birthday and thus become a less offensive 'Nelson Day'. This caused a heated discussion in *The Times* and Arnold White attacked the suggestion in the *Navy League Journal*.[28] In the end, neither the date nor the name of the festivity was changed. But in 1900, the year in which the Navy League had so drastically curbed its expenditure on the Trafalgar Day celebrations, its executive committee 'decided that they would dedicate one wreath to the French and Spaniards with a suitable inscription'.[29] As a result, the Navy League commemorated all French and Spanish dead of the battle, while, on the British side, only Nelson was commemorated. This does not appear to have troubled anybody, since the practice remained the same until the First World War, when the League started to commemorate the recently dead.

The propagandistic use of Nelson carried with it a constant financial burden for the Navy League. In order to rid itself of this problem it called for contributions and finally, in 1909, it created a special 'Trafalgar Fund'. This fund attracted so many contributions that the executive committee could invest the money in other projects, mainly their newly created 'Boy's Naval Brigades' (the forerunners of the Sea Cadets). After three years the League itself borrowed the considerable amount of £300 from the Trafalgar Fund; and this while it was still spending only about £50 on each of the annual Trafalgar Day celebrations from 1901 (except the celebrations for the centenary in 1905, for which it was ready to spend £200).[30] Since so many people were ready to invest in the 'Trafalgar Fund', rather than the Navy League itself, it appears that many felt more attracted to the commemoration of Nelson and Trafalgar than to the political ideas of the Navy League. Indeed, the *Manchester Guardian* commented that:

a little more ancestor worship would do us as a nation no harm . . . [and it] regretted that the public Nelson celebrations should have depended so much on an organization identified in the public mind with indiscreet and often unintelligent advocacy of increased naval expenditure.[31]

The public celebrations of Nelson reached a peak with the centenary of Nelson's most famous battle, Trafalgar Day 1905, for which the Navy League had arranged a short 'semi-religious' ceremony. Although only a part of the ceremony was overtly religious (the reading of a prayer), the whole event was hugely indebted to Christian symbolism of the saviour, reminiscent of Easter, including the notion of death and 'resurrection'. A journalist of *The Times* described the scene in Trafalgar Square, which was filled with a 'sea of people':

In silence all waited while the hands of St Martin's clock crept round to half-past 2 . . . At the first sound of the chime of the half-hour the flags at the four corners [of Nelson's monument], Union Jack, White Ensign, Red and Blue Ensigns, were solemnly lowered to half-mast, all men uncovering their heads, while the band of the Queen's Westminsters played the 'Death of Nelson'. As the music died away Bishop Welldon read the prayer 'To the memory of Nelson' – the preposition perhaps, might have been more prudently chosen . . . the bugles sounded the reveille . . . and, as the stirring call was blown slow and loud, the flags went up again. The ritual ended with the singing of the National Anthem . . . followed by cheers which rang and echoed and thundered around the square.[32]

Other organizations all over Britain and the Empire joined the Navy League in contributing their own celebrations of the centenary of Trafalgar. The massive commemorations included church services, concerts (regularly including Braham's 'The Death of Nelson'), dinners and, in Liverpool, even a public procession led by the lord mayor. Although the Admiralty did not officially support the event, the then First Sea Lord, John Arbuthnot Fisher, certainly approved of it. He made his admiration for Nelson and his appreciation of Trafalgar Day public when he insisted on being installed as First Sea Lord, in 1904, not earlier than 'on Trafalgar Day!'[33] Fisher contributed a preface about Nelson to a book that Arnold White, the initiator of the Trafalgar Day celebrations, wrote with Ester Hallam Moorhouse for the centenary.[34] Fisher had also learned years before how to use journalistic

15 Two-handled cup with rope-twist borders and handles (1905); the inscriptions read: 'Lord Nelson / Born 1758 Died 1805', 'England expects every man will do his duty', 'Doulton & Co. Ltd, Lambeth' © National Maritime Museum, London

pressure, particularly that exerted by Arnold White, in order to achieve his political aims.[35] Though clearly interested in exploiting Nelson and Trafalgar, Fisher, as in his earlier propagandistic co-operation with White, appears to have preferred to give the impression that the Admiralty reacted to popular pressure rather than making propaganda itself. Opposition to the event was voiced by very few people.[36] The public's interest in the Trafalgar celebration was manifested in many other ways than participating: postcards were produced for and of the different events across Britain, journals published articles and pictures of Nelson or Trafalgar and the souvenir industry profited from all these celebrations, producing a veritable outburst of commemorative production for 1905, the year of the Trafalgar centenary.

As the Trafalgar celebrations became ever more focused on Nelson and detached from current issues of naval policy, a variety of objects, ranging from exquisitely worked porcelain to paper napkins, were decorated with portraits of Nelson and other elements that could fittingly commemorate the centenary. The majority of the items focused on Nelson. One pottery reproduced its popular Nelson jugs of 1840 and Wedgwood reused its portrait-medallion with reference to the centenary. The newly designed pieces of commemorative ceramics were decorated with portraits of Nelson, usually copied from one of Abbott's portraits, and with naval elements, such as a battle scene, or simply elements that conjured up a maritime impression, such as ropes. Inscriptions were short, usually giving only names and dates (of Nelson's birth and death or those of the centenary). The longest piece of text was Nelson's famous signal at Trafalgar (now usually rendered as 'England expects every man will do his duty'). In comparison to the elaborate pieces from the early nineteenth century, the centenary ceramics were usually adorned with much simpler imagery and they completely dispensed with poetry or other lengthy written messages. Other items, such as statuettes or medallions, naturally contained even less elaborate textual elements. Artefacts in general thus focused on imagery, rather than written messages, in commemorating the centenary of the death of Nelson. A series of fifty 'Nelson' cigarette cards shows that the image of Nelson even served to attract buyers with very limited purchasing power. As the name of Nelson was developing into a trademark of national identity, it also started to attract commercial users. With the growth of brand marketing and imagery in newspapers, Nelson was beginning to be used to sell the usual products of early advertising: soap, washing powder and pills 'for all derangements of the Stomach'. Sometimes only Nelson's portrait was used. In other cases some reference to his name or to his fame or to 'England expects' was made, as in 'Nelson the Hero of Trafalgar and Pears Soap Have Become the Most Familiar Names in the English Language' or 'England expects that every man this day will do his duty and take Beecham's Pills.'

Interest in Nelson relics, paintings and engravings grew considerably as a result of the Royal Naval Exhibition of 1891 and the celebrations organized by the Navy League. In 1895 a descendant of one of Nelson's brothers sold his considerable collection of Nelsonia. At the sale '[e]very article was contested for with almost unparalleled eagerness, and so tumultuous was the excitement that it was scarcely possible to record the bids'.[37] Nelson's decorations, however, were acquired for the nation and were deposited in Greenwich Hospital. Unfortunately, the new publicity surrounding the Nelson relics also attracted thieves. In 1900 all but one of the jewels of Nelson's orders, together with some other relics, were stolen from Greenwich Hospital. Most of the pieces, including the stolen orders, were never recovered. With the desire for Nelson relics growing and the number of pieces limited, the production of fakes thrived and contributed considerably to Lady Llangattock's collection, which included Nelson's supposed glass eye (he never actually lost his eye, only the sight of it).

The most impressive Nelson relics were, of course, the ships that were connected with him. J. M. W. Turner was the first to alert the public to the way in which this part of Nelson's heritage was being treated, when he painted 'The Fighting Temeraire tugged to her last berth to be broken up, 1838' in order to show in what a dishonourable way this participant in the battle of Trafalgar had been treated by the Admiralty.[38] While contemporaries often simply admired the beauty of the painting without understanding its patriotic statement, the fate of the *Foudroyant* (Nelson's flagship after the battle of the Nile) caused much more publicity. When the Admiralty sold her to a German shipbreaker in the Baltic, it prompted a wave of public outrage, including a caricature using Turner's 'Fighting Temeraire'[39] and a poem by Arthur Conan Doyle entitled 'For Nelson's Sake', which finished: 'Take heed! And bring us back once more / Our Nelson's ship!'[40] The *Foudroyant* was recovered at immense cost, and was restored and sailed around the coasts of Britain, before it foundered in a storm off Blackpool in 1897. This drew public attention to the fate of the *Victory*, the most famous surviving ship of Trafalgar,[41] which served as a floating museum in Portsmouth harbour. The Society for Nautical Research, founded in 1910, set itself the task of preserving the *Victory*, a project which was postponed because of the First World War. On Trafalgar Day 1922 the 'Save the *Victory*!' fund was launched, but was severely curtailed by the economic crisis: 'On one occasion . . . Admiral [Sturdee] raised £65 in pennies.' When the appeal had raised £3,000, it was saved by the anonymous donation of £50,000 from the wealthy former shipowner James Caird, a gift which enabled the restoration work to start.[42]

It again took James Caird's support to get the project of a national museum going in order to house a major Nelson collection. While the army was served with the Imperial War Museum shortly after the First World War, the Royal Navy had to be content with the overcrowded Painted Hall in Greenwich Hospital. Combined financial (James Caird), political (Lord Stanhope) and scholarly (Geoffrey Callender) forces finally led to the passing of the National Maritime Museum bill in 1934 and the opening of the museum in 1937. Although the museum's name indicated that its subject would broadly include anything 'maritime', its collections still had a distinct naval focus, because they incorporated those of Greenwich Hospital and the Royal United Service Institute. The new National Maritime Museum had its focus on Nelson. It was organized chronologically and 'climaxed with Trafalgar and the death of Nelson, a display which included Turner's painting of the battle [of 1824], both Devis's and West's versions of Nelson's death [West's painting for Clarke and M'Arthur's biography], and the Nelson relics'. While the museum was modern in displaying the exhibits in spacious rooms, it remained traditional in its choice of exhibits, concentrating on paintings, engravings and relics.[43] The first director of the museum, Geoffrey Callender, wrote to its political father, Lord Stanhope, who intended to bring the museum under the auspices of the Board of Education: 'I do not think it is the task of the National Maritime Museum to teach and instruct . . . but rather to inspire pride and admiration.' Callender wished the museum to serve as a focal point of Britain's maritime identity, but this was criticized within the museum, not so much for its nationalism as for its neglect of the intrinsic significance of the different items. Specialist curators wished their collections to be at the centre of interest, rather than made subservient to some patriotic exhibition about Nelson.[44]

16 *'Kiss me and tell, Hardy'*. Reproduced by kind permission of *Private Eye*/Reeve. © Pressdram 2004, www.private-eye.co.uk

The Nelson Gallery nevertheless survived into the years after the Second World War and the death of Callender as an 'integrated display', including 'paintings, models, relics, charts, uniforms, and other material used to illustrate a subject or theme'.[45] Whereas Nelson relics may have been disregarded by scholarly museum personnel, they were popular enough among thieves. In 1951 the diamond chelengk, which Nelson had received from the sultan of Turkey after the battle of the Nile and which he had worn on his hat, was stolen from the National Maritime Museum and broken up. Two years later, after a radio programme had attracted attention to the collection at the Nelson Museum in Monmouth, thieves raided that place as well.

More recently the National Maritime Museum, as prime repository of Nelson relics, souvenirs and paintings, has found a new approach to 'Britain's most popular naval hero'.[46] The museum's collection of Nelson material appears to focus on manuscripts rather than material artefacts and relics. Its Nelson exhibition of 1995 to 2005 to cover the 'Nelson Decade' before the bicentenary of the battle of Trafalgar, also revealed a new approach. While it followed the now more generally accepted pattern of an 'integrated display', it no longer aimed at 'inspir[ing] pride and admiration', but rather sought to

17 Contemporary advertisement for 'Nelson's Revenge Premium Ale'

inform. The display leads from historical facts to the legendary status of Nelson. The Royal Naval Museum in Portsmouth, incorporating the *Victory*, also rearranged its Nelson exhibition and distanced itself from an all too patriotic approach by putting 'emphasis on the human aspects of the story', producing models of Lady Hamilton and Captain Hardy and, recently, a new wax figure of Nelson himself.[47] The second half of the twentieth century also witnessed many private Nelson exhibitions, often produced by Nelson enthusiasts. In 2002 a new museum in Great Yarmouth opened, housing a Nelson memorabilia collection.[48]

In the political sphere, since the Second World War Nelson has rarely been used to represent the navy or notions of national identity.[49] The celebrations of Trafalgar Day have lost prominence and the political content they may once have had. Nevertheless, some remnants of the tradition, invented by the Navy League, have survived. Hundreds of Sea Cadets (successors to the members of the Boy's Naval Brigades and all that remains of the now defunct Navy League) still parade in Trafalgar Square every 21 October. In Portsmouth, the Sea Cadets and the Royal Navy join in a commemoration and take part in a traditional 'Seafarers' Service' at Portsmouth cathedral. In Edinburgh, Nelson's signal is hoisted every 21 October (unless it is a Sunday) on the local Nelson Monument, overlooking much of the city. Trafalgar Dinners are held by different clubs and societies all over Britain, and these always include a toast to 'The Immortal Memory'. If Nelson has remained part of the political discourse at all, it is mainly in cartoons, which usually make use of his characteristic appearance (eighteenth-century naval uniform, empty sleeve, sometimes an unhistorical eye-patch, sometimes on the top of his column in Trafalgar Square, London) and his most famous expressions. In one cartoon, which referred to discussions about homosexuals in the armed forces, Nelson is portrayed dying in the arms of his captain, saying: 'Kiss me and tell, Hardy'.

The use of Nelson for advertisements usually involves reference to his outer appearance, as in Admiral Insurance, which shows a stylized one-armed Nelson, holding a telescope to his eye. Since the reference to the person is obvious in 'Nelson's Revenge. Premium Ale' from Woodforde's Norfolk Ales, a black-and-white rear view of Nelson's head and shoulders in combination with a stylized image of the *Victory* and some muzzles of guns suffice.

The bicentenary of the battle of Trafalgar in 2005 will certainly be commemorated on a very large scale. Nelson's iconic status in the collective memory of the British ensures that he will probably go on being used to convey political as well as commercial messages that do not necessarily have anything to do with his life, achievements or opinions.

9

Fictionalizing Nelson

In searching for the essence of Nelson's life and personality, fictional approaches were able to go into more detail than visual imagery, exhibitions and the propagandistic use of Nelson. At the same time they have much greater licence than scholarly biographers. This chapter examines how aspects of Nelson's life and death have been increasingly fictionalized in theatrical performances, novels and films over the last two hundred years.

In immediate response to the battle of Trafalgar and Nelson's death, a massive amount of poetry about Nelson was produced. In theatres, at concerts, at dinners, in magazines, in books, on broadsheets and on elegant engravings poems about the battle of Trafalgar and the death of Nelson were recited, sung and printed. Everybody with the slightest inclination towards poetry, from politicians (George Canning and John Wilson Croker) to 'a Young Lady Eight Years of Age', produced odes, dirges and stanzas in memory of the battle and the hero's death. Naval officers and sailors joined the ranks of acknowledged poets, such as Charles Dibdin, Richard Cumberland and the then poet laureate Henry James Pye. Some authors rhymed in Latin, French or Greek. A hundred years later Henry Newbolt commented: 'Probably no other national event has ever produced so large and so direct a movement to expression in verse.'[1]

Theatres, too, reacted immediately to the news of the battle of Trafalgar and Nelson's death. On the evening of 6 November 1805, the day on which the news spread in London, Drury Lane and Covent Garden Theatres staged commemorative pieces. They combined well-known patriotic elements, such as the song 'Rule Britannia', with poetry composed on the occasion by some 'prompt and patriotic pen'. The new poetry had a strong effect on the audience, which showed 'the corresponding emotions of sorrow'. Covent Garden had even arranged some scenery, including portraits of naval heroes and the 'English fleet . . . riding triumphantly in the perspective'. In the foreground 'Naval Officers and Sailors' were grouped 'in attitudes of admiration', when 'a medallion descended, representing a half-length [portrait] of the Hero of the Nile, surrounded with rays of glory'. According to the *Naval Chronicle* the 'effect was electrical, and the house resounded with the loudest plaudits and acclamations'.[2] Covent Garden went on developing its 'loyal Musical Impromptu' into a play in its own right, giving it the title *Nelson's Glory*. Drury Lane did not remain behind and staged *The Victory and Death of Lord Viscount Nelson* by Richard Cumberland to music by King and Braham, with Braham also performing. This piece was also more of a combination of different solemn representations than the depiction of developing action. A 'grand Sea View, in which two Fleets are represented as towards the close of an engagement', a descending figure of fame, 'a scroll on which appear the words, "England expects every one will do his duty"', and a rising 'illuminated figure of Lord Nelson' formed the scenery. The whole performance 'was received with tumultuous applause'.[3]

The obvious public demand for such commemorative pieces led theatres to develop their repertoire in this field. On 7 December 1805 the King's Theatre misjudged the public demand when it went so far as to show in *Naval Victory, and Triumph of Lord Nelson* 'the immortal Nelson . . . in the cabin of the *Victory*, in the convulsions of his last moments'. Whereas theatre-goers could not get enough idealizations of 'the immortal Nelson', they did not want to be confronted with the reality of his death. In immediate reaction to this dramatization of Nelson's death 'a general cry of "off, off" prevailed'. Even after Braham had promised the audience that the scene would be omitted in the next performance, tempers did not cool down entirely. Although the audience had 'rapturously applauded' the first scene, 'representing the battle', it now answered to Braham's assurance that if any scene 'was objectionable . . . [it] should be omitted' with 'cries of "all, all" from the Pit and several parts of the House'. A contemporary critic was not surprised at this vehement reaction, commenting: 'The scene was too strong for the feelings of those who loved and admired him.'[4]

Lower-class artists and consumers, too, enjoyed an interpretation of Nelson's part in the battle of Trafalgar in dramatic form. *Trafalgar; the Sailor's Play. In 5 Acts*, though often clumsily worded, explored the event from a variety of angles. Nelson was shown addressing 'his Admirals and Captains' as well as his 'Brave Shipmates'. He repeatedly gained a 'roar of applause from the Men', for example by appealing to their rough sense of humour with some crude sexual innuendo: 'I feel the longings of a woman to place you close aboard their largest ships for my own.' The actual battle was represented in a scene from 'the middle gun deck of the *Victory*'.[5] In fiction about sailors Nelson seems to have become increasingly part of the world of 'Jack Tar', particularly in the years after the scandalous publication of his letters to Lady Hamilton made him an unacceptable subject to respectable society. In John Mitford's *Adventures of Johnny Newcome in the Navy* Nelson frequently crosses the protagonist's path and he is portrayed, together with Lady Hamilton, as the sailors' friend and the two are even the subject of a print in the book (see plate

9).[6] In a note the author pointed out that Nelson and Lady Hamilton went to harbour taverns together, dressed as ordinary sailors, 'mingling in the sailors' pleasures, listening to their songs, and generally retiring unknown'.[7] Nelson was also shown close to his men in a popular play, *Nelson; or, the Life of a Sailor* by Edward Fitzball, first produced in 1827 and afterwards repeatedly performed during the middle decades of the nineteenth century. Following the pattern of the typical melodrama, the characters were stereotypical: the protagonist, a sailor appropriately called 'Jack' (in reference to 'Jack Tar'), is honest and faithful, as is his sweetheart Rachael, whose father, a Jew called 'Moses', is avaricious and speaks English with a strong accent, while honourable Nelson is the pattern of an ideal commander. He is proud of his 'brave boys', generous in allowing them 'to have their wives and sweethearts aboard' when in port, tough when wounded, and compassionate with all the wounded, including the enemy: 'in distress all men are brothers'.[8]

Frederick Chamier's novel, *Ben Brace: the last of the Agamemnons*, was also popular during the middle decades of the nineteenth century and it also portrayed Nelson from the point of view of an ordinary sailor. Ben Brace, the first-person narrator, was modelled after Nelson's servant Tom Allen,[9] though with the significant difference that he accompanies Nelson during his whole career and not merely for a few years. The novel relied heavily on Southey's *Life of Nelson* and avoided delving into the controversial issue of Nelson's involvement in the defeat of the Neapolitan revolution by stating: 'I don't really exactly understand it.'[10] Nelson's affair with Lady Hamilton is brushed aside to some extent, but Ben Brace makes frequent references to '*her*', usually reflecting the critical views of the time he was writing, but in one early passage he also defends her against 'the great people [who] have been pleased to abuse Lady Hamilton right and left, yet I say, she had more heart, more courage, than a whole regiment of Neapolitan soldiers. She was a wonderful woman; she did not know what fear was.'[11] Brace's account of Nelson's death, built on Beatty's version, introduces two major fictional elements: a conversation with Brace and a rather unheroic end: 'his under jaw fell, and Nelson of the Nile was no more! . . . I saw the glassy stillness of his eye – the dead cold paleness of his forehead – the fluttering tremor which shook his whole frame.'[12] By the 1830s, at least, popular fictional accounts clearly had no qualms about describing Nelson's death.

After half a century in which no noteworthy novels or plays about Nelson were produced, writers of fiction started to explore Nelson's masculinity. This subject was generally on the mind of those dealing with Nelson at the time. It manifested itself particularly in the search for masculine attributes in portraits of Nelson. One biographer, writing at the turn to the twentieth century, missed what he called 'Nelson's battle face' and observed that 'in most of his portraits the sensitive mouth, the curving lips, the set of his eyebrows' only told 'of the emotional side of Nelson's character'.[13] Arnold White and Ester Hallam Moorhouse agreed that no portrait reflected 'the marvellous battle-light which shone in his face when in the presence of the enemy'.[14] Though not in such crude terms, later authors, too, have distinguished between the 'feminine' and the 'masculine' portrayals of Nelson. In their search for the most authentic portrayal of him, critics have tended to prefer the virile to the mild Nelson. One author judged portraits according to whether one could 'imagine the daredevil fighter' in them and he asked about Abbott's famous picture: 'Who can see the fighter there?'[15] This search has continued to the present. Agreement now exists in the assessment of the two pictures by William Beechey and John Hoppner, both painted in 1801 (see plates 10 and 11). Oliver Warner was the first to remark: 'They are of particular interest as emphasising the masculine and feminine side of his nature'. He went on to contrast Beechey's portrayal of 'a virile, confident, even masterful man' to Hoppner's picture, showing 'a face full [of] suffering and sensibility, delicate, sympathetic and vivid'.[16] When the National Portrait Gallery acquired the oil sketch for Beechey's portrait of Nelson, the staff were thrilled, as Richard Ormond remembers: 'Here was a naval commander we could believe in, tough, energetic and resourceful, with the wound above his right eye clearly visible, an image startlingly at odds with the weak tea and sugar dished up by Abbott.'[17] In his thorough study of *The Nelson Portraits* Richard Walker notes: 'Hoppner's Nelson, with its coyly tilted head and sugary expression, has an effeminacy distasteful to this hard-bitten age.'[18] Even Beechey, however, had observed at the time that Nelson's 'cheek had rather an Infantine [sic] plumpness'.[19]

When British novel writers started to exploit the subject of Nelson with some force at the end of the nineteenth century, they did so at first only in the field of boy's literature, ignoring visual indications of feminine traits in Nelson. These books, which explicitly addressed boys (and not girls), followed the pattern of masculinity in British boy's literature that had developed at that time, featuring ideals of patriotism and stoicism. The authors portrayed Nelson as the embodiment of a masculine warrior: as using 'terse seaman language' and as someone who 'became in a measure intoxicated with the sound of battle, like the war horse who scents the combat from afar'.[20] In crisis situations he remained visibly unmoved: 'Nelson's face did not soften in the least. It was like a mask of steel.'[21] He was part of a world in which 'true courage, manliness, muscle, dash and go were appreciated to their fullest extent'.[22] This world of 'manliness' in which Nelson moved was quite distinct from the weak and effeminate spheres of shore life. The boy's books consequently concentrate on depicting the hero at sea; one author proclaims: 'My Nelson is Nelson on the quarter-deck', assuming that the 'young fellows for whom I write . . . infinitely prefer the sailor's cutlass to a lady's fan'.[23] In these books for boys Nelson is depicted primarily as a fighter. His fighting affirms his masculinity and serves as a pattern for the initiation into manhood of the boys in the novels. One novelist described his protagonist's 'accession of manhood' as his 'initiation into the terrors and the grandeur of naval warfare'.[24] The novels had Nelson lending a helping hand in this process of initiation into a man's world. He encourages boys to join the navy and he welcomes them as his 'lads' into the world of men. According to these novels for boys, Nelson's authentic character can flourish only so long as the separation of gender spheres is maintained. One novelist described how Nelson's 'whole demeanour altered in a moment' as soon as his wife appeared. In her presence, Nelson recommends the protagonist of the story, a young boy, not to join the navy, but to 'plant cabbages' instead, while in her absence he is enthusiastic about his profession.[25] One of his early loves is described as the 'haul[ing] down [of] his flag to a girl'.[26] Clearly women have to be kept at a distance and even Lady Hamilton, who never actually appears in person in any of these novels, is mentioned merely as a supportive female or inspiration for Nelson.

The British novels for boys, as well as the plays at the beginning of the twentieth century, tend to present Nelson very much as the great hero. His first appearance in these works is usually elaborately staged, with him surrounded by a cheering crowd, with a description of his eminence or with a conversation concerning him. Nelson himself, once he starts speaking, often maintains this atmosphere of distance by merely making curt remarks. One successful play, set in the early twentieth-century household of a naval officer, even included an apparition of Nelson, prepared by elaborate stage directions, which demanded a darkening of the stage and a spotlight on the figure of Nelson.[27] Once on stage, Nelson admonishes the naval officer's wife to let her husband go to do his duty and, in a second apparition, he calls on the officer himself to follow the example of those 'who have passed'.[28] The desire to recapture Nelson's spirit found its expression in so many fictional patriotic representations that it annoyed George Bernard Shaw. He wrote, a year after the widely celebrated Trafalgar centenary,[29] about Nelson, 'the intensely English Englishman', in comparison to 'the intensely Irish Irishman' Wellington: 'it seems impossible that any other country than England could produce a hero so utterly devoid of common sense, intellectual delicacy, and international chivalry as Nelson'.[30] This verdict seems to have been at odds with the pre-First World War chorus of adulation for Nelson.

In addition to patriotic novels and plays, a romantic fictional approach to Nelson also started as the nineteenth century gave way to the twentieth. Douglas Sladen's novel *The Admiral. A Romance of Nelson in the Year of the Nile* went through further, and cheaper, editions under the more outspoken title *The Admiral. The Love Story of Lord Nelson and Lady Hamilton*. Building on many historical sources and an invented 'journal', supposedly written by Nelson himself, Sladen represented the relationship between Nelson and Lady Hamilton in a positive light. In doing so, he followed the ideals of gender roles current in his day, at least at the beginning of his book. Nelson is described as a man of strong masculine character, who displays in battle 'his fighting smile of serene superiority'.[31] At the same time, Sladen attributed to him 'delicate sensibilities'.[32] While Nelson's wife Fanny fails him, because she proved to be 'totally unable to satisfy such an intense, imaginative, romantic temperament as the Admiral's',[33] Lady Hamilton shows herself as the very model of a supportive woman. She cares for the wounded Nelson 'with a woman's tender solicitude for sickness' and she shows 'a woman's reverence for a hero'.[34] Towards the end of the novel, however, Nelson's relationship with Lady Hamilton is described as 'companionship' and Nelson praises his lover in his 'journal' as a strong woman in her own right: 'Had Emma been a sea-captain, she would have been as Daring as Foley at the Nile.'[35]

The first full-length feature film about *Nelson*, produced in 1918, made ample use of elements that had already been developed in British prose fiction. The frame of and general motivation for the film was a propagandistic effort on behalf of the navy. In the first scene, Admiral Sydney Fremantle, a leading member of the Navy League, appears and, in summarizing the importance of the navy in British history, gets a boy so interested in the subject that the admiral suggests that he read Southey's *Life of Nelson*. The actual story-line is then told through recurrent flashbacks. Young Nelson is shown in a boyish struggle for manliness, climbing trees and falling out of them, engaged in pillow-fights with his boarding-school mates and also being 'the victim of brutal horse play then the fashion in the Navy'.[36] Once initiated into the manly world of the navy, Nelson becomes a pattern of fighting virility. His future wife, Fanny, in feminine contrast, is shown sewing. Though she is also shown caring for the wounded Nelson, a disconnected inter-title comments: 'Like most men of genius, Nelson craved for warm-hearted appreciative response. Unfortunately his wife lacked the power to supply this.' This prepares the scene for Lady Hamilton. She is first shown as the coquettish wife of the British ambassador to Naples. When she learns about the gravity of the political and military situation of the British, however, she becomes serious and turns into a patriotic supporter of the British cause. When she sees Nelson's empty sleeve on his second visit to Naples, she becomes, more specifically, Nelson's supporter, though only after her husband's death does she become his lover. Nelson, in the meantime, is shown as a caring superior, who 'loved his men better than honours'. As the battle of Trafalgar approaches on 21 October 1805 the images switch between Lady Hamilton at home and Nelson aboard ship, thus depicting the relationship as romantic. After the patriotic opening of the battle, with Nelson's signal 'England expects' and hat-waving sailors, Nelson's death scene is depicted very much in the style of Devis's painting (see plate 5).[37] The scene is embellished with him holding and beholding a medallion of Lady Hamilton. The closing comment, 'There will never be another hero like Nelson', is followed by the encouraging message that he has followers, including the enthusiastic reader of his biography. Modern battleships seen firing at sea complete the message that the Royal Navy maintains the spirit of Nelson.

Later novels and films went on, at least in part, to portray Lady Hamilton in a positive fashion, particularly by using the idea of Nelson transforming Lady Hamilton into a patriotic lady. E. Barrington's novel of 1925 about *The Divine Lady. A Romance of Nelson and Lady Hamilton* added some elements that were designed to explain why Nelson was so attracted by Lady Hamilton's patriotism. According to this book, Lady Hamilton supported Nelson on various occasions. Towards the end of the novel, however, Barrington produces a critical treatment of Nelson's affair with Lady Hamilton and concludes that his adulterous affair led to unhappiness. The novel was used as the basis for an American film, in 1929, which seems to have followed a rather unconvincing storyline, because one critic remarked on the difficulty of striking 'a balance between History on the one hand and squeamish morality on the other' and that the result was '[e]verything but a persuasive story'.[38]

Avoiding the intricacies of Nelson's affair with Lady Hamilton, British films of the 1920s focused rather on Nelson's professional career. Cedric Hardwicke, in *Nelson* (1926), presented an acclaimed portrayal of Nelson as commander, while a production of 'British Instruction Films' – about *Naval Warfare 1789 to 1805* – dealt exclusively with naval encounters. British novels now also started to exploit the naval setting of Nelson. The admiral himself has a short appearance in Joseph Conrad's *The Rover*. In this story he is described as a kind and sickly man with a 'nervous' energy that expresses itself in constant walking (up and down the room) and a drive for action. Nelson himself is quoted as saying:

> This is anxious work . . . It is killing me . . . I have hardly enough breath in my body to carry me on from day to day . . . But I am like that . . . I will stick to my task till perhaps some shot from the enemy puts an end to everything.[39]

It appears that the image of Nelson as the ever active, never doubting naval commander was so strong that it did not allow for much fictional licence. C. S. Forester decided, therefore, to construct a parallel character, tailored in part on Nelson and called Horatio Hornblower, who had the bad luck never to have served under Nelson. Later authors followed this idea, producing series about naval men during the French wars, in which Nelson never actually makes an appearance. British pieces of fiction, mostly plays, that went on to develop the story of Nelson's relationship to Lady Hamilton in the 1930s struggled unsuccessfully with the story. Though they portrayed Nelson's wife in a negative fashion, they did not romanticize Lady Hamilton either.

Negative aspects in the depiction of Nelson's affair with Lady Hamilton mostly vanished with the outbreak of the Second World War and the nation's need for an endearing and entirely admirable national hero. The most enduring of the patriotic interpretations of Nelson's story and also the most famous film about him is Alexander Korda's *That Hamilton Woman* (in Britain: *Lady Hamilton*), shot in Hollywood in the autumn of 1940. The film contained clearly propagandistic elements, among which the speech that scriptwriters Walter Reisch and R. C. Sherriff wrote for Nelson (played by Laurence Olivier) stood out. In this speech Nelson appeals to the lords of the Admiralty not to trust Napoleon (here read Hitler), culminating in the remark: 'you cannot make peace with dictators'. Korda was aware that '[p]ropaganda . . . can be bitter medicine. It needs sugar coating – and Lady Hamilton is a very thick coating of sugar indeed'.[40] The Lady Hamilton coating was provided by the most positive elements of twentieth-century novels and plays about the famous love affair, particularly Lady Hamilton's patriotic support for Nelson. Nelson's appearance in her life does not lead her solely into the typically female role of supporting a man, but also makes her 'change morally for the better as her wardrobe shift[s] radically from the low cut dresses of her Hamilton period to the high collared dresses and shawl-clad wardrobe of her country life as Nelson's "wife" and mother to their beloved daughter'.[41] Reisch and Sherriff portray Lady Nelson in a distinctly negative fashion and allow Captain Hardy to remind Nelson only once of what people will say. But when Nelson replies, 'I will not see those I love and owe loyalty to left alone', Hardy mutters that he understands him. The portrayal of Nelson himself focused on two major conflicts: the tensions between his profession and his emotional needs ('I have not seen her [his wife] for seven years. I wonder why sailors ever marry') and the moral struggles that resulted from his love for Lady Hamilton ('I know that I must not come back and I know that nothing in the world can keep me away'). The romantic message of the film is underlined by the fact that the protagonists were played by a notorious (and originally adulterous) couple of the day: the recently married Laurence Olivier and Vivien Leigh.

Such romanticization of the adulterous Nelson–Hamilton affair did not escape the self-censorship of Hollywood's film industry. The responsible censor Joseph Breen protested that the script was 'treating the adulterous relationship as a romance, instead of as a sin' and insisted on changes. Korda eventually gave up his original idea of 'cutting back and forth between Nelson's cabin on HMS *Victory* and Emma's bedroom at their country home' on the day of the battle of Trafalgar, as had occurred in the British *Nelson* film of 1918. He did add a final scene that showed Lady Hamilton in prison at the end of her life, in order to satisfy Breen's demand that the adulterous parties 'must be punished'. And he shot another scene, which he cut out again when the film was exported; this scene, following one of Breen's suggestions, showed Nelson's parson father admonishing his son for his adultery.[42] As a result some critics were 'disappointed by Korda's chaste handling of the Nelson–Hamilton affair'. Other critics disliked the obvious propagandistic elements, and Korda was just about to justify his position when the USA entered the Second World War and, as a consequence, siding with the British became acceptable.[43] From the beginning, however, the film was popular with the public and it achieved great success in such places as the Soviet Union and South America.

The British post-war novels and plays about Nelson followed earlier fictional patterns without producing any notable artistic work until the late 1960s.

Novels for children or adults were concerned with Nelson's masculinity, showing him as a man who escapes from his dominating wife into male bonding with his stepson or as a man who overcomes his weaknesses to achieve authority. Other novels recycled the Nelson–Hamilton story without introducing any revealing new elements. The libretto for a *Nelson* opera, though traditional in portraying Nelson as lacking a masculine appearance and 'bewildered' by Lady Hamilton's advances, also introduces Earl Minto and Captain Hardy as influences on Nelson's decision to go to sea in 1805.[44] This was developed into the setting for a whole play by Terence Rattigan.

Rattigan's *Bequest to the Nation* (performed as a television play under the title *Nelson: A Study in Miniature*), which was later, with some variations, made into a film, focuses on Nelson at the height of his fame in 1805 and on Nelson's affair with Lady Hamilton. The spectator of the play as well as the film must wonder what attracts Nelson to his lover, since she is portrayed as drunk and vulgar: 'I know you think me a vulgar, drunken slut . . . I don't give a fart for being thought what I am.'[45] Nelson is even portrayed as recognizing his lover's unattractiveness: 'Do you think I relish the gutter-talk, don't wince at the vulgarity, and have lost the capacity to smell liquor on the breath? Do you think there isn't a moment in each day that I don't feel blasted with shame?' To Captain Hardy's question why then does he endure such days, he answers: 'because after the days there are the nights'. This purely carnal attraction leads Nelson to the conclusion, which otherwise cannot convince in the light of the repugnance he expresses for Lady Hamilton: 'You must understand that there is nothing in Emma I would change . . . because I love her.'[46] The play does not succeed in offering a convincing examination of an unusual love affair. Rattigan gives a hint that Nelson is very different at sea from how he behaves ashore (an opinion probably inspired by post-war biographical literature).[47] The printed version of the play and the film do not investigate this 'other Nelson' any further. He is not shown explaining his battle plans to the visiting captains (although this is hinted at) and the episode on the battle of Trafalgar that is included in the film merely deals with Nelson's vanity in wearing his orders and with his death. Nelson is shown in his professional context only when he speaks to the First Lord of the Admiralty. The actual conversation develops very unprofessionally, however. Nelson makes constant references to his lover and behaves overbearingly, treating his superior with insolence. As a result, Rattigan, instead of unravelling Nelson's personality, creates an enigma.

John Arden and Margaretta D'Arcy, in their play *The Hero Rises Up*, found a different approach in order to demolish ideas of romance and heroism in the story of Nelson. They chose as their setting the events in Naples of 1799. In front of an unfolding scene of atrocities, Nelson is portrayed as intent on destruction and keen on disregarding orders: 'I was the first naval commander who understood – and put into practice – the theory of the entire and total destruction of the enemy fleet, at whatever cost to my own. A destruction made possible by my enthusiastic disregard of everybody's orders.'[48] In view of this approach to Nelson as a 'naval commander', the allusion elsewhere to a different Nelson who is trusted by his crews appears even less convincing than in Rattigan's play.[49] Arden's and D'Arcy's portrayal of Nelson as an aggressive warrior at sea is combined with a display of dominating virility ashore. Drawing on the revelation that Nelson had had an adulterous affair in Leghorn around the turn of 1794–95, he is now depicted as promiscuous, desiring Lady Hamilton merely as an additional conquest to his wife: 'Not one woman: two: I'm a hero.'[50] In order to attract a man with such an attitude towards women, both Lady Hamilton and Lady Nelson show their obedient side. The two women positively determine the course of events only once, when they force Nelson to decide between them against his will, since he would have preferred to have them both. Only after his death do they both offer themselves to him, so that Nelson can finish the play remarking from eternity: 'what more can a sailor want?'[51] The stricture on Nelson's affair with Lady Hamilton was recognized by a contemporary critic of 'this unexpectedly reactionary play' as 'stern morality'.[52]

More than twenty years after Arden and D'Arcy, Susan Sontag, in her novel about Sir William Hamilton, *The Volcano Lover*, also focused on events in Naples in her portrayal of Nelson. Her protagonists are stereotypically referred to as 'the Cavaliere' (Sir William Hamilton), 'the Cavaliere's wife' (Lady Hamilton) and 'the hero' (Nelson). Having styled Nelson 'the hero', Sontag describes somebody aspiring to the Victorian ideal of a hero: 'He wanted not to let himself down . . . He had wished to be taller . . . He did not want to feel weak . . . He dreamed that he had both arms . . .' – merely to dismantle the false image: 'War confiscated parts of his body . . . The hero does not look like a hero . . . the hero is a maimed, toothless, worn, underweight little man'.[53] The dismembered 'hero', naturally vain and in need of admiration, in his constant drive for recognition, is then drawn into Neapolitan affairs. In an account based on several false assumptions,[54] Sontag expounds 'the hero['s] . . . merciless' deeds, concluding repeatedly (though in varying words): 'Eternal shame on the hero!'[55] Her version of 'the hero' is successfully torn from his pedestal.

The Naples subject has remained at the centre of fictional treatments of Nelson until most recently. The four-part television series about Nelson, *I Remember Nelson*, had Naples as one of its four subjects, all of which were described from the viewpoints of different people. Nelson himself thus remained at a distance and none of the episodes succeeded in developing an understanding of Nelson himself. Where the search for an understanding of Nelson can lead was shown in Barry Unsworth's *Losing Nelson*, which won its author the Booker Prize. In this novel Unsworth chose not to deal primarily with Nelson, but rather to describe somebody obsessed with Nelson, who tries to write a biography of his hero. This approach enabled Unsworth to reflect on what biographers are looking for in Nelson and what kind of problems they encounter in writing about him. Charles Cleasby, the protagonist in the book, increasingly identifies with Nelson, whom he starts to refer to as 'Horatio'. He links Nelson to his own national identity ('he was English to the core')[56] and he tries to see him as a representative of the hard kind of masculinity he aspires to himself (*Never show what you feel*),[57] though he is unsettled by 'something feminine' in the portrait of Nelson's father and he is reminded of Nelson's emotional side by his uncomfortably independent-minded secretary.[58] While Cleasby manages to escape the issue, at least temporarily, by referring to an 'obvious broad division in Nelson's case . . . between sea-life and land-life',[59] he keeps struggling with Nelson's involvement in the defeat of the Neapolitan revolution. Although he feels supported by 'manly' Mahan, he is haunted by Badham, whom he recognizes in a Neapolitan historian who confronts his own views on Naples and Nelson: 'There are no heroes out there, Mr Cleasby, there are only fears and dreams and the process of fabrication.'[60] Cleasby's defence of Nelson is doomed to fail.

Stephen Fry gave an amusing interpretation of the desire to see Nelson represented in purely romantic fashion. His contribution to the film *Lucky Break* is *Nelson. The Musical*. This piece, supposedly written by an unworldly prison warden, is introduced in order to give the inmates a chance to escape. Naïvely worded, it contains the basic elements of love and patriotism: Nelson sings to Lady Hamilton: 'Sail with me, leave with me, Say you'll always sail the world with me'; and Hardy sings to the dying Nelson: 'You gave your life that we could live and might be free; a land you loved so much, you gave the Nelson Touch.'

The artistic Nelson Touch has encouraged authors for two hundred years to write novels and plays and to produce films about Nelson. What mostly inspired them was his affair with Lady Hamilton, which so intriguingly combined romance and morally dubious behaviour. An additional, thoroughly controversial element is provided in Nelson's story by his involvement in the defeat of the Neapolitan revolution. Works about Nelson often struggle in their effort to depict Nelson's masculinity. While pre-First World War fiction tends to reassert Nelson's manly behaviour, fictional treatments that focus on Lady Hamilton's role in Nelson's life and the events in Naples usually regard him as weakened, if not emasculated. An exception is the play by Arden and D'Arcy, which managed to construct an assertively virile lover. Overall, the image of Nelson that emerges from novels, plays and films is that of a man dominated by his emotions and often enigmatic in his actions.

10

Views from across the Channel

Following the analysis of how Horatio Nelson's life has been interpreted and represented in Britain, this chapter explores the treatment of Nelson's life and career in France, Spain and Germany, countries which have been Britain's European competitors for naval power since Nelson's time. It examines how French, Spanish and German authors and artists have attempted to shape their own image of Nelson in ways that were different from those offered in biographies and fiction written by British authors.

The strongest immediate reaction outside Britain to the battle of Trafalgar and the death of Nelson can be observed in Spain. This reaction reflected the prevailing prejudices against the British. In contrast to the Spanish self-image of the heroic and humane Spaniards, the British were regarded as piratical, brutal and uncivilized. A tale of the *Public Entry of Admiral Nelson in the court of Pluto, on 23rd October of this year* was published in Cadiz, the port from whence the combined Franco-Spanish fleet had so recently left for the battle of Trafalgar and to which its shattered remains returned after the battle. This tale described the views and behaviour of Nelson and his men as enjoying and causing devastation. The general picture of the British was reflected in the poem that Nelson declaimed at the end of the story. In it, he openly conceded that 'the motive of the war was weak, null and void' and praised the recent battle as 'What a well-ordered action! / What a gentlemanly combat! / What an action! What a butchery! / What a barbarity! What a devastation!'[1] The outbreak of the Peninsular War in 1808 brought more pressing matters to the minds of the Spanish than making sense of the battle of Trafalgar and evaluating Nelson. The struggle against French occupation and military cooperation with the British also complicated the perceptions of the British enemy at Trafalgar. In their 'War of Independence' the Spanish destroyed what had remained of the French fleet at Cadiz after the battle of Trafalgar and they fought their former ally in part side by side with the British, their former enemy. As a consequence of the diplomatic reversal of alliances, neither the battle of Trafalgar in general nor Nelson in particular were subject to any historical interpretation in Spain for more than forty years.[2] The only exception was a short story, published in 1835, in which its authoress described the human suffering caused by the battle, while referring to 'the brilliant star of Nelson'.[3]

French silence about the battle of Trafalgar was broken after the fall of Napoleon. There was a clear public need to explain the defeat at Trafalgar. Most of the treatment of the battle therefore consisted of defending and accusing different high-ranking French officers who had taken part in the battle, while no serious attention was paid to Nelson's contribution to the outcome. He was often simply referred to as a 'genius' or 'the great Admiral Nelson',[4] but neither his tactics nor his personality were examined more closely. If authors believed that the French should try to imitate the successful British, and Nelson in particular, they did not do so by investigating Nelson's life and battles, but by recommending what were regarded as typical British characteristics of strict discipline and harsh punishments, applied to officers in particular.[5] French authors avoided exploring Nelson's professional ability any further and focused on his death when dealing with the battle of Trafalgar. The *Mémoires de Robert Guillemard* gave a dramatic account of how the author of the memoirs shot Nelson during the battle of Trafalgar.[6] These fictitious memoirs were so convincingly written that many, especially in Britain, took them to be authentic.[7] However, texts written by French historians did not examine the life and personality of Nelson much more thoroughly. Instead, it started to become popular to stress Nelson's 'blind hate' of the French.[8] Much more critical was *Histoire Criminelle du Gouvernement Anglais* of 1841. It elaborated on and hinted at Nelson's supposed misdeeds in Italy, not only in Naples, but also in Leghorn and Palermo. Using sources which were neither very detailed nor very specific, the former prime minister of France, Louis Adolphe Thiers, developed an image of Nelson in his influential work about the *History of the Consulate and the Empire of France under Napoleon*, published in twenty-one volumes from 1845 onwards. There Nelson is portrayed as a man of dash, but 'narrow-minded in things foreign to his heart'. This view of Nelson's character also had an impact on the assessment of Nelson's tactics, in which, according to Thiers, 'Nelson . . . had contracted the habit of advancing boldly, without observing any order but that which resulted from the relative swiftness of the ships, of dashing upon the enemy's fleet'.[9] He attributed victory in the battle of Trafalgar, which he regarded as of no great importance, not to Nelson's professional abilities, but to the number of three-deckers in the British fleet and the weakness of his enemies, particularly the Spanish.

Thiers' description of the Spanish officers and men who fought at the battle of Trafalgar as cowardly and incompetent caused vehement protests in Spain, where his work was translated and published in three separate editions in the 1840s. The Spanish protests led to a revival of interest in the battle, and in its wake also, though to a lesser degree, to a renewed interest in Nelson. Several publications about the battle of Trafalgar, notably the book by Manuel Marliani, examined not only the Spanish, but also the French and British sources, to challenge Thiers' criticism of the role played by the Spanish in the battle. It is hardly surprising that a new evaluation of the Franco-Spanish relationship was at the centre of this discussion and there was little clear analysis of Nelson and his tactics. In their cursory assessment of Nelson, Spanish authors recognized him as an 'illustrious English leader whose eulogy is made by pronouncing his name',[10] but they also criticized him. This criticism focused on his relationship with Lady Hamilton, but it did not deal with Nelson's involvement in the defeat of the Neapolitan revolution. Marliani described Nelson's relationship with Lady Hamilton as the 'ugly spot [on Nelson's] existence'. Lady Hamilton in turn was described as 'the fatal enchantress, unworthy object of the passionate cult of such a great man' and a 'detestable woman'. Marliani was particularly appalled by Nelson leaving her and his 'adulterous daughter whom he had with her' as his legacy to his king and country and he remarked approvingly that 'England repudiated this immoral legacy'.[11] While Spanish authors adopted the image of the dashing man who enjoyed luck in battle and possessed deplorable weaknesses, they addressed more openly his relationship with Lady Hamilton and were prepared to attribute some outstanding qualities of imagination to Nelson.

At the same time a French author also began to investigate Nelson in more detail. In his *Guerres Maritimes sous la République et l'Empire*, published in 1847, E. Jurien de la Gravière focused on Nelson's professional career. He used Nicolas's edition of *The Dispatches and Letters of Lord Nelson* and as a result stressed Nelson's qualities of leadership. But in general, he only reproduced the characterization of Nelson that had been previously developed in France, describing Nelson as being possessed of a 'blind and fanatic zeal' and his tactics as having consisted less in new ideas than in throwing overboard 'all that the old tactics had in prudent and wise rules'.[12] Jurien de la Gravière also shared his countrymen's stress on obedience. He used Nelson's early career as an example of how obedience should be inculcated into young minds and he largely ignored Nelson's disobedience at the battles of Cape St Vincent and Copenhagen. He saw Nelson's 'ardent initiative' against his admiral in the West Indies as an omen of bad things to come, hinting at Nelson's future role as the 'adulterous lover of Lady Hamilton and murderer of Caracciolo'.[13] Much less balanced than Jurien de la Gravière's depiction was Alphonse-Marie-Louis Prat de Lamartine's *Nelson*, published in 1853. Lamartine's account makes several mistakes in the chronology of events, confusing, for example, the battle of Copenhagen in 1801 with the bombardment of that city in 1807, and he offers not much more on Nelson than on Lady Hamilton. Lamartine wrote much about the influence of Lady Hamilton on Nelson, which he attributed to the 'uncultivated' mindset of the admiral. The 'insanity' of his passion, according to Lamartine, made Nelson lose his 'reason and virtue'.[14] This view of Nelson was used and built on in novels by Alexandre Dumas.

Dumas, 'the King of Romance', found himself in a uniquely suitable position to exploit the subject, when in 1860 Giuseppe Garibaldi made him director of the National Museum at Naples, with 'the very freest access to the State Papers of the defunct dynasty'.[15] On the basis of his tendentious and in parts manipulated edition of documents from the royal archive, *I Borboni di Napoli*, Dumas went on to produce three novels that deal with the events in Naples in 1799. Two of these novels deal with the events themselves by focusing, as their titles betray, on *La San Felice*, as representative of the republicans, and *Emma Lyonna* (Lady Hamilton), as representative of the royalists.[16] These two novels, in spite of their 'inordinate length, made a big impact on the French reading public', and are now usually published together under the title of the first (*La San Felice*).[17] The third novel, *Souvenirs d'une favorite*, is written in the form of memoirs of the dying Lady Hamilton. The different approaches of the novels have an impact on their contents. While the treatment of the revolutionary events in Naples in *La San Felice* is very critical of the royalists, the supposed memoirs take a much more complex view of Lady Hamilton as well as of Nelson. Nevertheless, it is possible, to some degree, to generalize about Dumas' treatment of Nelson.

Dumas derived his knowledge of Nelson mostly from Lamartine's biography. His characterization of Nelson therefore remained rather stereotyped. Dumas' only reflection on Nelson's life at sea showed him repeatedly returning wounded from some encounter or other. In general terms, Dumas depicted Nelson as a 'man of the people, born far from the court' and therefore as somebody who 'felt . . . more profoundly than those born in a superior condition, the fascination that the royal smile exercises'.[18] As a rough seaman without gentlemanly demeanour and with a tendency to throw himself passionately into the arms of women, Nelson, in Dumas' view, was clearly inexperienced in the two spheres he was entering in Naples: politics and female society. According to Dumas, these two spheres were dangerously connected in late eighteenth-century Naples by a network of intrigue, at the centre of which sat the queen of Naples and Lady Hamilton.

Dumas showed how Nelson fell prey to both these women, because he had already been 'madly in love with Lady Hamilton' since their first meeting in 1793. On his return to Naples after the battle of the Nile, in 1798, he became even 'more in love, more mad, more insane'.[19] The connection of love with insanity shows Nelson as losing his self-control to a dominant woman. In Dumas' version of events, Nelson himself admits to Lady Hamilton that she is exercising a dangerous ascendancy over him: 'You will drive me mad'; and he asks her to 'lead' him: 'you know that I cannot see anything else, when I see you'.[20] In order to portray Nelson as a man robbed of his masculine strength, Dumas employed a strategy developed in French literature during the nineteenth century: an interpretation of lesbianism. Honoré de Balzac in *La Fille aux yeux d'or* (*The Girl with the Golden Eyes*, published in 1833) had been the first to portray a lesbian 'as monster: a mysterious, perverse, jealous, vengeful, and powerful female animal', who humiliated 'the male sense of masculine supremacy' and was in the end punished for her libidinous lifestyle.[21] A few years before Dumas started writing about Naples, the subject of lesbian-ism was revived in French literature by the publication of Charles Baudelaire's controversial *Les Fleurs du mal* in 1857, which had originally been announced as *Les Lesbiennes* (*The Lesbians*) and which contained the famous poem about 'Femmes damnées' ('Damned Women'), dealing with lesbian love.

Dumas exploited this pattern in French literature by making Nelson appear as the dupe of calculating lesbians. These lesbians are moulded into the shape developed for them in French nineteenth-century literature. The queen of Naples keeps Lady Hamilton overnight, sings 'verses of Sappho' to her, undresses and kisses her.[22] Following the pattern that lesbians were of 'licentious stock', Lady Hamilton is described as the illegitimate daughter of an English nobleman.[23] Further corrupted by the frivolous Miss Arabell, a modern 'Sappho', she begins to threaten male gender roles, appearing 'virile' and desiring to play 'Lady Macbeth or Cleopatra' in real life.[24] Both the queen of Naples and Lady Hamilton dress as 'amazons' and they confess to each other that they are disappointed by their male lovers.[25] Their lesbian activities are thus expressions of frustrated heterosexual love. The women's latent lesbian-ism makes them 'rivals in conquest to men'[26] and unreliable in their heterosex-ual relationships. The queen of Naples is not only a rival to Nelson for Lady Hamilton's affections, but also through her a dominating force undermining Nelson's control over his own actions. She thus threatens his virility. The queen encourages Lady Hamilton at one festivity in her salon to sing a song '*À la femme aimée*' ('To the Beloved Woman'), accompanying herself on a 'lesbian lyre', which is said to have belonged to the 'muse of Mythilene [a town on Lesbos, where Sappho lived]'. This love-song ends with the poetess dying 'without expiring, of desire and of love'. As Lady Hamilton falls at the end of the performance she is caught in the queen's arms, while Nelson stands by 'trembling'. The queen, ever in control of the situation, takes a laurel crown from Lady Hamilton's head and puts it on Nelson's. On leaving, she declares: 'in my absence, it's Emma who is the queen'; and to Nelson she says: 'Tell her to dance the shawl dance for you that she has been dancing for me.'[27] In this atmosphere of delusion, Nelson appears to be dominated by emotion and to be inaccessible to reason. Like 'Ulysses' in the arms of 'Circe', Nelson disobeys an order to leave Naples with the argument, suggested by Lady Hamilton, that he cannot leave the queen of Naples.[28] Drawn ever more into the politics of the queen of Naples, Nelson ruthlessly supports the defeat of the Neapolitan rev-olution. In his description of these events, Dumas is remarkably imprecise, though priding himself on changing from the role of novelist to that of histo-rian. Making little effort to examine the documentary evidence, he insists that Nelson 'bombard[ed] Naples', describes Nelson as keen on catching rebels and confidently asserts that Nelson forced the Neapolitan court martial to condemn Admiral Caracciolo to death.[29]

Only in *Souvenirs d'une favorite* did Dumas go on to describe Nelson's life after the events at Naples in 1799. Here Nelson himself and his relationship to

Lady Hamilton undergo a remarkable change. Whereas Lady Hamilton confesses her guilt at not having stopped Nelson at Naples and at having separated Nelson from his wife, Nelson, thus comfortably freed from all responsibility, recovers not only his heroic stature, but also his status as a virile man: 'It was now him, on the contrary, who had all the power over me', confesses Lady Hamilton.[30] Her wild spirit thus subdued by masculine determination, she becomes faithful and even establishes some kind of respectable family life with Nelson. When he dies tragically, she is doomed to fall back into her old dissolute lifestyle. Dumas' depiction of Nelson thus attempted to demonstrate the importance of men's dominance over women and the danger of a loss of virility through the loss of this dominance to potentially amoral females.

Dumas' unwieldy treatment of Nelson's involvement with Lady Hamilton and his role in the defeat of the Neapolitan revolution were not only widely read; they also had an impact on how other French authors depicted Nelson. This influence can be noticed well into the twentieth century. The account of Nelson's responsibility for the execution of the Neapolitan admiral Caracciolo became widely known as a result of Dumas' treatment, and this led Victor Hugo to remark on 'a column to Nelson, with Caraccioli's ghost pointing the finger at it!'[31] Particularly popular became the idea of Nelson being mixed up in a network of intriguing lesbians, with the queen of Naples and Lady Hamilton competing in viciousness. This interpretation, however, remained predominantly French. A 'cruelly abridged' British version, published in the run-up to the Trafalgar centenary, did not attract much attention.[32] The Spanish author Manuel Cubas used Dumas as a source for his account of Lady Hamilton in his book about *Famous Courtesans*, published in 1893. Although he followed Dumas' interpretation of Nelson as being duped by a vicious woman, who in the end finds her due punishment, he did not include any hint of lesbianism in his account.

Spanish fiction about Nelson has focused mainly on the battle of Trafalgar and it has produced the most famous, most widely read and most enduring interpretation ever written about the battle: a 130-year-old best-seller, still available in at least three different pocket book editions in Spain. This is Benito Pérez Galdós' novel *Trafalgar*. Galdós, arguably the most famous Spanish author of the nineteenth century, was thirty years old when he wrote the novel in 1873 as the first of a series of *Episodios Nacionales* (National Episodes), which would, in the end (that is in 1912), amount to forty-six volumes. Galdós was driven to start this monumental series by the prevailing political instability in Spain at the time. Since the uprising that had overthrown Queen Isabel II in 1868, Spain had been in a state of turmoil: provisional government, republican insurrections, regency and revolutionary movements followed each other. Finally, Spain acquired a new monarch, Amadeo I, who abdicated while Galdós was writing *Trafalgar*. When Galdós sat down to begin his *Episodios Nacionales*, his aim was to alert his compatriots to the condition of contemporary Spain and to offer an outlook on the future. For that purpose he set out to describe historic events in the country's fairly recent past from the viewpoint of ordinary people, the protagonist in *Trafalgar* being a fourteen-year-old orphan. Most historians of literature who have dealt with Galdós' novel *Trafalgar* agree that he wanted to send out a message of peace and harmony to a country which he thought ought to strive to establish a meritocratic society and yet a stronger sense of its own national identity. Because Galdós' ideal of patriotism was one which saw different nationalities coexisting peacefully, he neither condemned nor glorified any particular nation.[33]

The presentation of Nelson in *Trafalgar* shifts as Galdós' protagonist in the novel, Gabriel, expands his initial narrow views on war and nationhood into more balanced ideas about peace and national identity. At the beginning, Nelson is referred to by Gabriel's adult friend, Marcial, an invalid sailor, who presents his experiences of naval warfare as a big adventure story. Marcial, in his idiosyncratic nautical language, calls Nelson *Señorito*, which according to Galdós' explanation 'indicated a certain esteem or respect', and wishes Nelson to bring a lot of 'timber' into which to shoot cannonballs.[34] Marcial's respect for the British admiral takes a more serious turn when he explains Nelson's plan of battle to his fellow sailors, shortly before the action begins. With his comment that 'to this gentleman everything seems easy' he provokes some murmuring among his listeners.[35] Even in Galdós' description of the battle itself, which lacks the overenthusiasm of Marcial, the author shows respect for 'the genius of the great Nelson'.[36] During the course of the battle, a new and softer view of Nelson emerges. Gabriel witnesses, when his ship is taken by the British, how a British officer speaks about Nelson's death and bursts into tears. The first-person narrator breaks the line of the story here and inserts a short account of Nelson's death. Galdós omitted here any allusions to Lady Hamilton, although he drew on Marliani, who had so strongly condemned Nelson's adulterous relationship. Instead of detracting from his subject with a moralistic message about marital fidelity, Galdós focused on the dramatic aspect of the death of 'the first seaman of our century',[37] thus conveying more powerfully the loss to the British and consequently strengthening his own anti-war message. The indirect portrayal of Nelson in *Trafalgar* – through other people's comments – shows that he is generally regarded with respect, which fits into Galdós' concept of mutual respect and peaceful coexistence between nations. Although Nelson is only a minor figure in Galdós' *Trafalgar*, thanks to the great success of the book, the respectfully positive way in which he is treated has left an indelible mark on the Spanish image of Nelson.

The Germans developed an interest in Nelson only after their unification in 1871 and the foundation of their national navy, but thereafter several authors examined the life and personality of Nelson very thoroughly. Two biographies, published in 1880 and 1883 respectively, surpass in depth and detail any French or Spanish texts about Nelson published during the nineteenth century. Both biographies came closest to the British image of Nelson at this time.[38] The non-British influence was reflected most in German views about Nelson's role in Naples and his relationship with Lady Hamilton. Althaus and Werner, in their separate studies, agreed in their criticism of Nelson's actions in Naples and both accepted that Nelson's daughter Horatia was a product of his relationship with Lady Hamilton. The two authors disagreed, however, in their assessment of Nelson's relations with Lady Hamilton. Whereas Reinhold Werner regarded Lady Hamilton as a 'demonic influence' on Nelson, Friedrich Althaus described Lady Hamilton in a very positive fashion and claimed that Nelson and Lady Hamilton 'doubtless' felt mutually attracted to each other.[39] In their assessment of Nelson as a naval officer Althaus and Werner largely agreed with one another. Like Jurien de la Gravière, they acknowledged Nelson's ability as a leader of men, but, unlike French authors, they both praised Nelson's critical thinking and even his acts of disobedience. Werner (an admiral himself) particularly commended Nelson's critical observations on the Admiralty's habit of tearing crews apart in order to redistribute them to different ships, and he regarded Nelson's disobedience in the West Indies concerning the navigations laws as the act of a 'dutiful man'.[40] Althaus went even further in approving of Nelson's acts of disobedience. He described Nelson's often criticized disobedience of Admiral Keith in 1799 as 'courageous'.[41] In order to examine the question of disobedience more generally, he quoted a passage from a letter in which Nelson stated: 'to say that an officer is never, for any object to alter his orders, is what I cannot comprehend'. Althaus eulogized this attitude as: 'the indignation of a heroic soul who values the daily rule as nothing in comparison to the necessity of appropriate action'.[42]

German fictional adaptations of Nelson's life tended to focus more on the events in Naples, but even they contained patriotic elements. A *Nelson* play of 1903 included some conversations of ordinary sailors, some of them Germans who served in the Royal Navy. One of the Germans points out that British successes at sea are partly due to their own German involvement and a British coxswain admits that the Germans used to be a 'powerful seafaring people' in the days of the 'Hansa'.[43] Even Nelson himself acknowledges the German contribution to British might, and he eagerly preaches to his wife about 'patriotic duty', very much in the spirit widely encouraged at the beginning of the twentieth century.[44] His patriotic spirit fails him, however, when he enters the corrupting atmosphere of the Neapolitan court. The play underlines Nelson's moral decline, including by his own acknowledgement his dependence on Lady Hamilton.[45]

The subject of Lady Hamilton was a particular favourite in Germany. The most successful German adaptation of the Nelson and Lady Hamilton story was Heinrich Vollrat Schumacher's two-volume novel about *Lady Hamilton* and *Nelson's Last Love*.[46] Schumacher drew heavily on Dumas in the first volume and the beginning of the second volume, although he appears to be slightly more sympathetic to Lady Hamilton, portraying her as a victim of circumstances and showing her as disgusted by the lesbian approaches of

Miss Arabella Kelly and the queen of Naples. As soon as Nelson appears, the story takes on a different slant. He is portrayed as the honest person who helps Lady Hamilton to free herself from her corrupt circumstances and to live a more honest life. When she meets Nelson in Naples in 1793, she turns patriotic and wants to become like him, 'a man, a warrior!'[47] His sincerity softens her distrust of him, for which she apologizes, having 'lived among Italians'.[48] On Nelson's second arrival in Naples in 1798, his admiration for her patriotism finally wins her over in a double sense: to love Nelson and to become a moral person. While he needs her physical support to overcome his different ailments, he helps her to enter a world of patriotism and integrity. Nelson's involvement in the defeat of the Neapolitan Republic is, for the first time in a piece of fiction, defended and the blame for later atrocities is shifted onto the king of Naples. Only in ordering Caracciolo's execution is Nelson described as having gone too far, and in this matter Lady Hamilton is, contrary to all earlier depictions, portrayed as trying to stop Nelson reaching this decision. In contrast to the reformed Lady Hamilton, Nelson's wife proves to be harsh and demanding, so that her generous husband appears justified in deserting her. For the two lovers: 'Nothing was now left to complete their happiness.'[49] Nelson's death leaves Lady Hamilton defrauded of her pension, instead of falling into deserved decline, as earlier novels had portrayed her later life.

Schumacher's interpretation of Nelson's relationship with Lady Hamilton was made into an internationally successful German film in 1921. Producer, scriptwriter and director Richard Oswald used an all-star cast for his *Lady Hamilton*. Conrad Veidt, who had just gained world fame for his role as the somnambulist in *Das Cabinett des Dr. Caligari*, played Nelson. Unfortunately, it is now difficult to reconstruct faithfully his portrayal of Nelson. In making the film, Oswald deviated from his own script and many of the scenes that were originally intended seem never to have been filmed. It also appears that different versions of the film were cut. A Russian copy presents a mostly romantic version of events, while a surviving series of incoherently combined scenes in a German version includes depictions of the trial, execution and reappearance of the corpse of the Neapolitan admiral 'Caraciollo'. Judging from the scenes that have come down to us, Nelson undergoes a certain change during the course of the action. In Naples he appears rather helpless, lost in front of the stunning scenery and vibrant intrigues that develop in the film. When Nelson is shown, he is portrayed as weakened by his wounds, almost staggering, with a lecherous expression on his face, or he seems bewildered, nervous and besotted, wildly kissing a miniature of Lady Hamilton or, later, the original. After Lady Hamilton has demanded from Nelson a promise never to see his wife again, the film for its short final scenes presents a family idyll with Lady Hamilton and her baby, Nelson kissing his lover and caressing his little daughter. Nelson's death is represented in a short scene. According to the script, the author had intended an appearance of the head of the dead 'Caraciollo in the water', which would make Nelson exclaim:

'Don't throw me into the water'; but in the actual film Nelson only stares and points with trembling hand into empty space, so that the spectator is left wondering what may be haunting him.[50]

In other works of German fiction, produced in the 1920s, Nelson remained the admiral under the command of a woman. An operetta by the popular composer Eduard Künneke depicts Lady Hamilton as dominating the events – and in the end also dominating Nelson. Nelson's submission is only the culmination of a lecherous desire for Lady Hamilton, a turn of events probably inspired by Oswald's film. When Nelson first meets her, he is described as 'panting'.[51] Such ridicule made Nelson an ideal subject for an absurd portrayal of the kind fashionable at the time: *Lady Hamilton or the Posing-Emma or from Servant Girl to Beefsteak à la Nelson. A just as Fantastic as Well as Short-Story-Rocking Proliferating Parody; Most Industriously and Most Fleshly Pictured by George Grosz.*[52] This Dadaist novel, instead of focusing, as other novels had done, on how Lady Hamilton seduced her successive lovers, described how these successive lovers tried to get rid of her. Nelson achieves his final goal by blowing up the *Victory* (and himself) at the battle of Trafalgar: 'All other stories about the death of the admiral are legends, as they develop all too easily around such a great man.'[53]

Historical treatments of Nelson in France, Spain and Germany focused from the end of the nineteenth century until the eve of the First World War mainly upon the battle of Trafalgar. The international discussion of the event led to a more balanced interpretation of the battle. In France, Edouard Desbrière published an extensive edition of documents relating to the battle, for which he had also mustered the support of the Spanish admiral, Pelayo Alcalá Galiano. The latter, who was related to three captains who had served at Trafalgar, published his own account of the battle in a study of nearly a thousand pages. The importance of Nelson's most famous battle was generally acknowledged, even if his person did not arouse such interest. This scholarly treatment of the battle of Trafalgar appears to have led both Spanish and German authors to a greater admiration for Nelson, while French authors stuck to their traditional image of Nelson as narrow-minded (if not incompetent), uncultured, dangerously insubordinate and hating the French.

The ambivalent perception of Nelson in Spain as a genius of naval warfare, on the one hand, and a slave to his lover's will, on the other, led to a particularly Spanish interpretation of Nelson as quixotic. When the influential Spanish philosopher Ortega y Gasset claimed in his *Estudios sobre el amor* (*Studies about Love*), originally published as a newspaper series, that 'in the choice of a loved woman men reveal their essential character', a reader contradicted him, giving as examples of men loving undeserving women Don Quixote (who loved Aldonza Lorenzo) and Nelson (who loved Lady Hamilton).[54] This comment, actually published in 1941 in the book containing the *Estudios sobre el amor*, seems to have inspired a genuinely Spanish view of Nelson's ability to love. In his *Nelson: A Sentimental Life* of 1944 Juan

Cabal wrote about the way in which Nelson loved his wife: 'Like *Don Quixote*, he invented his *Dulcinea*' (Quixote's highly idealized version of his beloved Aldonza Lorenzo).[55] José del Rio Sainz, in *Nelson* (published in 1943), compared Nelson to the most famous figure of Spanish literature in a more comprehensive sense. He referred not only to Nelson's first true love as his Dulcinea, but also described Nelson himself when disobeying his commander-in-chief in the West Indies as a Quixote, thus conjuring up the image of the proud knight fighting against windmills.[56] In seeing a quixotic single-mindedness in Nelson's love affairs as well as in his professional conduct, del Rio Sainz managed to consolidate the two main traits that Spaniards had detected in Nelson: the passionate lover and the purposeful hero. Unfortunately, this was done in such an allusive manner that it did not have much impact on the overall interpretation of Nelson.

German authors shared an admiration for Nelson's insubordination and independent action. Even Admiral Alfred von Tirpitz referred admiringly to Nelson putting his telescope to his blind eye at the battle of Copenhagen in order not to see his superior's signalled order.[57] A collection of biographies of warriors, entitled *Führertum* and published in several editions in the 1930s, treated Nelson as an example of a leader (*Führer*). The text about Nelson stressed that 'Nelson's strong, free and discerning apprehension of warfare' was in contrast to 'the ceremonious, schematic way of the old tactics'. The collective authors went on to stress that Nelson was by no means carried away by some kind of 'impetuosity', but instead prepared his attacks very carefully.[58] The examination of the professional side of Nelson praised his leadership qualities, particularly his habit of keeping his subordinates informed of his plans, as well as his own habit of independent action. Nelson's spirit, according to German authors of the 1930s, had been lost in Britain and had passed on to other nations, particularly the Germans.

Interpretations of Nelson with a pronounced national outlook all but disappeared in Germany, as well as in Spain, in the second half of the twentieth century, as information about the admiral was taken from biographies, translated from English. Compared to the Spanish and Germans, however, the French have maintained their image of Nelson relatively independent of the image established by the British. More recent French publications have usually repeated the traditional French image of Nelson. No translations of British biographies of Nelson were published in France, although in 1990 a substantial biography of *Nelson* by Jacques de Langlade was published. The author, a specialist in British nineteenth-century literature and art, made ample use of British primary as well as secondary sources. As a result, traditional French perceptions, such as unease at Nelson's acts of disobedience, were challenged. Langlade, however, did maintain the prevailing French view of the negative influence of Lady Hamilton on Nelson and of the weakness of his opponents, and he still refrained from exploring Nelson's tactics.

Fictional treatments of Nelson in France and Germany kept focusing on his relationship with Lady Hamilton rather than elements of Nelson's professional career, let alone the political aspects of Nelson's actions in Naples. French and German authors wrote novels about the love affair, one of which even explicitly doubts the authenticity of Dumas' evidence. Even when they follow the traditional approach of blaming Nelson for the events in Naples, they do not make the subject a central aspect of their story. Thus, freed from controversial political issues, the story was made into a film in 1968: *Lady Hamilton zwischen Schmach und Liebe* (*Lady Hamilton between Disgrace and Love*). In this German–French–Italian co-production, Nelson is presented as a swashbuckling hero, fighting off, with sword in his only surviving hand, revolutionaries in Naples and murderers sent out by Caracciolo. The hanging of Caracciolo, shown in the film, is therefore easily explained as justified punishment for attempted murder. Nelson's honourable, though also openly erotic, appearance in Lady Hamilton's life frees her from the overtly lesbian approaches of the queen of Naples and leads her into a respectable, though short-lived, family life, as in earlier filmic treatments of the Nelson–Hamilton story.

A thoughtful portrayal of Nelson in his professional context is offered in Sten Nadolny's best-selling German novel about the polar explorer, John Franklin. Nadolny describes Nelson shortly before the battle of Trafalgar: 'He appeared like a man filled with love – love of glory, and love for his own kind. And soon there was no one who didn't want to be of Nelson's kind.' John Franklin decides not to 'be infected by this'. When he addressed his men, years later, however, it 'suddenly occurred to him that Nelson's address . . . had begun with the same words', thus he becomes aware of the ambiguities of professional dedication.[59]

In conclusion, it can be said that although the images of Nelson in France, Spain and Germany have shown a tendency to merge with the British view, distinct national perceptions have had a marked influence on how Nelson has been presented and seen in France, Spain and Germany over the last two centuries. The French image of Nelson has been the most negative, traditionally focusing on Nelson's involvement in Neapolitan affairs and his relations with Lady Hamilton. Both these aspects have been strongly influenced by the writings of Alexandre Dumas on the subject. French historians have additionally expressed suspicions of Nelson's acts of disobedience, and they have regarded Nelson's naval achievements as the result of mere dash and good fortune. For the Spanish, Nelson has mostly been seen as the formidable enemy at Trafalgar, thanks mostly to the famous novel about this battle by Galdós. As an enemy Nelson has gained respect over the years and his abilities have emerged in more detail in studies produced throughout the twentieth century. The Germans became seriously interested in Nelson relatively late and only as they started to develop their own national navy. They then, however, developed a broad interest in his life and personality. They largely followed the British portrayal of Nelson, though with a special emphasis on the idea of the single-minded leader, combined with a fairly relaxed attitude about Lady Hamilton and a modestly critical attitude towards Nelson's involvement in Naples. In other words, foreign perceptions of Nelson have been shaped more by the needs of these societies than by the reality of what Nelson had in fact achieved.

Conclusion

This book has offered a twin approach to the subject of Horatio Nelson. On the one hand, it has explored the controversies surrounding the man himself and, on the other, it has shown how posterity has created and exploited these controversies, thereby offering different and sometimes conflicting interpretations of the hero.

The first part of this book has presented new insights into the most crucial and controversial aspects of Nelson's life. These insights have been achieved by asking new questions of and applying new methods to the relevant primary sources and by showing how the most controversial aspects of Nelson's life and career have been interpreted over time. These different approaches to this British hero have made it possible to challenge those prejudices that have so distorted the image we have of him and as a result we were able to gain a more authentic viewpoint. This can be seen in any of the major elements of Nelson's life. Instead of regarding his acts of disobedience as expressions of heroic individualism or shameful disregard of orders, they have been shown as the result of difficult deliberations about responsible action in complex circumstances. Instead of glorifying Nelson's success in battle or claiming that success was the result of mere dash, Nelson's complex tactics have been analysed carefully. Instead of conveniently siding with Nelson's critics in matters of his involvement in the defeat of the Neapolitan revolution or refusing to deal with the subject in any detail, Nelson's actions have been examined in their multi-layered context. Instead of romanticizing Nelson's relationship with Lady Hamilton, or disregarding it as not worthy of serious historical deliberation, it has been analysed within a framework that has benefited from the advances in gender history. Instead of merely copying parts of surgeon Beatty's account of Nelson's death, the end of his life has been presented using hitherto neglected sources that have revealed much about Nelson's suffering in his final hours. Rather than focusing either on his private or his professional actions and conduct, an interpretation of Nelson's personality has been offered that considers his character in both its private and professional contexts. As a consequence of this approach not only has much been discovered about Nelson himself, but also much has become clearer about the development of his image in historical literature over the past two centuries.

In discussing the major aspects of Nelson's life and career, it has been shown how biographers and naval historians have presented these elements and how they have often struggled to explain them. For different reasons they have not always managed to examine the most important aspects of Nelson's life thoroughly enough. Sometimes the events were too complex to be easily understood and explained or detailed research in a particular field was lacking, as, for example, in the case of Nelson's involvement in the defeat of the Neapolitan revolution and, to a lesser degree, in the case of his tactics. In other cases authors have shrunk from further investigation because of a reluctance to face up to moral issues that challenged traditional concepts of the 'hero': in Nelson's relationship with Lady Hamilton and in his acts of disobedience, for example. Often the treatment of Nelson's life has been determined by an author's overall assessment of Nelson: whether they wished to hold him up as a pattern to be emulated by succeeding generations or whether they wanted to dismantle his heroic image. Such problems are not easily overcome and the story of Nelson's life and interpretations of it probably mean that he will remain a controversial figure. Nelson's life challenges us to deal with such fundamental questions as courage, love, war and death. It also requires us to see how Nelson has been linked to Britain's whole maritime identity. His personality and achievements therefore remain constantly fascinating and the evidence for them remains so open to different interpretations that there will always be ample scope for controversy.

The second part of this book has shown how representations of Nelson have been offered outside traditional historical literature. It has been shown how artists created his visual image and how increasingly varied forms of representation have been found to portray him to the public over the course of the last two hundred years. This analysis has included a thorough overview of early visual representations, before going on to explore other forms of iconography. For the first time, the manifold propagandistic efforts to present Nelson have been examined in order to show how political, patriotic and business interests interacted to shape Nelson as an icon. In addition to an ever increasing visual presentation of Nelson, imaginative fiction has found new ways of interpreting the hero. Finally, this book has shown how the French, Spanish and Germans have shaped an image of Nelson that often differed remarkably from British interpretations.

Both parts of this book have shown that the appeal of Nelson, enduring as it has proved to be, has also undergone changes in intensity as well as in quality throughout the last two hundred years. These changes have meant that various portrayals of Nelson have often been far removed from the historical personality on which they are based. Depictions of Nelson have sometimes relied on historical imagination, and they have often appeared in fictional representation and material iconography. Nelson's death at the height of the battle of Trafalgar prompted a powerful reaction in biographical literature and in different art forms, such as material artefacts and poetry. Interpreted as a saviour of Britain, Nelson caught the public's imagination and aroused a profound sense of gratitude. The resulting idealized views of Nelson, however, as well as contemporary moral standards, were deeply upset by the publication of some of Nelson's letters to Lady Hamilton, in 1814. As a consequence Nelson was neglected for a period of time. Only from the late 1830s onwards did friends and fellow naval officers manage to revive an interest in Nelson by publishing works about him and, perhaps more importantly, by starting the subscription for the erection of Nelson's Column on Trafalgar Square. Another phase of limited public interest in Nelson during the second half of the nineteenth century ended with parallel efforts to restore him to public attention by exploiting imagery and iconography. Shortly after naval historians had started researching Nelson seriously, he was popularized by the *Royal Naval Exhibition* in 1891, the focus of which was, in great part, on Nelson, and the Navy League's celebrations of Nelson at the anniversaries of the battle of Trafalgar from 1895 onwards. Nelson was moved to the core of British national, if not imperial, identity and firmly installed as a national hero. The quality of historical investigation into Nelson's life and career and the scale of his popularity both reached a peak in the years around the centenary of the battle of Trafalgar in 1905.

Nelson was brought so much into public consciousness in the years before the First World War that imagery as well as iconography dealing with him remained present throughout the twentieth century, presenting a challenge to those interested in him to find interpretations to put before the public. The isolated treatment of Nelson, promoted as part of the cult of the hero, was further emphasized as Nelson was increasingly presented in a manner that took him out of his naval context in the many works produced in the twentieth century. While novels, plays and films explored his love affair with Lady Hamilton and criticized his involvement in the defeat of the Neapolitan revolution, biographic literature scrutinized his personality, in a desire to break with Victorian hero-worship and to profit from new psychological insights. Much effort has been made to investigate his most disputed and controversial actions, such as his acts of disobedience, his tactics at the battle of Trafalgar, his involvement in Naples and his love affair with Lady Hamilton, but his personality has remained enigmatic and a fascinating mixture of masculine and feminine attributes. Since the nineteenth century, biographers, observers of Nelson's portraits and authors of novels and plays have been intrigued and even confused by what they perceive as elements of femininity in the successful warrior. The difficulty of explaining Nelson in simple terms guarantees a continuing struggle to understand the man, while it opens different iconic interpretations – from roughness in 'Nelson's Revenge Premium Ale' to the sensitive issue of gays in the military. The different aspects that excite popular and scholarly interest in Nelson and the continuing controversies about them promise further imagery and iconography.

Notes

Prologue: Nelson's funeral

1 Robert Southey, *The Life of Nelson* (2 vols., London: John Murray, 1813) [hereafter: Southey (1813)], ii, 272.

2 *The Times*, 7, 9 and 14 November 1805; *Naval Chronicle*, 14 (1805), 386.

3 A. Y. Mann, *The Last Moments and Principal Events Relative to the ever to Be Lamented Death of Lord Viscount Nelson* (London: Symonds, 1806), p. 10.

4 *The Times*, 11 November 1805.

5 *The Times*, 6 December 1805.

6 H. Draper, *National Distresses counterbalanced by National Mercies: A Funeral Sermon on the Death of . . . Lord Nelson* (second edition [n.p.: published by the author, 1805]), p. 3.

7 *Naval Chronicle*, 14 (1805), 487–91: 'extract [from a Thanksgiving] Sermon . . . [given in] Trinity Chapel, Conduit Street, [by] Rev. J. S. Clarke', 488, 491.

8 *Naval Chronicle*, 14 (1805), 502.

9 *The Times*, 5 and 6 December 1805.

10 James Stanier Clarke and John M'Arthur, *The Life of Admiral Lord Nelson, K.B. from His Lordship's Manuscripts* (2 vols., London: T. Cadell and W. Davies, 1809) [hereafter: Clarke and M'Arthur], ii, 459, using William Beatty, *Authentic Narrative of the Death of Lord Nelson* ([London]: T. Cadell and W. Davies, 1807) [hereafter: Beatty], p. 72.

11 Southey (1813), ii, 271–2.

12 *The Times*, 25 November 1806.

13 *The Times*, 7 November 1805.

14 *The Times*, 13 November 1805.

15 The *Sun*, 14 November 1805; quoted in: Timothy Jenks, 'Contesting the Hero: The Funeral of Admiral Lord Nelson', *Journal of British Studies*, 39 (2000) [hereafter: Jenks], 422–53, at 426–7.

16 *The Times*, 30 November 1805.

17 Jenks, 436, referring to *Bell's Weekly Messenger*, 1 December 1805.

18 *The Times*, 13 December 1805.

19 *The Times*, 23 December 1805.

20 The National Archives of the United Kingdom (formerly: Public Record Office), LC 2/37, f. 1.

21 Anthony Wagner, *Heralds of England. A History of the Office and College of Arms* (London: Her Majesty's Stationery Office, 1967), p. xxiv.

22 Julian Litten, *The English Way of Death. The Common Funeral Since 1450* (London: Robert Hale, 1991), pp. 174–7.

23 John Wolffe, *Great Deaths. Grieving, Religion, and Nationhood in Victorian and Edwardian Britain* (published for The British Academy, Oxford: Oxford University Press, 2000), p. 16; in the event, all seven sons of George III attended the funeral (*The Times*, 10 January 1806).

24 Jenks, 427–8.

25 *The Times*, 30 December 1805.

26 *The Times*, 1 and 2 January 1806.

27 *The Gentleman's Magazine*, 75 (1805), 1168.

28 George H. Pollock, 'Mourning and Adaptation', *International Journal of Psycho-Analysis*, 42 (1961), 341–61, 343–4, quoting Sigmund Freud.

29 Lily Lambert McCarthy, *Remembering Nelson* ([Portsmouth]: privately published in the United Kingdom, 1995) [hereafter: McCarthy], pp. xix, 89, 95.

30 *The Times*, 6 January 1806.

31 *The Times*, 7 January 1806; *Naval Chronicle*, 15 (1806), 49–50.

32 *The Times*, 8 January 1806.

33 *Naval Chronicle*, 15 (1806), 52.

34 *Gentleman's Magazine*, 76 (1806), 66.

35 *The Times*, 9 January 1806.

36 Quoted in Richard Davey, *A History of Mourning* (Jay's: London, [n.d.]) [hereafter: Davey], p. 75.

37 *Gentleman's Magazine*, 76 (1806), 66.

38 *The Times*, 9 January 1806.

39 Joshua White, *Memoirs of the Professional Life of the late Most Noble Lord Horatio Nelson* (third edition, considerably enlarged, London: James Cundee, 1806) [hereafter: J. White], supplement, pp. 39–40.

40 Castalia Countess Granville (ed.), *Lord Granville Leveson Gower (First Earl Granville). Private Correspondence 1781–1821* (2 vols., London: John Murray, 1916), ii, 155.

41 Quoted in Davey, p. 77.

42 *Naval Chronicle*, 15 (1806), 225.

43 J. White, supplement, pp. 63–5, quoting from the *London Gazette*.

44 *Gentleman's Magazine*, 76 (1806), 71.

45 College of Arms, Funeral of Viscount Nelson MSS, f. 122.

46 J. White, supplement, p. 65, quoting from the *London Gazette*.

47 *Naval Chronicle*, 15 (1806), 333.

48 *The Times*, 21 January 1806.

49 *The Times*, 17 January 1806.

50 *Glasgow Herald*, 15 January and 4 August 1806.

51 Quoted from contemporary newspaper in Gillian Russell, *The Theatres of War. Performance, Politics, and Society, 1793–1815* (Oxford: Clarendon Press, 1995) [hereafter: G. Russell], p. 82; Nelson Museum, S10.

52 Nelson Museum, S12; G. Russell, p. 84.

53 Attempts by Linda Colley and G. Russell to interpret it politically have been contested by Jenks and in my own thesis.

1   The disobedient officer

1 *The Dispatches and Letters of Vice-Admiral Lord Viscount Nelson*, ed. Nicholas Harris Nicolas (7 vols., London: Chatham Publishing, 1997–98, reprint of first edition 1844–46) [hereafter: Nicolas], i, 175.

2 Nicolas, i, 149.

3 Nicolas, i, 114.

4 *Nelson's Letters from the Leeward Islands and other Original Documents in the Public Record Office and the British Museum*, ed. Geoffrey Rawson with notes by Professor Michael Lewis and engravings by Geoffrey Wales ([n.p.]: Golden Cockerel Press, 1953) [hereafter: Rawson], pp. 33–9.

5 Nicolas, i, 110; Rawson, p. 28.

6 Rawson, pp. 29, 30.

7 Nicolas, i, 114.

8 Nicolas, i, 116–18, 129–30, 126.

9 Rawson, p. 42.

10 Nicolas, i, 159.

11 Rawson, pp. 45–6.

12 Nicolas, i, 157–8.

13 James Harrison, *The Life of the Right Honourable Horatio Lord Viscount Nelson* (2 vols., [London]: C. Chapple, 1806) [hereafter: Harrison], i, 102.

14 Southey (1813), i, 86–7.

15   G. Lathom Browne, *Nelson. The Public and Private Life of Horatio, Viscount Nelson as told by Himself, His Comrades, and His Friends* ([n.p.]: Trident Press International, 1999, reprint of original 1891 edition) [hereafter: Browne], p. 34.

16   Motto to Nelson's life and to the book by Douglas Sladen, *The Admiral. A Romance of Nelson in the Year of the Nile* (London: Hutchinson and Co., 1898) [hereafter: Sladen], title page, pp. vii, 226; *The Times*, 25 December 1846.

17   John Knox Laughton, *Nelson* (London: Macmillan, 1895) [hereafter: Laughton (1895)], pp. 34–5.

18   *Letters and Papers of Professor Sir John Knox Laughton, 1830–1915*, ed. Andrew Lambert ([London]: The Navy Records Society, 2002), p. 113.

19   C. S. Forester, *Nelson* (London: John Lane/The Bodley Head, 1929) [hereafter: Forester, *Nelson*], pp. 45, 47.

20   W. M. James, *The Durable Monument* (London: Longmans, Green and Co., 1948) [hereafter: James, *Durable Monument*], p. 46.

21   Richard Hough, *Nelson* (London: Park Lane Press, 1980), p. 36; Roger Morriss, *Nelson. The Life and Letters of a Hero* (London: Collins and Brown, 1996) [hereafter: Morriss (1996)], p. 46.

22   Andrew Lambert, *Nelson. Britannia's God of War* (London: Faber and Faber, 2004), p. 21; John Sugden, *Nelson. A Dream of Glory* (London: Jonathan Cape, 2004) [hereafter: Sugden (2004)], p. 271; an exception is Joseph Callo, *Nelson in the Caribbean. The Hero Emerges, 1784–1787* (Annapolis, MD: Naval Institute Press, 2003), p. 91.

23   Nicolas, ii, 341.

24   M. A. J. Palmer, 'Sir John's Victory: The Battle of Cape St Vincent Reconsidered', *The Mariner's Mirror*, 77 (1991), 31–46.

25   This episode is dealt with in Chapter 3.

26   Nicolas, iii, 415.

27   Nicolas, iii, 409–10, fn.

28   Nicolas, vii, cxcii.

29   Theodore Roosevelt, *Literary Essays* (New York: Charles Scribner's Sons, 1924), p. 331; similarly, Admiral of the Fleet [John Arbuthnot] Lord Fisher, *Memories* (London: Hodder and Stoughton, 1919), p. 111.

30   Forester, *Nelson*, p. 165.

31   Laughton (1895), p. 140.

32   A. T. Mahan, *The Life of Nelson. The Embodiment of the Sea Power of Great Britain* (first published 1897; London: Sampson Low, Marston and Co., 1899) [hereafter: Mahan, *Life*], p. 400.

33   Ludovic Kennedy, *Nelson's Band of Brothers* (London: Odhams Press, 1951) [hereafter: Kennedy], p. 180; although it may be worth noting that Keith himself did not see this priority: he wanted to use Nelson's squadron *either* for the defence of Minorca *or*, in case the French fleet united with the Spanish (which it did not), 'for the purpose of co-operating with me against the combined force of the Enemy' (Nicolas, iii, 414, fn).

34   Ernle Bradford, *Nelson. The Essential Hero* (London: Macmillan, 1977), p. 140; David Walder, *Nelson* (London: Hamish Hamilton, 1978) [hereafter: Walder], p. 332.

35   *The Times*, 1 May 1801.

36   Harrison, ii, 295.

37   J. White, p. 191.

38   Clarke and M'Arthur, ii, 270.

39   Southey (1813), ii, 123–4; Nicolas, iv, 308–9 (the narrative of Stewart starts on 299).

40   J. Ralfe, *The Naval Biography of Great Britain* (4 vols., London: Whitmore and Fenn, 1828) [hereafter: Ralfe], ii, 188.

41   Robert Southey, *The Life of Nelson* (London: John Murray, 1831) [hereafter: Southey (1831)], p. 146; on pp. 146–7 Southey describes how Captain Domett (sic, not Otway) unsuccessfully tried to convince Sir Hyde to communicate with Nelson before making his signal.

42   [A. and M. Gatty], *Recollections of the Life of the Rev. A. J. Scott, D. D. Lord Nelson's Chaplain* (London: Saunders and Otley, 1842) [hereafter: *Recollections of . . . Scott*], p. 70. An extract from Scott's diary at the time, p. 71, does not contain any reference to such an arrangement.

43   George Edinger and E. J. C. Neep, *Horatio Nelson* (London: Jonathan Cape, 1930) [hereafter: Edinger/Neep], p. 269.

44 Dudley Pope, *The Great Gamble* (London: Weidenfeld and Nicolson, 1972), particularly pp. 407, 410–11.

2 The commander

1 *Naval Chronicle*, 3 (1800), 157–87, 176; Nelson's report is in Nicolas, ii, 340–3; the eye-witness account used was Colonel John Drinkwater Bethune, *A Narrative of the Battle of St. Vincent* ([n.p.]: William R. Blackmore, 1969, identical with the second edition of 1840, which contained on pp. 25–54 the first edition of 1797).

2 Clarke and M'Arthur, ii, 77.

3 I am grateful to Prof. Roger Knight for the information contained in this paragraph.

4 [Edward Berry], *Authentic Narrative of . . . Nelson . . . [at the] Battle of the Nile* (Edinburgh: James Simpson, 1798) [hereafter: Berry's *Narrative*], pp. 12–13; extracts also in Nicolas, iii, 49–53; Brian Lavery, *Nelson and the Nile. The Naval War against Bonaparte 1798* (London: Chatham Publishing, 1998) [hereafter: Lavery], p. 155.

5 Again, I owe this information to Prof. Roger Knight.

6 See Terry Coleman, *Nelson. The Man and the Legend* (first edition, London: Bloomsbury, 2001; new revised edition, London: Bloomsbury, 2002) [hereafter: Coleman], p. 161.

7 For a detailed discussion of the public reaction to Nelson's victory at the Nile, see Marianne Czisnik, 'Nelson and the Nile: The Creation of Admiral Nelson's Public Image', *Mariner's Mirror*, 88 (2002) [hereafter: Czisnik, 'Nile'], 41–60.

8 For these see Chapter 5.

9 *Naval Chronicle*, 3 (1800), 183.

10 Berry's *Narrative*, p. 18.

11 [Anon.], *The Authentic History of the Gallant Life, Heroic Actions, and Sea Fights, of . . . Nelson* (London: Anne Lemoine and J. Joe, [1805]), pp. 18–19.

12 Lavery, p. 156, points out that Nelson did not have a close relationship with Louis before the battle.

13 Southey (1813), i, 232.

14 Those elements that did *not* undergo major changes are: (1) Nelson being hit by a piece of langridge shot; (2) Captain Berry catching Nelson; (3) Nelson waiting his turn.

15 Harrison, ii, 3.

16 Clarke and M'Arthur, ii, 84; the developed version, usually mentioning a 'flap' of skin; P. D. Gordon Pugh, *Nelson and His Surgeons. Nelson Chirurgique* (Edinburgh and London: E. and S. Livingstone, 1968), p. 24, quotes the record of the surgeon who treated Nelson: 'Brought the edges of the wound together', *not* that he brought a flap of skin back into position; see also: T. C. Barras, 'Nelson's Head Injury at the Battle of the Nile', *Nelson Dispatch*, 2 (1987), 217.

17 Lavery, p. 191, points out that the secretary was not treated.

18 Clarke and M'Arthur, ii, 84 (frequently copied since).

19 Nicolas, iii, 55, gives a wrong quotation from Clarke and M'Arthur.

20 Lavery, p. 191.

21 Browne, p. 198, quoting from his *Life of Nelson* ([n.p.]: Society for Promoting Christian Knowledge, 1851).

22 Mahan, *Life*, p. 300.

23 Duncan, Archibald, *The Life of the Right Honourable Horatio Lord Viscount Nelson* (London: James Cundee, 1806), p. 81.

24 *The Times*, 17 April 1801; *The Times* had reprinted the *London Gazette* of 15 April 1801 about the battle of Copenhagen on 16 April 1801.

25 The Danish admiral at the battle of Copenhagen argued thus: *Naval Chronicle*, 5 (1801), 342. This has remained controversial. For a recent Danish view, see Ole Feldbæk, *The Battle of Copenhagen 1801. Nelson and the Danes* (Barnsley, South Yorkshire: Leo Cooper, 2002), pp. 195, 197.

26 These four ideas were deduced from the memorandum by Julian S. Corbett, *The Campaign of Trafalgar* (London: Longmans, Green and Co., 1910) [hereafter: Corbett (1910)], p. 347.

27 The following exposition of Nelson's tactics at the battle of Trafalgar is a summary of my article about 'Admiral Nelson's Tactics at the Battle of Trafalgar', *History*, 89 (2004), 549–59.

28 Nicolas, vii, 89.

29 Lists of the signals given in the British fleet, in immediate preparation for the battle of Trafalgar, can be found in Corbett (1910), pp. 454–63 and [Anon.], *Report of a Committee Appointed by the Admiralty to Examine and Consider the Evidence Relating to the Tactics Employed by Nelson at the Battle of Trafalgar. Presented to Parliament by Command of His Majesty* (London: His Majesty's Stationery Office, 1913) [hereafter: Admiralty Committee], pp. 92–103.

30 While these manoeuvres followed Nelson's plan as set forth here (that his and Collingwood's flagships should lead their respective lines), they contradict Corbett's idea of Nelson's plan. In order to explain the resulting difference between Nelson's original plan and the actual battle, Corbett (1910), p. 374, claimed that Nelson had changed his mind and was engaging 'like any schoolboy' with Collingwood in a race to be the first into battle. Corbett did not explain why the other ships did not join in this supposed race and accepted their supposedly new positions.

31 Admiralty Committee, p. x.

32 William Cuthbert Brian Tunstall, *Naval Warfare in the Age of Sail. The Evolution of Fighting Tactics 1650–1815*, edited by Nicholas Tracy (London: Conway Maritime Press, 1990) [hereafter: Tunstall], pp. 250–1, referring to the original in the National Maritime Museum, Tunstall collection, TUN/61 (formerly S/P/R/8).

33 Corbett (1910), pp. 370, 374, speculated as to whether Collingwood was yet fully in charge of his line, because Nelson still made some signals to Collingwood's ships, but the Admiralty Committee, xii, commented convincingly: 'The grant of divisional independence did not then, nor would it now, involve abandonment by the Commander-in-Chief of his right to give any order or direction that seemed to him proper at the moment.'

34 Admiralty Committee, p. xii.

35 I am indebted to Admiral Rémi Monaque for having pointed out to me that Villeneuve did not give a separate order to Gravina's reserve squadron.

36 Nicolas, vii, 90, 92.

37 Nicolas, vii, 241, note.

38 Tunstall, p. 251.

39 Corbett (1910), pp. 351–2.

40 Corbett offered different interpretations of a 'telegraph message from Nelson', made 'at 11.40': 'I intend to push or go through the end of the enemy's line to prevent them from getting into Cadiz' (recorded in the log of the frigate *Euryalus* which was meant to repeat his signals to the fleet, but in no other log). In *Fighting Instructions 1530–1816*, ed. Julian S. Corbett (London: Navy Records Society, 1905) [hereafter: Corbett (1905)], p. 309, he assumed that 'the signal was wrongly repeated by the *Euryalus*, and as made by Nelson it was really an intimation to Collingwood that he meant to cover the attack on the rear and centre by a feint on the van'. Corbett (1910), pp. 281–3, claims that the message 'can only have meant that Nelson had abandoned his plan of attack on the rear half of the enemy'. This second opinion forced Corbett to assume that Nelson at a later stage of the advance changed his mind back again. A simple explanation of the message may be that Nelson wanted to ensure that the ships following in his division would keep their course onto the van and not betray his feint by steering towards the centre of the enemy's fleet.

41 Admiralty Committee, pp. xiii, xiv; a letter from Rear-Admiral Dumanoir, who had been in command of the Franco-Spanish van, corroborates this; the letter was published in translation in *The Times*, 2 January 1806: 'The left column of the English, having Admiral Nelson at its head, bore at first at the French vanguard, which I commanded; but finding it probably too compact, they exchanged some shots with us, and then struck at the centre of our line, while Vice-Admiral Collingwood attacked our rear-guard. Having then no enemy to contend with, I tacked about.' Corbett (1905), pp. 308–10, and Corbett (1910), p. 382, thought that Nelson changed his mind and for a time actually wanted to attack the enemy's van; he deduced that from the account of Captain Blackwood, of the frigate *Euryalus*, who was still on board the *Victory* at the time and who remembered that Nelson had told him that he intended 'to push or go through the end of the enemy's line [the van] to prevent them from getting into Cadiz': Nicolas, vii, 148, 186; Tunstall, p. 258, suspected that Nelson's remark to Blackwood was 'purely informative'.

42 Admiralty Committee, p. xiv.

43 *Logs of the Great Sea Fights*, ed. Rear Admiral T. Sturges Jackson (2 vols., London: Navy Records Society, vols. XVI and XVIII, 1899 and 1900), vol. 2 [hereafter: Jackson], pp. 224–5 (part of a letter from Captain Harvey of the *Temeraire* to his wife, written on 23 October 1805); Geoffrey Bennett, *The Battle of Trafalgar* (London: Batsford, 1977), p. 156, quoting 'Midshipman Badcock of HMS *Neptune*': 'About ten o'clock got close to the *Victory*, and Captain Fremantle had intended to pass her . . . but . . . Lord Nelson himself hailed us . . . and said: "*Neptune*, take in your stuns'ls and drop astern; I shall break the line myself".'

44 Jackson, p. 219.

45 Admiralty Committee, p. xiii.

46 Corbett (1910), pp. 390, 391. Dumanoir wrote in his letter, *The Times*, 2 January 1806: 'On my coming up, I found the *Santissima Trinidada* and the *Bucentaure* dismasted of all their masts, and taken possession of by the English . . . There remained then on the field of battle, to which I was coming up with my assistance, only thirteen French and Spanish vessels, which had surrendered, and fifteen English vessels (one only dismasted). I was thus cut off from the rest of the Combined Fleet.'

47 Corbett (1905), pp. 335–50.

48 Charles Ekins, *Naval Battles from 1744 to the Peace in 1814, Critically Reviewed and Illustrated* (London: Baldwin, Cradock and Joy, 1824), pp. 267, 273.

49 William James, *The Naval History of Great Britain, from the Declaration of War by France in 1793 to the Accession of George IV* (first edition 1822–24; 6 vols., a new edition with additions and notes, London: Richard Bentley, 1859, which is a reprint of the edition of 1826) [hereafter: W. James (1826)], iii, 468, 469.

50 Thomas [Cochrane], Tenth Earl of Dundonald, *The Autobiography of a Seaman* (2 vols., London: Richard Bentley, 1860), i, 88, 89.

51 Vice-Admiral P. H. Colomb, 'The Battle of Trafalgar', *United Service Magazine*, XIX, new series (vol. CXXV, old series) (September 1899), 578–95, particularly 580, 584.

52 Jackson; Corbett (1905).

53 Corbett (1905), pp. 282–313, especially pp. 300, 306 (about Nelson not fulfilling his own plan) and p. 312 (about 'mad perpendicular attack').

54 James R. Thursfield, *Nelson and Other Naval Studies* (London: John Murray, 1909) [hereafter: Thursfield (1909)], pp. 12–81, 'Trafalgar and the Nelson Touch' (published in the autumn of 1905 in *The Times*).

55 Corbett (1910).

56 Donald M. Schurman, *Julius S. Corbett, 1854–1922. Historian of British Maritime Policy from Drake to Jellicoe* (London: Royal Historical Society, 1981) [hereafter: Schurman], p. 128.

57 Admiralty Committee, p. viii.

58 Schurman, p. 128; Tunstall, p. 258.

59 See, for example, A. H. Taylor, 'The Battle of Trafalgar', *Mariner's Mirror*, 36 (1950), 281–321, at 283, and Gregory Robinson, letter to the editor, *Mariner's Mirror*, 37 (1951), 237.

3   Neapolitan imbroglio

1 These events are outlined in *Nelson and the Neapolitan Jacobins. Documents Relating to the Suppression of the Jacobin Revolution at Naples. June 1799*, ed. H. C. Gutteridge ([London]: Navy Records Society, 1903) [hereafter: Gutteridge], in his introduction on pp. xviii–xxi.

2 Lavery, p. 276.

3 George P. B. Naish, *Nelson's Letters to His Wife and Other Documents: 1785–1831* ([London]: Navy Records Society, 1958) [hereafter: Naish], p. 478.

4 Gutteridge, p. 19.

5 This has been argued by Gutteridge, p. xxxiv.

6 Nicolas, iii, 352, 355 and 357.

7 Gutteridge, p. xii.

8 Edward James Foote, *Captain Foote's Vindication of his Conduct, When Captain of His Majesty's Ship Sea-Horse, and Senior Officer in the Bay of Naples, in the Summer of 1799* (second edition, London: Hatchard, 1810) [hereafter: Foote], p. 125.

9 For a detailed assessment of the controversy concerning Ruffo's authority to sign the capitula-

tion, see Marianne Czisnik, 'Nelson at Naples: A Review of Events and Arguments', *Trafalgar Chronicle*, 12 (2002), 84–121 [hereafter: Czisnik, 'Naples'], at 95–6.

10   Gutteridge, p. 150.
11   In the nineteenth century it was hotly contested whether the rebels had started to embark or not, but this controversy proved fruitless. For a detailed assessment of this controversy, see Czisnik, 'Naples', 99–101.
12   Gutteridge, p. 143.
13   Gutteridge, p. 165.
14   For a discussion of (unjustified) doubts about Nelson's authority to act for the king of Naples see Czisnik, 'Naples', 102–3.
15   Gutteridge, p. 197.
16   Gutteridge, p. 265.
17   Nicolas, iii, 386 and Gutteridge, p. 217 (only the declaration); A. T. Mahan, 'The Neapolitan Republicans and Nelson's Accusers', *English Historical Review* 14 (1899), 483, suggests that these notes were written on 24 June and not on the 25th, as they are dated, because Nelson may have used sea time here, according to which the 25th started at midday of the 24th and ended on midday of the 25th. This use of sea time appears probable, because a note of '26 June' that Nelson sent to Ruffo has been proved to have been written on the afternoon of 25 June (land time).
18   Gutteridge, pp. 265, 266.
19   Gutteridge, p. 215 (Ruffo's view); some historians, however, have questioned Nelson's authority. For a detailed assessment of this controversy, see Czisnik, 'Naples', 104–5.
20   Gutteridge, p. 221.
21   Some authors have denied Ruffo's change of mind; for a detailed assessment of this controversy, see Czisnik, 'Naples', 107–9.
22   Gutteridge, pp. 231, 232.
23   Gutteridge, p. 233; Ruffo's letter on pp. 232–3.
24   This has been doubted with great efforts in hair-splitting by Badham; for a detailed assessment of his arguments, see Czisnik, 'Naples', 110.
25   British Library Add. MSS 34,963, ff. 53, 54 and 61.
26   Gutteridge, p. 336.
27   Gutteridge, p. 281.
28   It has been argued (unconvincingly) that he was included in the capitulation; for details of this line of argument, see Czisnik, 'Naples', 117–18.
29   It has been argued (unconvincingly) that the Neapolitan court was unfairly biased against Caracciolo and some authors have criticized the proceedings; for details of this line of argument, see Czisnik, 'Naples', 118–19.
30   Gutteridge, p. lxxvi.
31   Gutteridge, pp. lxxvi, 287–8.
32   Nicolas, iii, 404, 408 with note; see Chapter 1.
33   Minutes of Instructions to Lord Nelson, 20 August 1799, *The Nelson collection at Lloyd's. A Description of the Nelson Relics and a Transcript of the Autograph Letters and Documents of Nelson and his Circle and of Other Naval Papers of Nelson's Period*, ed. Warren R. Dawson (London: Macmillan, 1932), p. 322.
34   The *Morning Chronicle*, 4 February 1800.
35   Helen Maria Williams, *Sketches of the State of manners and opinions in the French Republic, towards the close of the eighteenth century, In a series of Letters* (2 vols., London: [no pub.], 1801), pp. 182–5.
36   Harrison, ii, 120. Foote saw this quotation in combination with Nelson's remark 'to which Captain Foote had put his name' (Harrison, ii, 99), which referred to the news of an 'Armistice' he had received at sea.
37   Foote, pp. 6, 58, 59.
38   Foote, p. 19.
39   Foote, pp. 21, 22, 23 (end), 24 (centre), 25 (end).
40   Foote, pp. 193, 194.

41 Foote, pp. 23, 24 (beginning and end), 25 (beginning).

42 Foote, pp. 59–60.

43 Foote, pp. 15, 38.

44 Gutteridge, p. xciv, note, referring to the log of the *Sea-Horse*, Foote's ship.

45 Foote, p. 39.

46 Southey (1813), ii, 46.

47 Henry Lord Brougham, *Historical Sketches of Statesmen who flourished in the Time of George III. Second Series* (London: Charles Knight, 1839) [hereafter: Brougham], p. 171.

48 Domenico Sacchinelli, *Memorie storiche sulla vita del Cardinale Fabrizio Ruffo* (Naples: Tipografia di Carlo Cataneo, 1836), for example on pp. 211, 218, 225 and 239.

49 Czisnik, 'Naples', 107–9, 110–11; see also Gutteridge, pp. xcvii–ci, who doubts the ultimatum, interview with Troubridge and *verbale* of Minichini.

50 F. P. Badham, *Nelson at Naples, A Journal for June 10–30, 1799, Refuting Misstatements of Captain Mahan and Professor J. K. Laughton* (London: David Nutt, 1900) [hereafter: Badham (1900)], p. 9.

51 Badham (1900), p. 24; F. P. Badham, 'Nelson and the Neapolitan Republicans', *English Historical Review*, 13 (1898), 261–82, at 266, 274 and 275; F. P. Badham, *Nelson and Ruffo* (London: James Finch and Co., 1905), his last publication on the matter, bases its main argument on presumptions, see particularly p. 31.

52 Micheroux's 'Compendio', in Gutteridge, pp. 116–17.

53 Gutteridge, pp. x, xcii, c–ci (inclined to blame Ruffo).

54 Tom Pocock, *Nelson and His World* (London: Thames and Hudson, 1968) [hereafter: Pocock (1968)], p. 79; Frank Knight, *The Hero. Vice-Admiral Horatio Viscount Nelson*, with decorations by John Lawrence (London: Macdonald, 1969), p. 97.

4   The love of his life

1 Nicolas, iii, 130.

2 Nicolas, iii, 210, 213.

3 *The Times*, 14 August 1799 and the *Morning Chronicle*, 15 August 1799.

4 The *Morning Chronicle*, 22 October 1799.

5 A daughter was born nine months later.

6 G. S. Parsons, *Nelsonian Reminiscences. Leaves from Memory's Log* (London: Saunders and Otley, 1843) [hereafter: Parsons], pp. 63–4.

7 Thomas Joseph Pettigrew, *Memoirs of the Life of Vice-Admiral Lord Viscount Nelson, K.B. Duke of Bronté etc. etc. etc.* (2 vols., London: T. and W. Boone, 1849) [hereafter: Pettigrew], ii, 161.

8 Coleman, p. 225.

9 Czisnik, 'Nile', 49–50.

10 *Journal kept during a Visit to Germany in 1799, 1800 [by Mrs. Melesina St. George, later: Trench]*, ed. the Dean of Westminster [printed for private circulation, also published in: 'No. CCXXI of the *Quarterly Review*'; hereafter: St George], p. 76; *Life and Letters of Sir Gilbert Elliot, First Earl of Minto from 1751 to 1806*, ed. Countess of Minto (3 vols., London: Longmans, Green and Co., 1874) [hereafter: Minto], iii, 147 (quoting from a letter written from Vienna by Lady Minto to her sister).

11 *Naval Chronicle*, 4, 429–30.

12 Ian R. Christie, *Myth and Reality in Late-Eighteenth-Century British Politics and other Papers* (London: Macmillan, 1970), p. 343.

13 The *Morning Chronicle*, 19 November 1800.

14 This process has only recently been revealed by the newly discovered letters of Lady Nelson to Nelson's agent Alexander Davison; see Colin White, 'The Wife's Tale: Frances, Lady Nelson and the Break-up of her Marriage', *Journal for Maritime Research*, October 2003, www.jmr.nmm.ac.uk (accessed 20 June 2005).

15 Pettigrew, ii, 68.

16 Naish, p. 345.

17 *The Collection of Autograph Letters and Historical Documents formed by Alfred Morrison (Second Series, 1882–1893) – The Hamilton & Nelson Papers*, [ed. Anon.] (2 vols., [n.p.]: printed for private circulation, 1893) [hereafter: Morrison], ii, 111, 117, 120 and 137.

18 Pettigrew, i, 424; Walter Sichel, *Emma Lady Hamilton. From New and Original Sources and Documents. Together with an Appendix of Notes and New Letters* (third edition revised, Edinburgh: Archibald Constable, 1907) [hereafter: Sichel], p. 513.

19 Morrison, ii, 118 and 120.

20 Morrison, ii, 117, 118, 125 and 142.

21 For example, Pettigrew, i, 447, ii, 16, 89, 138, 397, 477 and 510; Morrison, ii, 132, 145; Sichel, p. 513; and *The Letters of Lord Nelson to Lady Hamilton with a Supplement of Interesting Letters by Distinguished Characters*, [ed. Anon.] (2 vols., London: Thomas Lovewell and Co., 1814) [hereafter: 1814 letters], i, 113–18.

22 1814 letters, i, 92–3.

23 Morrison, ii, 115, 120, 122–3; Pettigrew, ii, 649, 651; and 1814 letters, i, 78.

24 Sichel, p. 513; Morrison, ii, 170.

25 Morrison, ii, 219.

26 Pettigrew, ii, 190.

27 Pettigrew, ii, 199 and 214.

28 Naish, p. 352.

29 Pettigrew, ii, 426.

30 Sichel, p. 517.

31 Jack Russell, *Nelson and the Hamiltons* (Harmondsworth: Penguin Books, 1972, first published 1969) [hereafter: J. Russell], pp. 46–9.

32 1814 letters, i, 133.

33 Brian Fothergill, *Sir William Hamilton* (Faber: London, 1969), p. 250.

34 Nicolas, vii, 370.

35 Sichel, p. 517 (Nelson's italics).

36 Harrison, i, 328.

37 Harrison, ii, 271.

38 Harrison, ii, 255.

39 Harrison, ii, 270–1, 276, 278–9, 280.

40 Harrison, ii, 280.

41 Harrison, i, 244–5.

42 Clarke and M'Arthur, i, 94, 109; ii, 46.

43 Southey (1813), ii, 28 and 91.

44 Southey (1813), i, 216; ii, 42; ii, 179.

45 1814 letters, i, 35–7 (not dated, March 1801). Nicolas, vii, 373–4, copied this letter, omitting its beginning, dating it 10 March 1801 and doubting its authenticity (this will be dealt with below).

46 1814 letters, i, 176–8, and i, 136–8. Also in Nicolas, vii, 377–8, who again doubts the authenticity of the letter.

47 [Anon], *Memoirs of Lady Hamilton* (second edition, London: Henry Colburn, 1815) [hereafter: *Memoirs of Lady Hamilton*], p. 180.

48 *Memoirs of Lady Hamilton*, p. 258.

49 *Memoirs of Lady Hamilton*, pp. 57, 76, 82–3.

50 *Memoirs of Lady Hamilton*, pp. 186–7.

51 *Memoirs of Lady Hamilton*, pp. 258–9, 276, 296.

52 *Memoirs of Lady Hamilton*, p. 304.

53 *Memoirs of Lady Hamilton*, p. 15.

54 *Memoirs of Lady Hamilton*, pp. 28, 32, 36, 51.

55 W. James (1826), ii, 311.

56 Edward Pelham Brenton, *The Naval History of Great Britain from the Year MDCCLXXXIII to MDCCCXXII* (5 vols., London: C. Rice, 1823–24), ii, 480 (copied and varied in other sources); Nelson was offered the dukedom on his return to Palermo, in August 1799.

57 Pryse Lockhart Gordon, *Personal Memoirs or Reminiscences of Men and Manners at Home and Abroad, During the Last Half Century. With Occasional Sketches of the Author's Life . . .* (2 vols., London: Henry Colburn and Richard Bentley, 1830) [hereafter: Gordon], ii, 394.

58 Gordon, ii, 384.

59 Gordon, i, 217, ii, 393–4.

60 Gordon, ii, 218–19, 219 fn. (account about pig from 'Mr. L—', most probably Charles Locke, who is also referred to as C—s L—e, i, 210, and who was very much at odds with Nelson and the Hamiltons – see J. Russell, pp. 114–15, 128, 131–2, 154–5, 178, 452).

61 Gordon, i, 210.

62 Parsons, p. 10.

63 Parsons, p. 61; further passages: pp. 9–12, 19, 41, 43.

64 Parsons, p. 12, italics in the original.

65 Parsons, p. 43.

66 Parsons, pp. 11, 63, also described Lady Hamilton as fearless and with strong opinions of her own.

67 Nicolas, vii, 373 and 377–80. For the quoted passages see footnotes 25 and 26.

68 Nicolas, vii, 389.

69 Nicolas, vii, 394.

70 Nicolas, vii, 391–2; a different account of the separation of Nelson from his wife is given in *The Diary of Joseph Farington*, ed. Kathryn Cave (16 vols., New Haven and London: Yale University Press, 1978–84) [hereafter: *Farington*], vii, 2659.

71 Pettigrew, i, v (first page of his 'Preface').

72 *The Times*, 17 and 22 August 1849.

73 *The Times*, 29 August, 30 August and 3 September 1849.

74 *The Times*, 2 June 1851.

75 *The Times*, 21 October and 11 November 1853, 3 April 1854.

76 *Letters and Despatches of Horatio, Viscount Nelson, K.B. duke of Bronte Vice-Admiral of the White Squadron*, ed. John Knox Laughton (London: Longmans, Green and Co., 1886) [hereafter: Laughton (1886)], vii, xx.

77 Morrison, ii, 123 (left out in Pettigrew, ii, 652).

78 Morrison, ii, 127.

79 John Cordy Jeaffreson, *Lady Hamilton and Lord Nelson. An Historical Biography Based on Letters and Other Documents in the Possession of Alfred Morrison, Esq. of Fonthill, Wiltshire* (2 vols., London: Hurst and Blackett, 1888) [hereafter: Jeaffreson], ii, 167.

80 Jeaffreson, ii, 161, 166.

81 Jeaffreson, ii, 161.

82 Jeaffreson, ii, 147, 152.

83 Jeaffreson, ii, 217.

84 Jeaffreson, ii, 219.

85 Jeaffreson, ii, 150.

86 Russell, W. Clark, *Horatio Nelson and the Naval Supremacy of England* (in series: 'Heroes of the Nations', ed. Evelyn Abbott, New York and London: G. P. Putnam's Sons, 1890) [hereafter: W. Clark Russell], p. 131.

87 James R. Thursfield, 'New Nelson Manuscripts', *Literature*, 19 and 26 February, 5, 12 and 26 March, 9 and 23 April 1898; Laughton (1895), pp. 127, 177; C. Reid Andrew, *A Rapid Review of the Life of Nelson* ('Rapid Review Library, No. 1', [London]: C. Arthur Pearson, 1905) [hereafter: Andrew], p. 104; Philip H. Colomb, 'Nelson', in *From Howard to Nelson: Twelve Sailors*, ed. John Knox Laughton (London: Lawrence and Bullen, 1899), pp. 435–68 [hereafter: Colomb, 'Nelson'], p. 449; W. Clark Russell, pp. 45–6; Mahan, *Life*, p. 317; W. H. Fitchett, *Nelson and his Captains* (London: Smith, Elder, and Co., 1902) [hereafter: Fitchett], p. 5.

88 Walter Runciman, *Drake, Nelson and Napoleon* (London: T. Fisher Unwin, 1919), pp. 96, 99.

89 See, for example, Sichel.

90 Mahan, *Life*, pp. 28, 36.

91 Colomb, 'Nelson', p. 448.

92 Fitchett, pp. 4–5.

93 Mahan, *Life*, p. 330.

94 Andrew, pp. 111–12.

95 Colomb, 'Nelson', p. 464.

96 Thursfield, p. 125.

97 Forester, *Nelson*, pp. 210–11, 242–3.

98   Minto, iii, 363.

99   Edinger/Neep, pp. 10, 235 (similarly, pp. 235–8), 292–5.

100 Edinger/Neep, p. 286.

101 Edinger/Neep, pp. 315–16.

102 Pettigrew, ii, 214.

103 C. J. Britton, *New Chronicles of the Life of Lord Nelson* (Birmingham: Cornish Brothers, [1947]) [hereafter: Britton], pp. 73, 74; the book is 'Dedicated to the memory of Emma Lady Hamilton whose faults the country remembered, and whose loving charms and the dead voice of duty the Nation forgot.'

104 James, *Durable Monument*, pp. 7–8.

105 W. M. James, *The Influence of Sea Power on the History of the British People* (Cambridge: Cambridge University Press, 1948), p. 27; the ideals of male friendship and of the admiration for the boy in late Victorian education is impressively dealt with in Jeffrey Richards, '"Passing the Love of Women": Manly Love and Victorian Society', in *Manliness and Morality. Middle-Class Masculinity in Britain and America, 1800–1940*, ed. J. A. Mangan and James Walvin (Manchester: Manchester University Press, 1987), pp. 92–122 (the admiration of boys is dealt with on p. 107).

106 Clemence Dane [alias Winifred Ashton], *The Nelson Touch. An Anthology of Lord Nelson's Letters* (London: William Heinemann, 1942), p. xii; the real name of the author is given on the first page of Michael Nash's foreword to the 1997–98 edition of Nicolas.

107 Frank Knight, *The Hero. Vice-Admiral Horatio Viscount Nelson* with decorations by John Lawrence (London: Macdonald, 1969), p. 99; James, *Durable Monument*, p. 151.

108 James, *Durable Monument*, p. 158; Christopher Lloyd, *Nelson and Sea Power* (London: English Universities Press, 1973), p. 10; and Pocock (1968), p. 47.

109 Tom Pocock, 'Tinkers, Poets, Whores and Scoundrels. The Italian Connection', in *The Nelson Almanac*, ed. David Harris (London: Conway Maritime Press, in association with the Warwick Leadlay Gallery, 1998), pp. 78–81, 80.

110 Walder, p. 309; the first was J. Russell, p. 96.

111 Oliver Warner, *A Portrait of Lord Nelson* (London: Chatto and Windus, 1958) [hereafter: Warner], pp. 165, 270–1.

112 Roger Morriss, '"No Common Being": Nelson's Character and Relationships', in *Nelson. An Illustrated History*, ed. Pieter van der Merwe (London: Laurence King, 1995) [hereafter: Morriss (1995)], pp. 114–43, at 123; Morriss (1996), p. 10.

113 Edgar Vincent, *Nelson. Love and Fame* (New Haven and London: Yale University Press, 2003) [hereafter: Vincent], pp. 301, 351.

114 Vincent, p. 350.

115 J. Russell, pp. 31–2.

5   A hero's death

1   J. Russell, p. 497.

2   Beatty, p. 22, note; Nicolas vii, 137 and 347–52.

3   Pierre Lorain, 'La balle qui tua Nelson', *Gazette des Armes*, 56 (1978), 18–25.

4   Beatty, pp. 69–71.

5   *Naval Chronicle*, 15 (1806), 38, 'statement . . . authenticated by Mr Beatty and Mr Bourke', the *Victory*'s surgeon and purser.

6   *Recollections of . . . Scott*, pp. 188–9; the complete account is on pp. 185–91 (only pp. 188–91 are from Scott himself; the whole passage is also in Nicolas, vii, 245–6, fn); the following narrative is based on Scott's account as well as Beatty's *Authentic Narrative* and the account in the biography by Harrison (ii, 501–4); if other sources are used, this is indicated.

7   A. Y. Mann, *The Last Moments and Principal Events Relative to the ever to Be Lamented Death of Lord Viscount Nelson. With the Procession by Water, and the Whole Ceremony of The Funeral. Intended as a Sequel to his Life* (London: Symonds, 1806), p. 7.

8   Dorothy Margaret Stuart, *Dearest Bess. The Life and Times of Lady Elizabeth Foster afterwards Duchess of Devonshire from Her Unpublished Journals and Correspondence* (London: Methuen, 1955, reprint) [hereafter: Stuart], p. 132.

9   [Anon.], *The Life of Horatio Viscount Nelson, Baron of the Nile, and Duke of Bronte, &c &c* (Halifax: J. Nicholson, 1805) [hereafter: Anon. (Nicholson)], p. 85.

10 Anon. (Nicholson), p. 85; Archibald Duncan, *The Life of the Right Honourable Horatio Lord Viscount Nelson, Vice-Admiral of the White* (London: James Cundee, and Liverpool: J. Nuttall, 1806) [hereafter: Duncan], p. 250; John Jones, *Biographical Memoirs of . . . Nelson* (Dublin: John Jones, 1805), p. 68; Frederick Lloyd, *An Accurate and Impartial Life of the Late Lord Viscount Nelson* (Ormskirk: [printer: J. Fowler], 1806), p. 201.

11 *Naval Chronicle*, 14 (1805), 463.

12 Beatty, p. 22, note. See also Nicolas vii, 137 and 347–52.

13 *Naval Chronicle*, 14 (1805), 413.

14 Duncan, pp. 51, 250 (death account).

15 *Naval Chronicle*, 15 (1806), 27.

16 *Naval Chronicle*, 15 (1806), 38.

17 Beatty, pp. 34–5.

18 ['The Old Sailor', Matthew Henry Barker], *The Life of Nelson, Revised and Illustrated with Original Anecdotes, Notes &c.* (London: Frederic Shoberl, 1836), p. 464, note; W. James (1826), iii, 445.

19 D. Bonner Smith, 'The Avenger of Nelson', *Mariner's Mirror*, 22 (1936), 470–4.

20 *Naval Chronicle*, 14 (1805), 414; *The Times*, 30 December 1805; [Anon.], *The Life of Admiral Lord Nelson, Baron of the Nile, &c. &c. &c.* (Birmingham: [printer: T. Martin, *c.* 1805]), p. 47.

21 *Naval Chronicle*, 14 (1805), 414.

22 *Naval Chronicle*, 15 (1806), 38–9.

23 J. Harrison, i, vii.

24 J. Harrison, ii, 501–4.

25 *Gentleman's Magazine*, 79 (1809), 404–5.

26 Clarke and M'Arthur, ii, 451.

27 William James, *The Naval History of Great Britain, from the Declaration of War by France in February 1793 to the Accession of George IV in January 1820 . . .* (5 vols., London: Baldwin, Cradock, and Joy, 1822–24, first edition), iii, 352.

28 W. James (1826), iii, 445 and 446.

29 *Recollections of . . . Scott*, pp. 188–90.

30 Nicolas, vii, 244–57 and footnote on p. 246.

31 Letters to the editor, *Mariner's Mirror*, 11 (1925), 96–7, 215–16, 427–8.

32 Kennedy, p. 324.

33 Edinger/Neep, p. 10.

34 It is also contradicted by contemporary evidence. Nelson's friend Gilbert Elliot noted on 10 November 1805: 'He was remarkably well and fresh too, and full of hope and spirit.' See Minto, iii, 374.

6   Nelson's character

1   Nicolas, iii, 361.

2   Sichel, p. 513; *The Collection of Autograph Letters and Historical Documents formed by Alfred Morrison (Second Series, 1882–1893) – The Hamilton & Nelson Papers*, [ed. Anon.] (2 vols., [n.p.]: printed for private circulation, 1893), ii, 170.

3   *Recollections of . . . Scott*, pp. 123–4.

4   Nicolas, vii, 71, note.

5   Nicolas, ii, 27.

6   Parsons, pp. 55, 244, 246 (twice).

7   Southey (1813), ii, 67.

8   Clarke and M'Arthur, i, 49; ii, 468 explicitly denied 'vanity' as a characteristic of Nelson's.

9   *Memoirs of Lady Hamilton*, pp. 177, 231.

10 Christopher Hibbert, *The Story of England* (first published 1992, London: Phaidon, 1999), p. 52.

11 Laughton (1895), pp. 24–5.

12 Lady Minto, writing to her sister from Vienna in 1800, Minto, iii, 147.

13 Minto, iii, 360.

14 Holland, Henry Edward Lord (ed.), *Memoirs of the Whig Party During My Time. By Henry Richard Lord Holland* (2 vols., London: Longman, Brown, Green and Longmans, 1852), ii, 19–22, 26.

15 See development of the discussion of Nelson's tactics at Trafalgar during the nineteenth century in Chapter 2.

16 Compare Gordon, i, 203, with *The Times*, 11 November 1800; for Gordon's prejudices against Lady Hamilton, see Chapter 4.

17 Mahan, *Life*, pp. 678–9, quoted this interview from *The Croker Papers. Correspondence and Diaries of the late Right Honourable John Wilson Croker*, ed. Louis J. Jennings (3 vols., London: John Murray, 1884), ii, 233–4, without giving his source (unlike Hibbert and Coleman), but with a calculation that the interview must have taken place between 10 and 13 September 1805. Croker noted down his conversation with Wellington 'Walmer, October 1st, 1834'.

18 *Lord Granville Leveson Gower (First Earl Granville). Private Correspondence 1781–1821. Edited by His Daughter-in-Law*, ed. Castalia Countess Granville (2 vols., London: John Murray, 1916), ii, 112 (letter from Lady Bessborough, of 12 September 1805, describing what she had heard from Lady Foster); Stuart, p. 155, gives a shorter account from Lady Foster herself.

19 It may also be considered that Nelson did not always appear impressive and Lord Minto described him in a letter written on the day Nelson left his home for Trafalgar (that is, not more than three days after he had met Wellington) as 'in many points a really great man, in others a baby' (Minto, iii, 370). I could not find any contemporary evidence of Nelson *talking* in a vain fashion.

20 See Chapter 5.

21 Nicolas, vii, 347–52. The quotation is taken from the index; the actual chapter is headed 'Nelson's "Fighting Coat"'.

22 Nicolas, vii, 347, 349.

23 Pettigrew, ii, 563. Thiers' work had been translated into English: see Chapter 10.

24 Laughton (1886), pp. xi, xiii.

25 Laughton (1886), pp. 24–5.

26 Jon Tetsuro Sumida, *Inventing Grand Strategy and Teaching Command. The Classic Works of Alfred Thayer Mahan Reconsidered* (Baltimore: Johns Hopkins University Press, 1997), pp. 36–9 gives many examples.

27 Mahan, *Life*, p. 24.

28 Mahan, *Life*, pp. 45, 52; for Mahan's ability to see Nelson's emotional side in his profession as well as in his private passion, see Chapter 4.

29 Theodore Roosevelt, *Literary Essays* (New York: Charles Scribner's Sons, 1924), pp. 326–33 (review of 'Captain Mahan's "Life of Nelson"'), pp. 328, 331; for Roosevelt's interest in exactly these occupations, and his evaluation of them as essential for a nation, see John M. Mackenzie, 'The Imperial Pioneer and Hunter and the British Masculine Stereotype in Late Victorian and Edwardian Times', in *Manliness and Morality. Middle-Class Masculinity in Britain and America, 1800–1940*, ed. J. A. Mangan and James Walvin (Manchester: Manchester University Press, 1987), pp. 176–98, at p. 178, quoting from Theodore Roosevelt, *Ranch Life*, p. 83).

30 Renalt Capes, *Poseidon: A Personal Study of Admiral Nelson* (London: Sidgwick and Jackson, 1947), p. vii.

31 See Chapter 5, where the development of the perception of Nelson as having two personalities is explored in more depth.

32 James, *Durable Monument*, pp. 7–8; similarly, pp. 201, 241, 301.

33 Warner, p. 220; the quotation is from Nicolas, iv, 92.

34 Morriss (1995), p. 142; Morriss (1996), p. 8.

35 Unlike after the battle of Cape St Vincent, Nelson did not use private means to get his views published in newspapers (some of his official reports were, obviously, published in the *London Gazette*). Even with regard to the criticism he attracted by his involvement in Naples, he made surprisingly little effort to defend himself (see Nicolas, iv, 232, and v, 43).

36 The lack of interest in tactical issues has been analysed in Chapter 2. The complexities of the demands on a commander remained virtually ignored in biographies of Nelson throughout the twentieth century and questions of leadership are completely out of fashion.

37 See the 'Introduction', in *Nelson. An Illustrated History*, ed. Pieter van der Merwe (Laurence King: London, 1995), pp. 8–10.

38 Christopher Hibbert, *Nelson. A Personal History* (London: Viking, 1994), p. 467, index under 'personality'; compare entries for 'ability' to those for 'self-esteem' and those for 'negotiator' to those for 'self-congratulation'.

39 Vincent; Sugden, (2004); Andrew Lambert, *Nelson. Britannia's God of War* (London: Faber and Faber, 2004).

7   Early visual representations of Nelson

1 See Chapter 5.

2 McCarthy, pp. 92, 94.

3 Morton D. Paley, *Energy and the Imagination. A Study of the Development of Blake's Thought* (Oxford: Clarendon Press, 1970) [hereafter: Paley], p. 174, quoting from *Discourses on Art* (San Marino, CA, 1959), p. 61.

4 Charles Mitchell, 'Benjamin West's *Death of Nelson*', in *Essays in the History of Art Presented to Rudolf Wittkower*, ed. Douglas Fraser, Howard Hibbard and Milton J. Lewine (London: Phaidon Press, 1967), pp. 265–73, and illustration XXXVIII, p. 271 [hereafter: Mitchell], (summarizing West's ideas from his *Philosophical and Critical History of the Fine Arts*).

5 Mitchell, p. 269; *Farington*, viii, 3058 (5 June 1807).

6 Mitchell, p. 268.

7 *Farington*, viii, 2837 (16 August 1806).

8 *Farington*, viii, 3064 (10 June 1807).

9 Clarke and M'Arthur, i, xxxvii.

10 James Hamilton, *Turner. A Life* (London: Hodder and Stoughton, 1997), p. 93.

11 David V. Erdman, *Blake. Prophet against Empire. A Poet's Interpretation of the History of His Own Times* (Princeton: Princeton University Press, 1954) [hereafter: Erdman], p. 416.

12 Paley, p. 195.

13 Paley, p. 196.

14 Mark Schorer, *William Blake: The Politics of Vision* (New York: Henry Holt and Company, 1946), p. 174.

15 Erdman, p. 417.

16 Paley, pp. 196, 199.

17 John and Jennifer May, *Commemorative Pottery 1780–1900. A Guide for Collectors* (London: Heinemann, 1972) [hereafter: May/May], pp. 96–101.

18 The correct version is: 'England expects that every man will do his duty.'

19 May/May, pp. 97–8.

20 McCarthy, p. 182 (no. 211).

21 National Maritime Museum, AAA 4988.

22 National Maritime Museum, objects 0020, 0042 and 0068.

23 McCarthy, pp. 113, 172–3, 120–1, 189.

24 John Alfred Langford, *A Chronicle of Birmingham Life* (2 vols., Birmingham: E. C. Osborne, 1868) [hereafter: Langford], ii, 305.

25 Matthew Cotes Wyatt, *Prospectus of a Model to the Memory of Lord Nelson, intended to adorn the habitations of those who appreciate his services* (London: [no pub.], 1808) [hereafter: Wyatt], p. 4.

26 Corporation of London Record Office Misc Mss 207.5 'Battle of Trafalgar', Common Council, 26 November 1805.

27 Langford, ii, 304, quoting from *Aris's Birmingham Gazette*, 19 November 1805.

28 Langford, ii, 302.

29 Robert Herrmann Schomburgk, *The History of Barbados* (London: Longman, Brown, Green and Longmans, 1848) [hereafter: Schomburgk], p. 246.

30 Edinburgh City Archive, Nelson Monument Committee Minutes, f. 6.

31 *Glasgow Herald*, 15 November 1805.

32 William Roscoe, *Lord Nelson's Monument, erected in the area of the Liverpool Exchange Buildings: completed October XXI. MDCCCXIII* ([n.p.: no pub., n.d., 1813?]) one page only.

33 *Nelson's Pillar. A Description of the Pillar, With a List of Subscribers* (Dublin: Published by order of the Committee, 1846) [hereafter: *Nelson's Pillar*], p. 14.

34 *Gentleman's Magazine*, 80 (1810), 414.

35 Schomburgk, pp. 245 and 147.
36 Rodney Mace, *Trafalgar Square. Emblem of Empire* (London: Lawrence and Wishart, 1976) [hereafter: Mace], pp. 29–31, 37, 41, 42, 45.
37 *Glasgow Herald*, 22 November 1805, 2 December 1805; *The Times*, 26 November 1805.
38 *Glasgow Herald*, 25 July 1806.
39 A monument in Norwich materialized only in the mid-nineteenth century for similar reasons.
40 Alison Willow Yarrington, 'The Commemoration of the Hero 1800–1864: Monuments to the British Victors of the Napoleonic Wars' (Ph.D. thesis, University of Cambridge, 1980) [hereafter: Yarrington], p. 104, referring to *Aris's Birmingham Gazette*, 30 December 1805; Langford, ii, 306.
41 Edinburgh City Archive, McLeod bundle 10, bay A, no folio number, *Description of the Monument . . . to the Memory of Lord Nelson*.
42 Wyatt (after whose design the monument was built), p. 5.
43 *Nelson's Pillar*, p. 17; [James Elmes], 'A critical Examination of the Architecture of the Nelson Column erected at Yarmouth, 1817–1819', *Annals of the Fine Arts*, 4 (1820), 511–43 [hereafter: 'critical Examination'], at 516.
44 Julie Rugg, 'From Reason to Regulation: 1760–1850', in *Death in England. An Illustrated History*, ed. Peter C. Jupp and Clare Gittings (Manchester: Manchester University Press, 1999), pp. 202–29, at p. 204.
45 Mace, pp. 257, 246; 'critical Examination', 521.
46 [Anon.], 'Of the Prevailing Taste for Isolated Columns as Public Monuments', *New Monthly Magazine and Literary Journal*, 1 (1821), 335–8 [hereafter: 'Prevailing Taste for Isolated Columns'], at 335, 336.
47 'critical Examination', 525.
48 'critical Examination', 528.
49 Joseph Rykwert, 'The Corinthian Order', *arena, The Architectural Association Journal*, 1966, 7–10, at 8, 9.
50 Reference in Mace, p. 101.
51 The *Illustrated London News*, 1 (1842), 266.
52 'Prevailing Taste for Isolated Columns', 336.
53 The *Illustrated London News*, 3 (1843), 289.
54 ['Stimulator'], 'Hints regarding the expected designs for the Nelson Testimonial', *The Art-Union*, 1 (1839), 46–7, at 47.
55 Yarrington, p. 82.
56 Cockerell quoted in David Irvin, 'Sentiment and Antiquity: European Tombs 1750–1830', in *Mirrors of Mortality. Studies in the Social History of Death*, ed. Joachim Whaley (London: Europa Publications, 1981), pp. 131–53 [hereafter: Irvin], at p. 135.
57 Quoted in Irvin, p. 137.
58 Quoted in Yarrington, p. 113.
59 P. D. Gordon Pugh, *Staffordshire Portrait Figures and Allied Subjects of the Victorian Era including the Definitive Catalogue* (first published 1970; new revised edition, Woodbridge, Suffolk: Antique Collector's Club, 1987), p. 9.
60 L. P. Le Quesne has recently challenged the view maintained particularly by Pugh; Le Quesne argues that such pieces were generally fashionable in the 1840s and 1850s: L. P. Le Quesne, *Nelson Commemorated in Glass Pictures* (Woodbridge, Suffolk: Antique Collectors' Club, 2001), p. 10. The massive production of cheap Staffordshire figures focused, however, on the portrayal of contemporary living personalities. The only exceptions are Nelson and Napoleon. Figures of Napoleon were usually produced as companion pieces to Wellington (as well as Nelson) and, at least in part, were produced for the export market: Asa Briggs, *Victorian Things* (London: B. T. Batsford, 1988), p. 148.

8   Transferring the image of Nelson

1 *The Times*, 2, 5, 17 December 1805, 11, 15, 23, 25, 27, 29, 31 January 1806.
2 Richard D. Altick, *The Shows of London* (Cambridge, MA and London: The Belknap Press of Harvard University Press, 1978) [hereafter: Altick], p. 436. For the attraction of St Paul's see the Prologue.

3   Altick, pp. 97, 136.

4   Joseph Allen, *Life of Lord Viscount Nelson, K.B. Duke of Bronté, &c.* (London: George Routledge and Co., 1853), p. 303n; the figurehead of the funeral car was preserved, however, and is on display in the National Maritime Museum.

5   Southey (1813), ii, 271–2.

6   *The Times*, 27 November 1805.

7   Entries of Richard Goodwin Keats and William Hoste in *The Dictionary of National Biography. Founded in 1882 by George Smith . . . From the Earliest Times to 1900*, ed. Leslie Stephen and Sidney Lee (22 vols., Oxford: Oxford University Press, 1885–1901, reprinted 1959–60), ix, 1297, and x, 1178 (both contributions are by John Knox Laughton); I am grateful to Jane Knight for alerting me to the note about Captain Keats.

8   For the origin of the wording of the toast, see Prologue.

9   Admiral Mark Kerr, *The Sailor's Nelson* (London: Hurst and Blackett, 1932), pp. 9–10.

10 David Ellison, 'The Battle of the Serpentine', *Nelson Dispatch*, 4 (1993), 206–8, quoting from the *Annual Register*.

11 Judy Egerton, *Turner. The Fighting Temeraire. With a Technical Examination of the Painting by Martin Wyld and Ashok Roy* (series 'Making and Meaning', London: National Gallery Publications, 1995) [hereafter: Egerton], p. 71.

12 Altick, p. 438, quoting from Benjamin Silliman, *A Visit to Europe in 1851* (New York, 1853), pp. 416–17.

13 Nicolas, vii, 250–2.

14 Letter from Nicolas to different newspapers of 1846, quoted in John Munday, 'The Nelson Relics', in *The Nelson Companion*, ed. Colin White (Annapolis, MD: Alan Sutton Publishing, 1995), p. 60.

15 Apart from the Naval Gallery at Greenwich Hospital there was the collection belonging to the Royal United Service Institution (founded in 1830), though this was opened 'normally . . . only to bearers of tickets signed by members, although the general public was admitted for three days at Christmas and Easter and on the anniversaries of Waterloo and Trafalgar' (Altick, p. 300).

16 [Anon.], *Official Catalogue and Guide [to the Royal Naval Exhibition]* (London: W. P. Griffith and Sons, 1891), p. xxxiv.

17 [Anon.], *Royal Naval Exhibition 1891. The Illustrated Handbook and Souvenir* (London: 'Pall Mall Gazette' Office, 1891) [hereafter: *RNE. Illustrated Handbook*], pp. 30–2.

18 *RNE. Illustrated Handbook*, p. 11.

19 *RNE. Illustrated Handbook*, pp. 13–14.

20 Martin Pugh, *The Tories and the People 1880–1935* (Oxford: Basil Blackwell, 1985), pp. 29, 214.

21 Anne Summers, 'The Character of Edwardian Nationalism: Three Popular Leagues', in *Nationalist and Racialist Movements in Britain and Germany before 1914*, ed. P. Kennedy and A. Nicholls (London: Macmillan, 1981), pp. 68–87, 84.

22 Sea Cadet Corps [hereafter: SCC], Minutes of the Executive Committee of the Navy League, vol. B, p. 111 (13 July 1896).

23 SCC, Minutes of the Executive Committee of the Navy League, vol. B, p. 140.

24 SCC, Minutes of the Executive Committee of the Navy League, vol. F, p. 3 (17 September 1900), vol. L/12, p. 4 (8 October 1906).

25 SCC, Minutes of the Executive Committee of the Navy League, vol. C, pp. 81, 99; vol. D, p. 111; vol E, p. 100; vol. F, p. 7.

26 *The Times*, 22 October 1900, p. 8.

27 *The Navy League Journal*, 1, no. 17 (November 1896), 7 (new series: 1, 137).

28 *The Times*, 20 October 1897, p. 12; 22 October 1897, p. 8; 23 October 1897, p. 11; 25 October 1897, p. 7; 27 October 1897, p. 11; *The Navy League Journal*, 1, no. 29 (November 1897), 2 (new series: 1, 268).

29 SCC, Minutes of the Executive Committee of the Navy League, vol. F, pp. 7–8 (24 September 1900).

30 SCC, Minutes of the Executive Committee of the Navy League, vol. P/17, pp. 60, 73, 75 and vol. [Q]/17a, p. 103; vol. [Q]/17a, p. 125; the amounts for the Trafalgar Day celebrations can be found

in: vol. F, p. 137, vol. G, p. 154, vol. H, p. 143, vol. I/9, p. 6, vol. J/10, p. 85, vol. J/10, pp. 92–3, vol. L/12, p. 129.

31 Gerald Jordan, 'Admiral Nelson and the Concept of Patriotism: The Trafalgar Centenary, 1905', *Naval History: The Seventh Symposium of the US Academy*, ed. William B. Cogar (Wilmington, DE: Scholarly Resources, 1988), p. 150, quoting from the *Manchester Guardian*, 23 October 1905.

32 *The Times*, 23 October 1905, p. 10.

33 *'Fear God and Dread Nought'. The Correspondence of Admiral of the Fleet Lord Fisher of Kilverstone*, ed. Arthur Marder (3 vols., London: Jonathan Cape, 1952–59), i, 320. The *Daily Mirror* reacted to Fisher's decision with a caricature, *The Anniversary of Trafalgar*; illustration given in R. H. Bacon, *The Life of Lord Fisher of Kilverstone. Admiral of the Fleet* (2 vols., London: Hodder and Stoughton, 1929) [hereafter: Marder], ii, opp. 64.

34 Arnold White and E. Hallam Moorhouse, *Nelson and the Twentieth Century* (London: Cassell, 1905) [hereafter: White/Moorhouse], pp. vii–xiii. The authors were legally barred from disclosing Fisher's name (p. v). One of Fisher's letters to A. White proves his authorship: Marder, ii, 62.

35 Ruddock F. Mackay, *Fisher of Kilverstone* (Oxford: Clarendon Press, 1973), pp. 242–3, 254.

36 A notable example being the reputable author of naval works, F. T. Jane; White/Moorhouse, pp. 295–7, where F. T. Jane was given a chance to argue his case.

37 Richard H. Holme, *Horatio Nelson: England's Sailor Hero* (London: Walter Scott Publishing Co., 1905), p. 412.

38 Egerton, p. 12; see also pp. 71, 90.

39 Kevin Littlewood and Beverly Butler, *Of Ships and Stars. Maritime Heritage and the Founding of the National Maritime Museum, Greenwich* (London and New Brunswick, NJ: Athlone Press, 1998) [hereafter: Littlewood/Butler], plate 11, between pp. 40 and 41.

40 [Anon.], *Nelson's Flagship the 'Foudroyant', 1789–1897* (Manchester: Codall, Lamb and Heighway, [1898]), pp. 20–1.

41 There remained also the *Implacable*, a French ship taken in the battle. She survived until after the Second World War, when she was blown up for lack of funds to maintain her. Her stern is kept at the National Maritime Museum (on display).

42 Littlewood/Butler, pp. 39–40.

43 Littlewood/Butler, pp. 89–90. The original paintings of the death scene by Devis and the *Immortality of Nelson* by West are kept at the National Maritime Museum.

44 Littlewood/Butler, p. 91.

45 Littlewood/Butler, p. 171.

46 Pocket plan provided for every visitor of the museum.

47 Colin White [curator of the Royal Naval Museum at Portsmouth], 'New Nelson and HMS Victory Displays at the Royal Naval Museum', *Nelson Dispatch*, 3(2) (April 1988), 24–6.

48 It deserves mention here that there have been several major exhibitions in Germany during the last twenty years that dealt in great part with Nelson: *Admiral Nelsons Epoche: Die Entwicklung der Segelschiffahrt von 1770 bis 1815*, ed. Dirk Böndel (Berlin: Museum für Verkehr und Technik, 1987); *Mythen der Nationen – ein europäisches Panorama: eine Ausstellung des Deutschen Historischen Museums; Begleitband zur Ausstellung vom 20. März 1998 bis 9. Juni 1998*, ed. Monika Flacke (Berlin: Deutsches Historisches Museuem, 1998); *Lord Nelson. Ein Triumphzug durch Europa* (Hamburg: Altonaer Museum, 2000).

49 An exception from this rule appears to be the 'Trafalgar Club' of the British National Party.

9 Fictionalizing Nelson

1 Henry Newbolt, *The Year of Trafalgar . . . With a Collection of the Poems and Ballads Written Thereupon Between 1805 and 1905* (London: John Murray, 1905), p. 187.

2 *Naval Chronicle*, 14 (1805), 498–9.

3 *The Times*, 12 November 1805; *Naval Chronicle*, 14 (1805), 500.

4 *The Times*, 9 December 1805.

5 *Gentleman's Magazine*, 77 (1807), 444–6, review of *Trafalgar; the Sailor's Play. In 5 Acts* (by 'no juvenile Bard').

6 John Mitford, *The Adventures of Johnny Newcome in the Navy. A Poem in Four Cantos. With*

Notes (second edition, London: published for the author and sold by Sherwood, Neely, Jones et al., 1819), pp. 46, 65, 71, 165–6, 169 [hereafter: Mitford].

7   Mitford, p. 166.

8   Edward Fitzball, *Nelson; or, the Life of a Sailor. A National Drama in Two Acts . . . First Performed at the Adelphi Theatre, Monday, December 3rd, 1827* (London: John Dicks, [1886]), pp. 8–9.

9   Frederick Chamier, *Ben Brace: The Last of the Agamemnons* (London: R. Bentley, 1836; the first of many editions) [hereafter: Chamier], p. 187, fn. Nelson was captain of the *Agamemnon* from January 1793 until June 1796, in which period he referred to his men as the 'Agamemnons'.

10 Chamier, p. 181.

11 Chamier, pp. 182, 286, 290–1, 294.

12 Chamier, pp. 282–4, 286.

13 Fitchett, p. 4.

14 White/Moorhouse, p. 13.

15 Britton, p. 84; examples of the Abbott pictures Britton refers to are in colour plates 2 and 3.

16 Warner (1958), p. 261; for illustrations of the two pictures see colour plates 9 and 10 (oil sketches, which as a kind of snapshot, taken immediately from Nelson, probably betray best the different portrayals of the two painters) and the cover of this book for a finished version of Hoppner's portrait.

17 Richard Walker, *The Nelson Portraits: An Iconography of Horatio Viscount Nelson, K. B., Vice Admiral of the White* ([Portsmouth]: Royal Naval Museum Publications, 1998) [hereafter: Walker], foreword by Richard Ormond (then Director, National Maritime Museum and formerly of the National Portrait Gallery), p. xviii.

18 Walker, p. 128; colour plate 9 and the cover of this book.

19 Quoted in Walker, p. 124.

20 Gordon Stables, *Hearts of Oak: A Story of Nelson and the Navy* (London: John F. Shaw and Co, [1893]) [hereafter: Stables], pp. 205, 210–11.

21 Frank H. Shaw, *In the Days of Nelson. A Story of the Battle of the Nile* (London: Cassell and Company, [1910]) [hereafter: F. Shaw], p. 221.

22 Stables, pp. 167–8.

23 Stables, pp. ix, x.

24 F. H. Winder, *With the Sea Kings. A Story of the Days of Lord Nelson* (London: Blackie and Son, [1894]), p. 312.

25 Stables, pp. 91–6.

26 Stables, p. 127.

27 W. P. Drury, *The Admiral Speaks. A Play in one Act* (Samuel French: London, 1912) [hereafter: Drury], p. 4 (giving places of performances in 1910 and 1911), 5, 16.

28 Drury, pp. 16 and 18.

29 For more about these celebrations, see Chapter 8.

30 George Bernard Shaw, *The Bodley Head Bernard Shaw. Collected Plays with their Prefaces* (7 vols., London: Max Reinhardt, The Bodley Head, 1971), ii, 807–71, 'Preface for Politicians, 1906' to 'John Bull's Other Island', ii, 817.

31 Sladen, p. 85.

32 Sladen, p. 26.

33 Sladen, p. 90.

34 Sladen, p. 105.

35 Sladen, pp. 137, 244; Captain Foley's ship led the British line at the battle of the Nile.

36 *Nelson. The Story of England's immortal Naval Hero.* The quoted passages are taken from the inter-titles.

37 For the discussion of this painting see Chapter 7.

38 *Variety*, 27 March 1929, quoted in John Sugden, 'Lord Nelson and the Film Industry', *Nelson Dispatch*, 2 (1985), 83–8, 84.

39 Joseph Conrad, *The Rover* (London and Toronto: J. M. Dent and Sons, 1923), pp. 55, 112, 272–7.

40 Quoted in K. R. M. Short, '"That Hamilton Woman" (1941): Propaganda, Feminism and the Production Code', *Historical Journal of Film, Radio and Television*, 11 (1991) [hereafter: Short], 3–19, 9.

41 Short, 12.
42 Short, 10–13.
43 Short, 5; Karol Kulik, *Alexander Korda. The Man Who Could Work Miracles* (London: W. H. Allen, 1975), pp. 249, 252–3.
44 Alan Pryce-Jones, *Nelson. Opera in Three Acts. Libretto by Alan Pryce-Jones. Music by Lennox Berkeley* (London: J. and W. Chester, 1954), pp. 13–14, 21, 36–7.
45 Terence Rattigan, *Bequest to the Nation* (London: Evans Plays, 1970) [hereafter: Rattigan], p. 68.
46 Rattigan, pp. 81–2.
47 Rattigan, p. 42. For a supposed contrast between Nelson at sea and ashore see Chapter 6.
48 John Arden and Margaretta D'Arcy, *The Hero Rises Up. A Romantic Melodrama* (London: Methuen, 1969) [hereafter: Arden/D'Arcy], p. 16.
49 Arden/D'Arcy, pp. 80, 93.
50 Arden/D'Arcy, p. 45; Warner (1958), pp. 91–3, had first published an account of this affair in a biography of Nelson.
51 Arden/D'Arcy, pp. 54–67, 101.
52 *Sunday Times*, 14 September 1969.
53 Susan Sontag, *The Volcano Lover. A Romance* (London: Jonathan Cape, 1992) [hereafter: Sontag], pp. 193–9, 189, 206.
54 Particularly Sontag, pp. 285–7.
55 Sontag, pp. 298, 319, 348–9, 419.
56 Barry Unsworth, *Losing Nelson* (London: Hamish Hamilton, 1999) [hereafter: Unsworth], p. 97.
57 Unsworth, p. 169.
58 Unsworth, pp. 56, 130–1.
59 Unsworth, p. 81.
60 Unsworth, pp. 243, 304.

10 Views from across the Channel

 1 ['D.A.S.A.'], *Entrada pública del almirante Nelson en la corte de Plutón el dia 23 de octúbre de este año* (Cadiz: Manuel Ximénez Carreño, 1805), pp. 4–7, 9–12; Nelson had taken a leading part in a bombardment of Cadiz in 1797.
 2 For the impact of the Peninsular War on the perception of the battle of Trafalgar in Spain, see Marianne Czisnik, 'La interpretación más conocida de la batalla de Trafalgar – la novela *Trafalgar* de Benito Pérez Galdós', in *Trafalgar y el mundo atlántico*, ed. Augustín Guimerá, Alberto Ramos and Gonzalo Butrón (Madrid: Marcial Pons, 2002), pp. 359–74 [hereafter: Czisnik, 'interpretación'].
 3 Fernán Caballero (the alias of Cecilia Böhl de Faber), 'Una madre', in *Obras de Fernán Caballero*, vol. iv (of v) (Madrid: Biblioteca de Autores Españoles, vol. 139, 1961), pp. 383–7, at p. 383; first published in *El Artista*, 2 (1835), 232–6.
 4 Mathieu Dumas, *Précis des Événemens militaires, ou Essais historiques sur les campagnes de 1799 à 1814* (Paris: Treuttel et Würtz, 1822), tome XII. Campaign of 1805: pp. vii, 201.
 5 This appears to have been inspired more by the execution of Admiral Byng in 1757 than by habits of British naval leadership in the days of Nelson.
 6 [Lardier], *Mémoires de Robert Guillemard, sergent en retraite, suivis de documens historiques, la plupart inédits, de 1805 à 1823* (2 vols., Paris: Delaforest, Bossange père, frères Baudouin, 1826–27), i, 31–3.
 7 Lardier, 'Lettre de l'auteur des Mémoires du sergent Robert Guillemard, publiés en 1826 et 1827, qui déclare que tout ce qu'il a raconté sur la mort du vice-amiral Villeneuve est une fiction, et que Guillemard est un personnage imaginaire', *Annales Maritimes et Coloniales*, année 1830, 2e Partie, tome 2, 184–7, at pp. 184, 186.
 8 I. F. G. Hennequin, *Biographie Maritime ou Notices Historiques sur la vie et les campagnes des marins célèbres français et étrangers* (3 vols., Paris: Regnault, 1835–37), i, 121–45 ('Nelson'), 137, 145.
 9 Louis Adolphe Thiers, *L'Histoire du Consulat et de l'Empire* (21 vols., Paris: 1845–62); translation into English by D. Forbes Campbell: *History of the Consulate and the Empire of France under Napoleon. Forming a Sequel to 'The History of the French Revolution'* (20 vols., London: Henry Colburn, 1845–62), vi, 72.

10 Francisco de Paula Quadrado y de-Roo, *Elogio histórico de don Antonio Escaño* (Madrid: Real Academia de la Historia, 1852), p. 32.

11 Manuel Marliani, *Combate de Trafalgar. Vindicación de la armada Española contra las aserciones injuriosas por Mr. Thiers en su Historia del Consulado y el Imperio* (Madrid: Impreso de orden superior, 1850), pp. 385, 386, 451.

12 E. Jurien de la Gravière, *Guerres Maritimes sous la République et l'Empire* (2 vols., Paris: Charpentier, 1847) [hereafter: Jurien de la Gravière], i, 4, 6.

13 Jurien de la Gravière, i, 37, 249.

14 A[lphonse-Marie-Louis Prat] de Lamartine, *Nelson* (Paris: L. Hachette, 1853) [hereafter: Lamartine], pp. 33, 35, 61.

15 F. W. J. Hemmings, *The King of Romance. A Portrait of Alexandre Dumas* (London: Hamish Hamilton, 1979) [hereafter: Hemmings]; Gutteridge, p. cv.

16 For the discussion of *I Borboni di Napoli*, see Chapter 3. The novels were written between 1863 and 1865, but first published only in 1876.

17 Hemmings, p. 198. For a combined edition, see Alexandre Dumas [père], *La San Felice. Établissement du texte, notes, postface, dictionnaire des personages par Claude Schopp* (Paris: Quarto, Gallimard, 1996) [hereafter: A. Dumas, *La San Felice*]. The text of this combined edition has 1,606 pages.

18 Alexandre Dumas [père], *Souvenirs d'une favorite* ([n.p.]: Feuilleton de l'Avenir National, 1865) [hereafter: A. Dumas, *Souvenirs d'une favorite*], p. 177.

19 A. Dumas, *La San Felice*, pp. 31–2.

20 A. Dumas, *Souvenirs d'une favorite*, p. 243; A. Dumas, *La San Felice*, p. 599.

21 Jennifer Waelti-Walters, *Damned Women. Lesbians in French Novels, 1796–1996* ([Montreal]: McGill-Queen's University Press, 2000) [hereafter: Waelti-Walters], pp. 20, 26–7.

22 A. Dumas, *La San Felice*, p. 47; A. Dumas, *Souvenirs d'une favorite*, pp. 128, 136–8, 227.

23 Waelti-Walters, p. 27 (about this pattern); A. Dumas, *La San Felice*, p. 39.

24 A. Dumas, *La San Felice*, pp. 43–6, 423, 425; A. Dumas, *Souvenirs d'une favorite*, pp. 35, 39–70.

25 A. Dumas, *La San Felice*, p. 472; A. Dumas, *Souvenirs d'une favorite*, pp. 129–31.

26 Waelti-Walters, p. 212.

27 A. Dumas, *La San Felice*, pp. 424–6.

28 A. Dumas, *La San Felice*, p. 601 (the heading of this chapter, pp. 596–604, is 'Ulysse et Circé').

29 A. Dumas, *Souvenirs d'une favorite*, p. 264; A. Dumas, *La San Felice*, pp. 1428–9, 1430.

30 A. Dumas, *Souvenirs d'une favorite*, p. 284.

31 Quoted in White/Moorhouse, p. 284; the story of Caracciolo is also at the centre of the condemnation of Nelson in Armand Dubarry, *L'Amiral Nelson adultère. Amours scandaleuses de l'Amiral Nelson avec lady Hamilton* (Paris: H. Daragon, 1905) [hereafter: Dubarry], p. v.

32 Alexandre Dumas [père], *The Lovely Lady Hamilton ('Emma Lyonna') or The Beauty and the Glory*, trans. Henry L. Williams (London: Shurmer Sibthorp, [1903]); Hemmings, pp. 198 and 223 (note 4).

33 Czisnik, 'interpretación', with further references.

34 Benito Pérez Galdós, *Trafalgar. Edición de Julio Rodríguez Puertolas* (Madrid: CATEDRA, Letras Hispanas, 1984, reissued several times since) [hereafter: Galdós, *Trafalgar*], pp. 91, 93.

35 Galdós, *Trafalgar*, p. 153.

36 Galdós, *Trafalgar*, p. 164.

37 Galdós, *Trafalgar*, p. 176.

38 Reinhold Werner, *Berühmte Seeleute. Zweithe Abtheilung. XVIII. und XIX. Jahrhundert. Paul Jones. Nelson. Farragut. Tegethoff* (Berlin: Otto Janke, [1883]) [hereafter: Werner], lists his sources in his unpaginated 'Vorrede'; Nelson is dealt with on pp. 116–344; Friedrich Althaus, *Admiral Nelson*, ed. Rudolf von Gottschall, *Der Neue Plutarch. Biographien hervorragender Charaktere der Geschichte, Literatur und Kunst. Achter Theil* (Leipzig: F. A. Brockhaus, 1880), pp. 137–288 [hereafter: Althaus].

39 Werner, p. 231; Althaus, p. 221.

40 Werner, pp. 128, 134.

41 Althaus, p. 233.

42 Althaus, p. 237; the quotation from Nelson can be found in Nicolas, iv, 90.

43 [Georg] Neudeck, *Nelson. Schauspiel in fünf Akten* (Dresden and Leipzig: E. Piersons Verlag, 1903) [hereafter: Neudeck], pp. 13–14.

44 Neudeck, pp. 39, 47–8.

45 Neudeck, p. 92.

46 English translations of these novels, first published in 1910–11, are Henry Schumacher, *The Fair Enchantress. A Romance of Lady Hamilton's Early Years* (London: Hutchinson and Co., 1912); Henry Schumacher, *Nelson's Last Love* (London: Hutchinson and Co., [1913]) [hereafter: Schumacher, *Nelson's Last Love*].

47 Schumacher, *Nelson's Last Love*, p. 14.

48 Schumacher, *Nelson's Last Love*, pp. 18–19.

49 Schumacher, *Nelson's Last Love*, p. 332.

50 The script (consisting of 173 scenes) is reprinted in: dif [Deutsches Institut für Filmkunde] – Filmkundliche Mitteilungen, Nr. 3/4, December 1971, 11–48, scene 170.

51 Richard Bars und Leopold Jacobson, *Lady Hamilton. Operette in drei Akten . . . Musik von Eduard Künneke. Vollständiges Regie- und Soufflierbuch* (Berlin: Arcadia Verlag, [1926]), p. 213.

52 Alfred Richard Meyer, *Lady Hamilton oder Die Posen-Emma oder Vom Dienstmädchen zum Beefsteak à la Nelson. Eine ebenso romanhafte wie auch novellenschaukelnde durchwachsene Travestie von Alfred Richard Meyer. Fleissigst und fleischigst bebildert von George Grosz* (Berlin: Fritz Gurlitt Verlag, [1923]) [hereafter: Meyer/Grosz]; the translation of the title is taken from Beth Irwin Lewis, *George Grosz. Art and Politics in the Weimar Republic* (Madison, Milwaukee and London: University of Wisconsin Press, 1971), p. 171.

53 Meyer/Grosz, p. 52.

54 José Ortega y Gasset, *Estudios sobre el amor* ([n.p.]: Biblioteca Básica Salvat, 1985), pp. 93–4; I am grateful to Alberto Lena Ordóñez for alerting me to this passage.

55 Juan Cabal, *Nelson. Vida sentimental* (Barcelona: Editorial Juventud, Colección 'Vidas y Memorias', 1944; second edition, Barcelona: Ediciones Planeta-De Agostini, 'Grandes Biografías,' 1966), p. 65.

56 José del Rio Sainz, *Nelson* (Madrid: Ediciones Atlas, 1943), pp. 30, 39, 64.

57 Alfred von Tirpitz, *Deutsche Ohnmachtspolitik im Weltkriege* (Hamburg and Berlin: Hanseatische Verlagsanstalt, 1926), p. 32; the book is one volume of Tirpitz's *Politische Dokumente* (*Political Documents*).

58 Manfred Fuhrke, Wilhelm Marschall and Friedrich Lützow, 'Nelson', in *Führertum. 26 Lebensbilder von Feldherren aller Zeiten. Auf Veranlassung des Reichskriegsministeriums bearbeitet von Offizieren der Wehrmacht und zusammengestellt von Generalleutnant von Cochenhausen*, ed. von Cochenhausen (third edition, Berlin: Verlag von E. G. Mittler und Sohn, 1937), pp. 280–305, at 297.

59 Sten Nadolny, *The Discovery of Slowness* (first published 1983 as *Die Entdeckung der Langsamkeit*; Edinburgh: Canongate Books, 2003), pp. 112, 196.

Select bibliography

This book is the product of extensive research into all the available evidence. A complete bibliography would be out of proportion to the limited scope of this text. The following bibliographical overview will give the interested reader the important sources, most of which will lead on to more detailed bibliographic information. Endnotes in the text have been used with restraint. Any passage in the book that relates to the posthumous image and iconography of Nelson is based on my doctoral thesis about 'Admiral Nelson. Image and Icon' (University of Edinburgh, 2004). Since this thesis is meticulously referenced, the sources used to trace the development of portrayals of Nelson in detail can be found there. Consequently, this book gives references only for all literal quotations and any elements that have been added to the contents of my thesis. The place of publication is London unless otherwise stated.

For the Prologue about Nelson's funeral, manuscript sources from the National Archives of the United Kingdom (formerly the Public Record Office) and the College of Arms have been used. These were supported and added to by contemporary newspaper articles, in particular from *The Times*, the *Naval Chronicle* and the *Gentleman's Magazine*. For a general introduction into funerary traditions, Julian Litten's book *The English Way of Death. The Common Funeral Since 1450* (Robert Hale, 1991) is recommended. The best treatment of Nelson's funeral itself is Timothy Jenks' article 'Contesting the Hero: The Funeral of Admiral Lord Nelson', *Journal of British Studies*, 39 (2000), 422–53.

The first part of this book is mostly based on primary sources and biographical literature about Nelson. Among the manuscript sources those held at the British Library and the National Maritime Museum stand out. The most valuable printed primary source is Nicholas Harris Nicolas's edition of *The Dispatches and Letters of Vice-Admiral Lord Viscount Nelson* (7 vols., Chatham Publishing, 1997–98, reprint of first edition 1844–46). Although the choice among the important biographies about Nelson is difficult, the most important works can be narrowed down to the following chronologically arranged books from the nineteenth century. Writing for Lady Hamilton, James Harrison presented with his *The Life of the Right Honourable Horatio Lord Viscount Nelson* (2 vols., C. Chapple, 1806) the first thorough biography. Because of the many fanciful additions that it contains, its more revealing parts have mostly been ignored. James Stanier Clarke's and John M'Arthur's biography, *The Life of Admiral Lord Nelson, K.B. from His Lordship's Manuscripts* (2 vols., T. Cadell and W. Davies, 1809), is much less important for its biographical qualities than for its accounts about and letters from Nelson. Unfortunately nearly all of these letters have been inaccurately printed and hence their contents have sometimes been distorted. Based on these early and in part unreliable sources, Robert Southey presented with his *The Life of Nelson* (2 vols., John Murray, 1813) the first popular biography of Nelson. Because of the damaging effect of the publication of some of Nelson's letters to Lady Hamilton, however, this biography became popular only from the mid-nineteenth century onwards and was published in innumerable editions until the end of the century. Using the renewed interest in Nelson, Thomas Joseph Pettigrew produced his *Memoirs of the Life of Vice-Admiral Lord Viscount Nelson, K.B. Duke of Bronté etc. etc. etc.* (2 vols., T. and W. Boone, 1849). This contains the most extensive collection of Nelson's letters to Lady Hamilton, but this has meant that it was avoided as a source by most later authors. The influential naval historian John Knox Laughton offered with his *Nelson* (Macmillan, 1895) a new interpretation of the great man, based on more advanced research, but also still marked by the struggle not to include Lady Hamilton in the story. A. T. Mahan's *The Life of Nelson. The Embodiment of the Sea Power of Great Britain* (first published 1897; second edition, Sampson Low, Marston and Co., 1899) offered a thorough analysis of Nelson's life, particularly its professional side. Its scholarly thoroughness, however, kept it from becoming widely read. Twentieth-century authors have mostly built on the sources published in the nineteenth century. Important new biographies were written by Carola Oman, Oliver Warner and Tom Pocock. The new millennium has started promisingly with several new biographies of Nelson by Terry Coleman, Edgar Vincent, John Sugden and Andrew Lambert. In addition to these sources, the following are of vital importance to chapters in the first part of this book in particular.

The most important additional source used for Chapter 1 is Geoffrey Rawson's edition of *Nelson's Letters from the Leeward Islands and other Original Documents in the Public Record Office and the British Museum* ([n.p.]: Golden Cockerel Press, 1953).

For Chapter 2 there are sources about the battle of Trafalgar to be considered. The most important of them is the *Report of a Committee Appointed by the Admiralty to Examine and Consider the Evidence Relating to the Tactics Employed by Nelson at the Battle of Trafalgar* (His Majesty's Stationery Office, 1913). Julian S. Corbett's edition of *Fighting Instructions 1530–1816* (Navy Records Society, 1905) and his book about *The Campaign of Trafalgar*

(Longmans, Green and Co., 1910) are important additional sources. A summarizing treatment of Nelson's tactics can be found in my article on the subject in *History*, 89 (2004), 549–59.

Undoubtedly the most important key to an understanding of Nelson's actions in Naples, dealt with in Chapter 3, is H. C. Gutteridge's edition of *Nelson and the Neapolitan Jacobins. Documents Relating to the Suppression of the Jacobin Revolution at Naples. June 1799* (Navy Records Society, 1903). Again I have offered an overview of this complex matter in an article ('Nelson at Naples – A Review of Events and Arguments', *Trafalgar Chronicle*, 12 (2002), 84–121).

For Nelson's relationship with Lady Hamilton, the subject of Chapter 4, several printed primary sources need to be considered in addition to Nicolas's edition of Nelson's letters. The earliest of these editions is the anonymously published, but generally reliable, collection of *The Letters of Lord Nelson to Lady Hamilton with a Supplement of Interesting Letters by Distinguished Characters* (2 vols., Thomas Lovewell and Co., 1814). A less extensive, but more reliable source than Pettigrew's biography, consisting in great part of extracts from Nelson's letters to Lady Hamilton, is Alfred Morrison's clumsily entitled *The Collection of Autograph Letters and Historical Documents formed by Alfred Morrison (Second Series, 1882–1893) – The Hamilton & Nelson Papers* (2 vols., [n.p.]: printed for private circulation, 1893). Additional letters can be found in Walter Sichel's biography of *Emma Lady Hamilton* (third revised edition, Edinburgh: Archibald Constable, 1907) and in George Naish's edition of *Nelson's Letters to his Wife and other Documents. 1785–1831* (Navy Records Society, 1958).

The most important source about Nelson's death, described in Chapter 5, is William Beatty's *Authentic Narrative of the Death of Lord Nelson* (T. Cadell and W. Davies, 1807). In addition to the neglected account of Nelson's death in Harrison's biography, the account in a letter by Alexander Scott ([A. and M. Gatty], *Recollections of the Life of the Rev. A. J. Scott, D. D. Lord Nelson's Chaplain* (Saunders and Otley, 1842), pp. 188–9) deserves to be more widely known.

For the second part of the book the collections of the National Maritime Museum in Greenwich, the Royal Naval Museum in Portsmouth and the Nelson Museum in Monmouth were the most important sources of pictures and material artefacts. The British Film Institute in London and the Bundesarchiv-Filmarchiv in Berlin offered important cinematographic material. As was the case for the Prologue, *The Times*, the *Naval Chronicle* and the *Gentleman's Magazine* were the most important printed primary sources.

For Chapter 7, essential secondary information was provided particularly by L. P. Le Quesne, *Nelson Commemorated in Glass Pictures* (Woodbridge, Suffolk: Antique Collectors' Club, 2001), Kathryn Cave's edition of *The Diary of Joseph Farington* (16 vols., New Haven and London: Yale University Press, 1978–84), John and Jennifer May's *Commemorative Pottery 1780–1900. A Guide for Collectors* (Heinemann, 1972), P. D. Gordon Pugh's works on *Naval Ceramics* (assisted by Margery Pugh, Newport, Mon.: Ceramic Book Company, 1971) and *Staffordshire Portrait Figures* (first published 1970; new and revised edition, Antique Collector's Club: Woodbridge, 1987), Rina Prentice's *A Celebration of the Sea. The Decorative Art Collections of the National Maritime Museum* (National Maritime Museum, 1994), Lily Lambert McCarthy's *Remembering Nelson* ([Portsmouth]: privately published in the United Kingdom, 1995), Rodney Mace's *Trafalgar Square. Emblem of Empire* (Lawrence and Wishart, 1976) and Alison Willow Yarrington's 'The Commemoration of the Hero 1800–1864: Monuments to the British Victors of the Napoleonic Wars' (Ph.D. thesis, University of Cambridge, 1980).

The sources for Chapter 8 relate either to exhibitions or propaganda. Important clues to the development of exhibitions in general are offered by Richard D. Altick's *The Shows of London* (Cambridge, MA and London: The Belknap Press of Harvard University Press, 1978), and for the preservation of the *Victory* and the development of the National Maritime Museum in partic- ular they can be found in exhibition catalogues and Kevin Littlewood and Beverly Butler's book *Of Ships and Stars. Maritime Heritage and the Founding of the National Maritime Museum, Greenwich* (London and New Brunswick, NJ: Athlone Press, 1998). The propagandistic activities of the Navy League can be best traced in its archive, which is kept by the Sea Cadet Corps in their office in London. Also important are the *Navy League Journal* and the valuable essay about 'The Character of Edwardian Nationalism: Three Popular Leagues' by Anne Summers, in *Nationalist and Racialist Movements in Britain and Germany before 1914*, ed. P. Kennedy and A. Nicholls (Macmillan, 1981), pp. 68–87. An essay that specifically deals with 'Admiral Nelson and the Concept of Patriotism: The Trafalgar Centenary, 1905' has been published by Gerald Jordan in *Naval History: The Seventh Symposium of the US Academy*, ed. William B. Cogar (Wilmington, DE: Scholarly Resources, 1988). It is a valuable source, although the author's conclusions are not shared in this book.

The fictional treatments used for Chapter 9 are too numerous to be listed here and unfortunately there is so far little secondary literature about fictional treat- ments of Nelson and none that would be a general introduction to written fiction about Nelson. The most important secondary sources about films that deal with Nelson are John Sugden's 'Lord Nelson and the Film Industry', *Nelson Dispatch*, 2 (1985), 83–8, and K. R. M. Short's '"That Hamilton Woman" (1941): Propaganda, Feminism and the Production Code', *Historical Journal of Film, Radio and Television*, 11 (1991), 3–19. A valuable overview of portraits of Nelson is given in Richard Walker's *The Nelson Portraits: An Iconography of Horatio Viscount Nelson, K.B., Vice Admiral of the White* ([Portsmouth]: Royal Naval Museum Publications, 1998).

The most important sources considered in Chapter 10 can be grouped according to the countries in which they were first published. The historical literature that most influenced French views on Nelson was Louis Adolphe Thiers' *L'Histoire du Consulat et de l'Empire* (21 vols., Paris: 1845–62), E.

Jurien de la Gravière's, *Guerres Maritimes sous la République et l'Empire* (2 vols., Paris: Charpentier, 1847), A. de Lamartine's *Nelson* (L. Hachette: Paris, 1853) and Edouard Desbrière's *La campagne maritime de 1805* (Paris: [Service Historique de l'État-Major de l'Armée], 1907). Even more influential were two novels by Alexandre Dumas (père) about the events in Naples in 1799, put together in *La San Felice. Établissement du texte, notes, postface, dictionnaire des personages par Claude Schopp* (Paris: Quarto, Gallimard, 1996) and Dumas' supposed memoir of Lady Hamilton, *Souvenirs d'une favorite* ([n.p.]: Feuilleton de l'Avenir National, 1865). Based on various historical works, particularly Manuel Marliani's *Combate de Trafalgar. Vindicación de la armada Española contra las aserciones injuriosas por Mr. Thiers en su Historia del Consulado y el Imperio* (Madrid: Impreso de orden superior, 1850), the famous Spanish author Benito Pérez Galdós determined the Spanish image of Nelson in his novel *Trafalgar*. The German image of Nelson was not determined by any work as popular as the novels by Dumas and Galdós and no single text alone reflects their image of the British hero.

Index